PUTTING PHILOSOPHY TO WORK

PUTTING PHILOSOPHY TO WORK

TOWARD AN ECOLOGICAL CIVILIZATION

JOHN B. COBB, JR.
WM. ANDREW SCHWARTZ
EDITORS

ANOKA, MINNESOTA 2018

Putting Philosophy to Work: Toward an Ecological Civilization

© 2018 Process Century Press

Process Century Press
RiverHouse LLC
802 River Lane
Anoka, MN 55303

Process Century Press books are published in association with the International Process Network.

Cover: Susanna Mennicke

VOLUME XV: TOWARD ECOLOGICAL CIVILIZATION SERIES
JEANYNE B. SLETTOM, GENERAL EDITOR

ISBN 978-1-940447-33-9
Printed in the United States of America

TABLE OF CONTENTS

We live in the ending of an age. But the ending of the modern period differs from the ending of previous periods, such as the classical or the medieval. The amazing achievements of modernity make it possible, even likely, that its end will also be the end of civilization, of many species, or even of the human species. At the same time, we are living in an age of new beginnings that give promise of an ecological civilization. Its emergence is marked by a growing sense of urgency and deepening awareness that the changes must go to the roots of what has led to the current threat of catastrophe.

In June 2015, the 10th Whitehead International Conference was held in Claremont, CA. Called "Seizing an Alternative: Toward an Ecological Civilization," it claimed an organic, relational, integrated, nondual, and processive conceptuality is needed, and that Alfred North Whitehead provides this in a remarkably comprehensive and rigorous way. We proposed that he could be "the philosopher of ecological civilization." With the help of those who have come to an ecological vision in other ways, the conference explored this Whiteheadian alternative, showing how it can provide the shared vision so urgently needed.

The judgment underlying this effort is that contemporary research and scholarship is still enthralled by the 17th century view of nature articulated by Descartes and reinforced by Kant. Without freeing our minds of this objectifying and reductive understanding of the world, we are not likely to direct our actions wisely in response to the crisis to which this tradition has led us. Given the ambitious goal of replacing now dominant patterns of thought with one that would redirect us toward ecological civilization, clearly more is needed than a single conference. Fortunately, a larger platform is developing that includes the conference and looks beyond it. It is named Pando Populus (pandopopulous.com)in honor of the world's largest and oldest organism, an aspen grove.

As a continuation of the conference, and in support of the larger initiative of Pando Populus, we are publishing this series, appropriately named "Toward Ecological Civilization."

-John B. Cobb, Jr.

OTHER BOOKS IN THIS SERIES

PREFACE

John B. Cobb, Jr.

PHILOSOPHY SUFFERED A MAJOR SETBACK with the advent of modernity. "Philosophy" means the "love of wisdom." Wisdom is understanding matters that are important to human beings. It is never absolute knowledge. It certainly does not claim inerrancy or infallibility. The wise person knows that her or his understanding is subject to change with more thought and experience. For Socrates wisdom begins when you know that you do not know.

Modernity has been characterized by what John Dewey taught us to call the "quest for certainty." From the perspective of the quest for wisdom, this was not a wise choice. Descartes made this new quest explicit. Because he thought he could answer with certainty the questions that philosophers were discussing, he called his work philosophy. Philosophy was redefined in terms of the topics it treated rather than its aim. What had been "philosophy" was redefined as "speculation." The idea of "wisdom" was marginalized. To avoid "speculation" those who called themselves philosophers narrowed their topics more and more. Rather than affirming truths, they analyzed meanings. Rather than talking about the world, they limited themselves to some aspect such as language. Those who took this

1

path tried to identify questions about language that other students of language were not asking. Even with all of this narrowing of subject matter, they failed in their quest for certainty. The "philosophical" students of language claim to help in the achievement of clarity. But it is rare that anyone who is not identified as a philosopher or would-be philosopher finds the work very useful.

It is, of course, obvious that my critical comments are generalizations that have many exceptions. I have abstracted one feature of modern philosophy from a far richer and more complex body of writing and asserted that the more this feature is pushed, the narrower the subject matter that can be dealt with, and the less the relevance of the discussion.

Further, I am far from alone in critiquing the quest for certainty. Especially in recent decades, many philosophers have done this. The French postmodernists have devoted much of their time to deconstructing the confident assumptions of earlier generations. The larger impact of the movement to find certainty has usually been to support skepticism and even nihilism. In other words, philosophy has played a considerable role in the shaping of the contemporary "mind."

This quest to undo and deconstruct and analyze away every supposed certainty is quite different from the quest for wisdom. In some respects the quest to undo can help us to prepare the way for the quest for wisdom. The wise rejection of all claims to certainty allows one to seek one's way carefully and reasonably in constructing the most plausible views responsive to basic questions. In short, a wise rejection supports a careful, critical, "speculative" path.

Scientists have always followed this "speculative" path. They propose and test hypotheses. Some of them are refuted by evidence and, accordingly, are rejected. But those that are not refuted are not held to be certain. They are, at least ideally, always to be reconsidered as new relevant evidence is gained. But the fact that the resulting theses are not certain does not mean that scientists do not have sufficient confidence to build on them. The vast progress that science has made on many fronts is based on working with well-tested hypotheses. Why should philosophers not follow an analogous method today as they did prior to the demand for certainty?

I am not saying that the scientists are themselves engaging in the quest for wisdom. From the beginning of modernity they undertook to be "value-free." For centuries, like all human beings, they certainly had values and were open to discussing them as a separate topic. But the quest for certainty split the world between the objects of scientific study and the values so important to subjective human beings. Given that split, wisdom has had no foothold, since all our humanly important questions involve at once questions about what reality is like and how we should think and feel and act given this information. There can be no wisdom about factual information alone or about values alone.

In the middle of the nineteenth century Charles Darwin opened the door to renewal of the quest for wisdom. He taught us that human beings are part of the nature studied by science. Cartesian dualism was no longer possible.

This paved the way for judging that, although science might proceed best by dealing only with what presents itself to us as the objects of sense experience, the full reality that it treats in this objectifying way also includes subjects who have emotions and purposes. Although one can learn a lot about a dog by studying the mechanical functioning of its body, to move, as Cartesians did, to the idea that the dog is a machine without emotion or purpose, was wrong. Our subjective feelings and purposes play a role in what we are and do, and evolutionary teaching strongly suggests that this is continuous with what other animals are and do. The dog suffered when it was tortured. It tries to escape such torture. It also tries to please its master. The dog's behavior is not accurately understood when these subjective factors are denied or ignored. The separation of facts and values is mistaken. Once this fact is taken seriously, the door is open to renewal of the quest for wisdom. True, we cannot know exactly what the dog feels or aims at. But we need not remain blankly ignorant. Our somewhat vague ideas can be indirectly checked and can be included in a broader, more realistic, nondual understanding of reality with implications for how we should live.

Many people understood this implication of the reality of evolution and have responded in this way. Some of them were philosophers who renewed philosophy in a way that is clearly continuous with what the great Greek thinkers had done. This was a great improvement over the dualisms and fragmentations that had resulted from the quest for certainty. Henri Bergson in Europe and William James in the United States may be the best known practitioners of the new quest for wisdom. They were taken seriously for a while, both in the universities and in the wider culture of their day. My teachers at the Divinity School of the University of Chicago were all neo-naturalists. That is, they all assumed that human beings are part of nature and that nature is misunderstood when it is reduced to matter in motion.

It takes nothing away from the wisdom of Bergson and James to state that Alfred North Whitehead developed the most rigorous and comprehensive philosophy of this movement. Bergson was a biologist and James, a psychologist. Their thinking was broad and universally relevant. But they were not really able to engage physics rigorously.

This proved a serious limitation because physicists had been accustomed to believing that, ultimately, biology and psychology could be explained in continuity with physics, and most people tended to accept its primacy. Everyone knew that at this stage of the development of the sciences, the full explanation had not been achieved. Biologists and psychologists had to introduce theories that went beyond what physics could explain. This was provisionally acceptable and even necessary. But it did not shake the deeper assumptions about the primacy of physics or suggest that physics was mistaken in its worldview. That worldview remained mechanistic. The ultimate explanation of biology and psychology would show that whatever distinctive features they seemed to have could eventually be replaced by physical factors.

Whitehead, as a physicist, called his vision the "philosophy of organism." He was able to show that although much could be understood about dogs (and cells, and atoms, and subatomic events) when the mechanical aspects of their functioning were studied, the evidence of contemporary physics pointed toward the primacy of organisms. This was already the case, he showed, with the emergence of field theory. Quantum theory accents this need. Whitehead's philosophy of organism undercuts the assumption that the primacy of physics justifies the primacy of mechanism. The primacy of organism entails the interconnectedness of all things and calls for what we now call ecological thinking throughout science. Whitehead's system can largely include, and be greatly enriched by, the work of Bergson and James and many other neo-naturalists.

Much to the loss of humanity, the deep-seated habit of considering the study of nature as composed only of objects led scientists, and universities in general, to marginalize and ignore the alternative view of nature. The quest for certainty ruled out discussion of alternatives to mechanism. Such alternatives were speculative, and "speculation" was a term of opprobrium. Dualism paved the way for fragmentation.

Once these neo-naturalist thinkers were excluded, nowhere in the university was there any effort to understand the whole. At the margins there has been some interdisciplinary work, and professional schools have never been able to limit themselves to the academic disciplines designed for value-free research. Liberal arts colleges have struggled to retain some concern for students and even for society. But all this has had little effect on university norms and their consequences for the university as a whole. What is most prized is value-free research conducted within the parameters and established assumptions of one discipline. In this research, many scholars think they can approximate certainty.

Some of us have thought that, despite the inability or unwillingness of universities to consider alternative assumptions to mechanism, it is important to keep more realistic views alive. I belong to the community that thinks that eventually thoughtful people will have to explore the alternative organic model for physics and philosophy. It will save them a lot of time if they will study

Whitehead. Given the dominant course of higher education and departments of philosophy, we understand the skepticism about the relevance of the organic model, but we think the change from the dominant mechanism to the organic alternative will have pervasive beneficial effects.

In June of 2015 we held a major conference on the campus of Pomona College, calling for all of us to work together toward ecological civilization. A secondary but important purpose was to persuade people that adopting Whitehead's philosophy of organism would help. To make that purpose explicit, we set aside one hour during the conference for presentations of Whitehead's relevance to each section of the conference. There were twelve sections. We envisioned making a book out of these twelve lectures. We planned the topics so that the lectures would illustrate how different features of Whitehead's thought are relevant to different topics. We hoped that a collection of these papers would persuade readers that the results of this profound quest for wisdom are relevant to all of our basic human concerns.

Matters rarely work out just as hoped. Not all the plenary speakers understood the assignments in just the way I described, and some of the best lectures fit other contexts better than this book and have already been published elsewhere. However, nine of the original lectures are included here along with three that have been written subsequently to fill in the gaps.

Each lecture stands on its own feet. Those who heard one did not hear the others. So one can read the lectures independently with assurance that they do not depend for their understanding on what precedes them in the book. It is a collection of separate and largely independent essays by very diverse authors, who approach their task in many different ways.

Nevertheless, the book is not simply a collection of papers given at the same conference. All of them undertake to provide a chapter in a book, and were planned to have continuity and unity. The sequence is designed to help develop a comprehensive view of Whitehead's system in a coherent development. We hope that the book as a whole will constitute a good introduction to Whitehead's philosophy for those who are focused on the "so what" question.

WHAT CAN TRIGGER TRANSFORMATION?

Catherine Keller

EDITORS' INTRODUCTION: *The Seizing an Alternative conference had one overarching goal: to bring together the best minds from as many fields as possible, both practical and academic, to confront the disastrous consequences of the Western worldview — the most urgent of which is climate change — and to offer an alternative. The alternative offered by presenters was the philosophy of Alfred North Whitehead, and their hope was that those persuaded by it would bring that understanding back to their professions, their disciplines, their settings. In short, the goal was to transform the way we think.*

Catherine Keller introduces this book (as well as her section of the conference) by focusing on an element of Whitehead's thought that opens the door to transformation by examining how our opinions are formed in the first place. As a philosopher, Whitehead was understandably concerned with claims people make in formulating arguments, and how they arrive at their positions. Logicians talk about "fallacies" — mistakes that are often made in argument. One may argue from a premise to a conclusion, for example, without noticing that there must be a second premise before the conclusion logically follows.

Whitehead thought that some of the most important mistakes made in reasoning have not been included in the logicians' list of fallacies. For example, he speaks of "the fallacy of the perfect dictionary." This is related to the issue of certainty emphasized in the Preface. Beginning with Descartes, some philosophers have thought they could make airtight arguments. But this would be possible only if the terms of the argument were not at all ambiguous. This would be possible only if each term could be defined unambiguously.

We can, of course, make progress toward clarifying our meaning. Whitehead is contributing to that process. But completing this task would depend on having a dictionary that provided unambiguous definitions, when, in fact, every definition can only be stated in terms of other words that are defined in terms of still other words. There is no escaping ambiguity in linguistic expressions. Since the premises of any argument have some ambiguity, absolute proof of any verbally formulated thesis is impossible.

Whitehead also identified "the fallacy of misplaced concreteness." He pointed out that we often treat our ideas as if they were actual things. For example, I have an idea of "pleasure." I might ask a group to discuss this topic. If one observes the discussion, one will often find that some speakers talk about pleasure as if it existed in itself as an actual thing. For clarity's sake, we need to recognize that although pleasurable experiences certainly occur, "pleasure" is an idea abstracted from these experiences. If we treat it as if it exists or occurs in itself, we have committed the fallacy of misplaced concreteness.

This example has some importance in sharpening the precision of our speech. However, Whitehead was convinced that the consequences of this fallacy are far more extensive than this example would suggest. It is actually committed on a large scale and with respect to very basic aspects of our thought and life. Committing this fallacy gets our whole society into serious trouble. Recognizing it and adjusting our beliefs accordingly could free us from some of our most destructive behavior.

In the conference at which this lecture was presented, Section 1, "The Threatening Catastrophe: Responding Now," had seven "tracks" (i.e., working groups). Keller pointed out the relevance of this fallacy to each of them. Though the conference structure is generally not preserved in this book, the reader should have no difficulty appreciating her discussion. There has been a little editing to reflect the shift from speaking at the outset to looking back on the conference from the present.

WE NO LONGER NEED TO BE TOLD THAT WE FACE CATASTROPHE. It is time now ask what we can still do about it. It helps to know that we have company in our misery, and that we might yet confront the future in wide and fresh alliances. The 97% scientific consensus (yes, you know already) is that the climate is changing due to the rise of the planet's average temperature driven by greenhouse gases emitted by fossil fuels. We wonder how much time we have until the dire effects kick in — of extreme weather, melting glaciers, intensified wildfires, and droughts. We glimpse the probable human devastation, in terms of mass hunger and climate migrations, with the inevitable mobilization of racist defenses and imperialist aggressions, and intensified violence over dwindling resources. The climate issue is not one issue among many, nor does it diminish or supersede our human justice issues. It entangles them.

You know that the threat needs response now. But to change our collective ways of thinking and acting, to change government and corporate practices, seems to require long-term transformation — too much time, too much improbability. Word is, we may have about 15 years to shift practices that have been developing for centuries, entrenched since the coal-fired Industrial Revolution and locked in since 1980 and the capital-fired Reagan-olution. (Reagan never met a millionaire he didn't like or a tree that didn't look like all the others; but that now seems bland by present standards of destruction.) There is too much to change way too fast: as Hamlet lamented, the time is out of joint. Naomi Klein, in *This Changes Everything: Capitalism vs. the Climate,* writes in her introduction: "It means there is a whole lot of stuff that we have been told is inevitable and that simply cannot stand. And it means that a whole lot of stuff we have been told is impossible has to start happening right away."[1]

The change can seem impossible. But, she adds, "nothing is inevitable." As stated in this conference section's description: "We do not believe that the extinction of the human race is inevitable." Admittedly, that is a pretty low bar for hope. So maybe you also ask with John Cobb "what actions now have the best chance of reducing the inevitable die-off and providing grounds for a healthier and more sustainable civilization for the survivors?"

OK, so all of the conference tracks, in all different ways, dug and scratched for answers to that painful kind of question. This work takes courage. You might annoy the powers of denial. And it takes grieving what has been and will be lost. We don't get to hope by avoiding grief. But hope is not optimism or pessimism: The hopeful look like Pollyanna among pessimists and like spoilsports among optimists. Hope is the embrace of the possible in the face of what looks impossible. As did the terminating of legal slavery, or of the nuclear arms race, or of apartheid, or of bans on gay marriage.

Am I even sounding Pollyannaish to draw that kind of precedent for this crisis? After all David Griffin has titled his important climate change book: *Unprecedented*. We might at best say that we have precedents for facing the unprecedented. But this unprecedented CO_2 crisis does make us acknowledge that catastrophe on a global scale is to an unpredictable degree now predictably unavoidable. *That* is a serious downer.

And that is what *catastrophe* means — literally — in the Greek: down-turning. *Kata* means 'down.' And totally. A catastrophe is an irreversible down-going. It does *not*, however, mean the end of the world. Or even of the species. Much specialized work is needed in response to specific threads of threat. But it is only worth the pain because there is a further twist to the down-turning. Catastrophe can be what turns us *down-to earth*. Of course this may mean dust-to-dust: picture the permanent dust storm and drought of the earth in the movie *Interstellar*. But like so much post-apocalyptic imagination, that movie only finds salvation by rocketing off to start in another galaxy. The ultimate technological cop-out. It is the secular version of supernaturalist transcendence of the earth.

Dust to dust: the phrase liturgically means to facilitate mourning; to remind us that we are mortal, that we are like Adam, made of *adamah,* dirt, dust. It is not an image of dead matter but of the great recycling strategy of the planet. Turning down to earth is for us as a civilization now catastrophic because our philosophies, religions, and sciences have led us ever onward and upward, imagining ourselves to be minds transcendent of bodies, subjects mastering a world of objects: this is a posture of abstraction, with very concrete effects. Already in the 17th century Lord Chancellor Bacon declared the way of knowledge as power—over the earth and all its creatures. It was the great modern misreading of the dominion passage of Genesis 1. In its modern form, dominion funds the delusion of a smoothly separate subject dominating and profiting from a world of smoothly knowable objects. And what that subject *doesn't* know is how abstract his (well, mostly *his*) separation of himself from the actual world actually is. Nothing wrong with abstraction. But there is something delusional about confusing the abstract separateness with the concrete. And so this is getting at the odd notion I am supposed to introduce you to in this lecture: "the fallacy of misplaced concreteness." It is the habit we have of mistaking our abstractions for concrete realities. Of course this whole idea might sound pretty abstract. But it is my assignment.

By turning *up*—up, up, and away, in a delusional transcendence of our earth, our civilization has produced a catastrophic *down*-turning. That is ironic. So we need the reverse irony: catastrophe turning us down to earth in a way that does not wipe us out but transforms us. Of course seizing an alternative will, one way or another, involve a massive turning down—of the energy. But I also have imprinted on my mind something Cobb said to me when I was a student here, on a walk, 35 years ago: "What we need is enough ecological catastrophe that people wake up, and not so much that it is too late." Still true?

In other words, can catastrophe be a catalyst?

To trigger concrete action, however, talk of the climate remains too abstract for many: it gets mixed up with weather, or with those teensy numbers like 2 degrees. Ecology gets hidden ever more intentionally by getting itself abstracted from the human and economic realities in which it is all too concretely entangled. Here comes again the fallacy of misplaced concreteness. We mistake the notion of "the environment" for a smooth object of knowledge and manipulation, separable from our culture, ourselves. The very language of global warming, the Anthropocene, climate change, can get too smooth, can't it? Which is why Whitney Bauman prefers to call it "climate weirding."[2] The catastrophic weirding can, he thinks, be faced in a prismatic—not just green—and so queerly resilient way.

It is this colorful spectrum of issues and alliances that I think we are about here—that bears the hope of a livable way down-to-earth. Our alternative is not about a single issue. It may sometimes be tempting to say that climate change leaves all of our other movements and vital concerns—race, sexuality, class, war–in the dust. And *that* is the sort of self-defeating zero-sum game that progressives must unlearn really fast. I had to learn this about my feminism decades ago *vis à vis* race, sex, religion, and of course ecology. Our righteous single-issue simplifications are fighting stereotypes, but they become another way of misplacing our concreteness. Our concrete, embodied existence remains incredibly complex. Of course we can't help conveniently simplifying the world with abstractions; we use them several times a sentence. The problem is how they turn into cookie cutters, chopping the universe into us/them, man/woman, culture/nature, good/bad, humans/animals, etc., etc., etc.

Naomi Klein puts it succinctly: "The environmental crisis—if conceived sufficiently broadly—neither trumps nor distracts from our pressing political and economic causes: it supercharges each one of them with existential urgency."[3] For instance, she writes carefully about the colonial synergy of racism, classism, and the civilization built on extraction [starting with coal]. So our extractivist civilization offers up peoples and cultures along with their habitats as "sacrifice zones." The ethicist Cynthia Moe Lobedo works similarly on the "race debt of climate change."

To be really concrete: the particular entanglement of the non-human and human systems of the earth in the system of global, corporate capitalism, so-called neoliberal capitalism, is what is producing the catastrophe and is what must be changed.

Already in the 80s Cobb tracked this interlinkage in the ground-breaking work, *For the Common Good: Economics for Community, Ecology and a Sustainable Future.* He conspired with economist Herman Daly to expose how the discipline of economics has justified our system of increasingly unregulated capitalism. Everything that is not calculable in terms of growth and profit is called an "externality"—irrelevant to the system. That includes human well-being or misery, the beauty of a city or a landscape, species survival or extinction, ecological sustainability: all external to the purely numerical calculations that produce wealth. In this way, economics insulates itself from other disciplines, even politics, let alone ethics or ecology.

In other words, Daly and Cobb showed that neoliberal economics is the major planetary instance of—you got it—Whitehead's fallacy of misplaced concreteness. With money, we think we are trading in concrete goods and services, but capitalism reduces exchange to the quantifiable abstraction of money and washes everything else out of view. Like a tidal wave. The liberation theologian Joerg Rieger wrote *A Rising Tide* to expose the fallacy that the rising tide of economic growth lifts all boats. With Pacific Island states in immediate jeopardy, the metaphor of rising seas is getting rapidly less abstract! In the meantime the CO_2-addicted super-corporations continue through each regime to systematically extract themselves from social and democratic accountability. And a critical mass of the North American public either buys into the system or ignores—as too abstract—the economic links to racism, to the poisoning of their bodies and their futures, just trying to get through the concrete challenges of each day.

This does not sound hopeful. But here lies the secret of *This Changes Everything*. Klein recognizes that

> the kind of counter-power that has a chance of changing society on anything close to the scale required is still missing. It is a painful irony that while the right is forever casting climate change as a left-wing plot, most leftists and liberals are still averting their eyes, having yet to grasp that climate science has handed them the most powerful argument against unfettered capitalism since William Blake's "dark Satanic Mills" blackened England's skies (which, incidentally, was the beginning of climate change).[4]

The mining of coal fired up the Industrial Revolution and modern economics. But the point is that the planetary threat is now evident—and the economic causes are clear to anyone with eyes to see. So here is what she thinks: The double jeopardy of social injustice and global warming should not discourage us. Climate change, with its

> rising flood waters—could become a galvanizing force for humanity, leaving us all not just safer from extreme weather, but with societies that are safer and fairer in all kinds of other ways as well. . . . It is a matter of collectively using 'the crisis to leap somewhere that seems, frankly, better than where we are right now.'[5]

In other words, wait for it! This joint capitalist-climate crisis can trigger transformation. Catastrophe can turn into catalyst.

Klein expresses hope about the concrete means of transformation represented by "Blockadia." It exemplifies a real and happening set of social movements standing up to the fossil fuel extraction giants, a coalescence of multiple coalitions no longer waiting for governments to act or markets to find green solutions, but willing to put their collective bodies in the way of extractivist progress. She stresses the moral force of these emergent coalitions between first peoples and indigenous groups with environmentalists, farmers, and students around the world. Many of them are in the Pacific Northwest, like the activists of the SHell No! blockade. These are very concrete instances of creative entanglement, weaving a glocal web: the relationality is highly intentional. For instance, a statement of gratitude now up on the 350.org website was sent to the Northwest activists from the Pacific Climate Warriors who in traditional hand-carved canoes paddled into the port of Newcastle in Australia to thousands of people on land. This is catalytic agency bubbling up from below.

David Griffin adds another view on needed agency. *Unprecedented* offers a superbly—and concretely—deployable map of our climate situation. He does so in three sections: "Unprecedented Threats," "Unprecedented Challenges and Failures," followed by "What Is to Be Done?" He is mostly in synch with Klein on what the transition to clean energy and the abolition of dirty energy will involve. Yet for him activist movement from below is how we may provoke the needed action from above. He is asking the president [Obama at the time] to declare a national emergency. James Hansen has announced that "we have a planetary emergency" that could destroy civilization. Griffin draws the irrefutable inference: "Because the destruction of civilization would involve the destruction of the United States, the planetary emergency is obviously a national emergency." Emergency action is needed now. Then, for instance, "all fossil fuel subsidies will be turned into subsidies for the various types of clean energy." "A price [would] be put on carbon with a means to prevent the carbon fee from increasing overall costs to poor and middle-class citizens." He adds bullet points for roles that academics, activists, religious groups, and the media would play.[6]

Of course that top-down approach seems dangerous since the subsequent election: the deployment of the power of emergency would most certainly go the opposite direction.[7] Nonetheless on principle his vision does not contradict but complements Klein's emphasis on blockadia. He concretizes our political possibilities—which is not to say, probabilities.

Griffin's proposal is now itself supplemented by another trigger of transformation: a voice that seems to come from high above, but twists down into dramatic solidarity with the common. Whatever our religion or irreligion, we may now celebrate the fact that the most influential single voice of moral authority on the planet, that of the pope, released a new encyclical on June 16, 2015, subtitled *On the Care of our Common Home*. Francis proposes an "integral ecology" that encompasses concerns of economic justice, true human development, and global solidarity. (Not all Catholics are pleased: Rick Santorum wants the pope to "leave science to the scientists." Interesting, coming from a guy who thinks 97% of scientists are wrong about climate science; and ignores the fact that Francis is a trained scientist, holding a Master's in chemistry from the University of Buenos Aires.) And in the meantime, the process response — including a new book by Griffin — has been vigorously public and published.[8]

Cobb, Klein, Griffin, Francis: these are thinkers not confusing abstractions with actualizations, but mobilizing abstractions *for* actualization. And that is the Whiteheadian point. We do not need to shift from thought to action — we need to activate, to enact, our thinking of the common good.[9] What was once held in common was turned into commodity — and the very notion of the common, the commoner, the shared commons, was degraded as boringly average or threateningly socialist. So Klein writes at the conclusion of her book that: "any attempt to rise to the climate challenge will be fruitless unless it is understood as part of a much broader battle of worldviews: a process of rebuilding and reinventing the very idea of the collective, the communal, the commons, the civil, and the civic after so many decades of attack and neglect."[10]

Can we imagine and activate our planetary commons as a fabulous patchwork of local collectives, slowing down to earth and at the same time interacting in speedy global networks, constructing new kinds of relations and coalitions, holding governments responsible? Might we rise to the occasion of planetary emergency? And wouldn't such a new public becoming mirror and amplify the fast-slow becoming that occasions each of us? We then refuse to remain subjects cookie-cut into separate consumer units. You are not a separable knowledge/

power identity remaining abstractly the same through time: you are each a happening, an event of becoming. You are improvisational in the sense Jay McDaniel performs globally in the Jesus, Jazz, and Buddhism website.[11] For you are mindfully resourced by the radical complexity of relations, good, bad, and neutral, which make you up at this very moment, you in your becoming together: radical, from *radix,* root, entangled in each other. Those roots suggest a rhizome. Like the Pando grove in Utah.[12]

Each track in the conference was aimed at being an improvisational becoming. Very concretely here and now, aiming at concrete effects across the live collective that is the earth. To be catalysts in the face of catastrophe we need to collect our stories, parables, images, as well as abstractions (such as compose Whitehead's corpus) that are recognized as abstractions. Ideas then can serve not as distractions and extractions from the concrete, but as possibilities for actualization of the concrete. To be concrete in the discussion of misplaced concreteness, we will consider briefly each of the seven tracks that made up Section 1.

[1] Catastrophic Climate Change

This has been the focus of the above remarks, so I will add only this: with Tom Hayden teamed up with David Griffin, there was no danger that climate change would be abstracted from the ferment and evolution of social movements, from issues of race, of war and peace, and even (this is, after all, the author of the Hayden Act) of the concrete lives of misplaced animals.

[2] The Technological Response: Geoengineering

This track did not promote phantasmagoric last minute techno-fixes. Klein writes that the risks of geoengineering scenarios sound abstract but must be reckoned with now. "That's because if geoengineering were ever deployed, it would almost surely be in an atmosphere of collective panic with scarce time for calm deliberation. Its defenders concede as much. Bill Gates describes geoengineering as "'just an insurance policy'. . . We would very likely not be dealing with a single geoengineering effort but some noxious brew of mixed up techno-fixes—sulfur in space to cool the temperature, cloud seeding to fix the droughts it causes, ocean fertilization in a desperate gambit to cope with acidification, and carbon-sucking machines to help get off the geo-junk once and for all."[13] *Snowpiercer* depicts the risk postapocalyptically: it takes place in the aftermath of the techno-sci answer to global warming. The coolants brought on a deep freeze that rendered life on earth extinct, but for survivors on a train running on an ugly class hierarchy.

Nonetheless technology remains crucial to our "turning down" to earth—through breakthroughs in affordable solar and wind and other sensitive innovations. Kevin O'Brien and Forest Clingerman led reflections on technologies not abstracted from the complex body of the planet, but working cannily within its shifting, weirding, delicate interactions.

[3] The Threat of Massive Hunger

For most of us here, real hunger—as opposed to voluntary fasting or dieting—is itself an abstraction. Yet the desire for the next meal is as concrete a sensation as we mammals experience. The fallacy of misplaced concreteness exhibits its most agonizingly concrete symptom in this threat.

As Lester Brown puts it in *Full Planet, Empty Plates*: "Food is the weak link in our modern civilization—just as it was for the Sumerians, Mayans, and many other civilizations that have come and gone. They could not separate their fate from that of their food supply. Nor can we."[14] So can the food catastrophe turn to cata-lyst as more folk in the global North recognize our entanglement? The author of *Poison Spring* led this track. Evaggelos Vallianatos has exposed how the EPA actually colludes with the chemical-industrial complex to poison our lands and waters—our food sources—with ever more toxic chemicals.

And, of course (tangles within tangles) the great chemical-industrial fixes of fossil fuel-driven agribusiness are partly responsible for the changing climate of which drought is the most pressing effect, and then the acidification of the oceans, with seafood the main source of food for more than 3 billion people. "Feeding some 9 billion people by mid-century in the face of a rapidly worsening climate may well be the greatest challenge the human race has ever faced."[15] Can the concreteness of local alternatives make a serious difference?

[4] Just Peacemaking: Response to Threats of Catastrophe

Led by Paul Bube and Jay McDaniel, this track explored how just peacemaking is not—just peacemaking! Of course climate change and hunger mobilize folks for war. And nowhere does the insanity of our civilization haunt us more vividly than in the undead specter of nuclear war. Talk about the fallacy of misplaced concreteness: we displace sheer evil onto an enemy, and goodness onto ourselves, with such cookie-cutter stereotypes that we can contemplate annihilating them without harming ourselves. The alternative principle was given its greatest U.S. idiom by Martin Luther King: "Whatever affects one directly affects all indirectly."[16] He articulates an ontology for non-violence: "All life is interrelated, and we are all caught in an inescapable network of mutuality, tied in a single garment of destiny."[17] That inescapable network re-places the misplaced concreteness. It is not accidentally related to early process thought. Nor to Gandhi. As Jay McDaniel tracks it in *Gandhi's Hope,* multiple religions and cultures learn to move from catastrophic competition to catalytic cooperation.

[5] Economic System Transformation

Do we agree that Seizing an Alternative means the redirection of the economy toward a COMMON GOOD? Toward a sustainable future for humans living responsibly and diversely in our common home, *oikos* (that is the Greek for the eco of economy and ecology)? Climate weirding is outing the substitution of abstract quantities—like money—for the concreteness of the common good. So can we embrace the improbable hope of a new coalition between those seeking economic justice and those blocking corporate extractivism? Is there a pathway emerging, complex, uncertain, adventurous—winding along the edge of chaos? If there is, these trackers are among its trailblazers. This track, adventurously led by David Lewit, sought the path "to a humane, ecological, global economy by 2030." Does the number sound fallaciously concrete? I don't think so. It is naming the time that remains, the interval the changing climate may grant us in which to reinvent our planetary commons.

[6] Political Collapse

Nations with their deceptively absolute boundaries are the modern poster children for the fallacy of misplaced political concreteness. But the same fallacy, operating in the abstraction of the GDP, paradoxically empowers the corporate weakening of good domestic laws and protections. As politics is hijacked by capitalism, the life of nations falters between aggressive manipulations and reactionary resentments. And some states fail. And here a catastrophic concreteness shows its face in the interaction between climate change and failing states. Let me offer one example, a Huffington Post piece by Charles Strozier:

> As the Obama administration undertakes a highly public, multilateral campaign to degrade and destroy the militant jihadists known as ISIS, ISIL and the Islamic State, many in the West remain unaware that climate played a significant role in the rise of Syria's extremists. A historic drought afflicted the country from 2006 through 2010, setting off a dire humanitarian crisis for millions of Syrians. Yet the four-year drought evoked little response from [Bashar] al-Assad's government. Rage at the regime's callousness boiled over in 2011, helping to fuel the popular uprising. In the ensuing chaos, ISIS stole onto the scene, proclaimed a caliphate in late June and accelerated its rampage of atrocities.[18]

Read Parenti's *Tropic of Violence* for a map of the many situations in which reporting abstracts religious violence from underlying climate change issues. But with John Culp's dauntless leadership this group focused on promising movements and experiments—especially at the local level. Movements down to earth! Yes! And even more relief is on the catastrophe-horizon.

[7] Organizing for Change and Sustaining Involvement

The topic of this track was the experiential life of the environmentally aware and active person. How do you survive emotionally, morally, and spiritually when we are in the midst of a slowly, irrevocably unfolding disaster? Each person has to confront the bad news and what it means for life on earth. How are we to remain active and alive, whole and sane, in the face of the truth?" Roger Gottlieb seems never to cease interlinking the force fields of climate, global warming, disability, sexual injustice, religious violence, and doing so precisely in order to discern the delicate network of alternatives. Turning catastrophe into catalyst may require not just public action but some wild thinking, contemplative practices, nonhuman companionship, storytelling strategies, surprising affections.

These topics all require focused attention, but each calls for and contributes to all the others. This is all about our entanglement in an endless network of mutuality. We need the vision and the practice of our improvisational interrelatedness amidst what Whitehead calls the democracy of fellow creatures, or what Vandana Shiva calls planetary democracy. We all need to participate in collective grief-work. And hope-work. To become, together, triggers of transformation, away from the unsustainable, we need to sustain our own and each other's involvement—long term, so that we can respond now.

Klein considers the despondent question "How can you persuade the human race to put the future ahead of the present?" Her important answer: "you don't. You point out . . . that for a great many people, climate action is their best hope for a better present, and a future far more exciting than anything else currently on offer." [20]

ENDNOTES

1   Naomi Klein, *This Changes Everything: Capitalism vs. The Climate* (NY: Simon & Schuster, 2014), 28.

2   Whitney A. Bauman, "Climate Weirding and Queering Nature: Getting Beyond the Anthropocene" *Religions* 2015, 6(2), 742–54; doi:10.3390/rel6020742

3   Klein, 153.

4   Klein, 156-57.

5   Klein, 7.

6   David Ray Griffin, *Unprecedented: Can Civilization Survive the CO2 Crisis?* (GA: Clarity Press, 2015).

7   See my forthcoming *Political Theology of the Earth: Our Planetary Emergency and the Struggle for a New Public,* (NY: Columbia University Press, 2018), for a discussion of the authoritarian political theology of sovereign power "in the exception," i.e., in manipulation of emergency.

8   See Ignacio Castuera and John B. Cobb Jr., editors, *For Our Common Home: Process-Relational Responses to Laudato Si'* (Anoka, MN: Process Century Press, 2015) and David Ray Griffin, *Protecting Our Common, Sacred Home: Pope Francis and Process Thought* (Anoka, MN: Process Century Press, 2016).

9   For more on this, see Melanie Johnson-DeBaufre, Catherine Keller, and Elias Ortega-Aponte, editors, *Common Goods: Economy, Ecology, and Political Theology* (New York: Fordham Press, 2015); see also Stefano Harney and Fred Moten, authors, *The Undercommons: Fugitive Planning and Black Study* (Minor Compositions, 2016).

10   Klein, *This Changes Everything,* 460.

11   The JesusJazzBuddhism has been renamed Open Horizons (https://www.openhorizons.org/).

12   "Pando is the name of the largest organism on Earth, and one of the oldest—a quaking aspen that extends over 100 acres from a single root"; from the Pando Populus website: https://pandopopulus.com/.

13   Klein, 276–77, 279.

14   Lester R. Brown, *Full Planet, Empty Plates: A New Geopolitics for Food Scarcity* (NY: W. W. Norton & Company, 2012), 122.

15   Joseph Romm, "Desertification: The Next Dust Bowl," in *Nature* 478 (October 26, 2011): 450–51.

16 Martin Luther King, Jr., Letter from a Birmingham Jail, 1963 (https://www.africa.upenn.edu/Articles_Gen/Letter_Birmingham. html).

17 Martin Luther King, Jr., "Remaining Awake Through a Great Revolution," Oberlin College Commencement Address, June 1965 (http://www2.oberlin.edu/external/EOG/BlackHistoryMonth/ MLK/CommAddress.html).

18 Charles B. Strozier and Kelly A. Berkell, "How Climate Change Helped ISIS," in Huffington Post (September 29, 2014).

19 Jackie Kay, "Extinction," in *The Guardian* (May 15, 2015).

20 Klein, *This Changes Everything*, 156.

꒰ 2 ꒱

PHILOSOPHY IS NOT JUST FOR PHILOSOPHERS:

Breaking Philosophy Free of Philosophy for the Sake of the Planet

Wm. Andrew Schwartz

EDITORS' INTRODUCTION: *Catherine Keller has introduced us to the central concerns of the conference where these plenary addresses were delivered. What can we do to mitigate the suffering and reduce the losses that are now inevitable? How can we prepare now to build something better on the ruins of collapse? She noted that Naomi Klein pointed to the need for changes in the basic way we understand the world. A sub-theme of the conference and especially of these section plenaries was that Whitehead's philosophy can help.*

We began by showing that Whitehead warned against particular mistakes that have been made and are still being made on a massive scale, and we featured the fallacy of misplaced concreteness. Our dominant Western philosophies have tended to teach us to think of individual objects as fully actual in themselves. This means that we can abstract them from their context without changing them. This belief leads to an economic, political, religious, and cultural individualism that causes us to ignore or deny our interdependence and our need for one another and a healthy environment. We also suppose that mind is separable from matter and matter from mind. Facts are thought to be separable from values and values from facts. Our universities are divided up into disciplines that

27

reify their independent subject matters, when the problems we face as human beings know no such boundaries. Humanity desperately needs wisdom, but our "value-free" research universities are not organized to help us.

Whitehead does not just call our attention to the fact that we are making mistakes. He also develops a complex system of thought that provides a truly basic alternative. This is, of course, a philosophy. But it is philosophy in the classic sense, one that does not fit into the narrow confines of philosophy as an academic discipline. Given the belief of the conference organizers that a change of philosophy is crucial to a healthy response to the catastrophes we face, we placed a section on philosophy right after the treatment of immediate pressing issues. We want to show that the bias against philosophy is just as serious a problem as adherence to the wrong philosophy, that it actually allows the wrong philosophy to shape our thinking uncritically. We need to ask philosophical questions and to reflect carefully about alternative answers if we are to treat one another and other creatures differently. Only good philosophy can replace bad philosophy.

We unabashedly recommend Whitehead's thought as leading us in a better direction. We hope the discussions in chapters 3 through 12 will show some of the ways it supports our better intuitions. You can skip this chapter and still learn a good deal about Whitehead from later chapters. However, if you can lay aside any bias you may have against philosophy, you will not only find this chapter interesting and informative, but the rest of the book, too.

PHILOSOPHY HAS GOTTEN A BAD RAP. In the wake of the industrial revolution, and in the face of mechanistic thinking, "science" is presented as the champion of all disciplines. After all, it is the scientific method that has given us antibiotics, cars, cell phones, computers, and Netflix. What good is philosophy? Asking the same old questions for thousands of years, and getting no closer to answers—whether sporting long beards and togas, or short beards and corduroy jackets with patches on the elbows[1]—philosophers are widely considered irrelevant to modern society. Pondering paradoxes and intellectual puzzles doesn't produce tangible results that enhance our daily lives. In a 2016 Republican presidential debate, Senator Marco Rubio received applause from the audience when he said, "We need more welders and less philosophers."[2] People want utility. A college degree that yields a job. A job that yields an income. And, in our framework of capitalism, that means producing something of

"I understand 'food for thought,' but I still can't let you pay with your philosophy thesis."

"value"—something others would be willing to pay for. People want cars to go places, bridges to help get them there, and buildings for shelter upon arrival. All of these require welding—a skill that directly leads to the production of items deemed valuable by society. That means welders (and their skills) are deemed valuable. Companies are willing to hire people to be welders because they can make a profit selling goods produced by welders. It's a chain of supply and demand. Not many have the luxury of being paid a fulltime salary to sit around and ponder the meaning of life; because such musings don't appear to yield a desirable product. One might recommend that philosophers get into the transportation business—with all the hot air they produce, surely they can make a killing fueling hot air balloons, right?

But how do we define value? By what process do we decide which skills are valuable? Why should value be tied to goods, services, and monetary standards? Give me an argument for why we need more welders and fewer philosophers, and I'll show you a philosopher (with a mirror . . . because you are the philosopher). I believe part of the resistance to (or devaluing of) philosophy is a reaction to institutionalized philosophy as an academic discipline. But there is more to philosophy than linguistic Rubik's cubes. Arguably, philosophy—or at least assumptions that presuppose philosophical perspectives—rests at the heart of our civilization. What we need is not fewer philosophers, but to free philosophy from philosophy. I mean this in two senses: 1) to free philosophy, the practice, from the boundaries of philosophy strictly understood as an academic discipline, and 2) to free philosophy from the controlling hands of the philosophers—giving it to the people, since philosophy is not just for philosophers. Both of these points require further reflection. By freeing philosophy from philosophy, it becomes a tool for everyday life; a tool that can assist average citizens in challenging the core assumptions which undergird our present society on the verge of collapse, and exploring alternatives toward ecological civilization.

While I am a big fan of air-conditioning and frozen pizza (thank you, science), I believe philosophy is one of the few remaining resources that can help us seize alternatives in order to avoid (or at least survive) global catastrophe. This is not because we need to inject philosophy into a situation void of philosophical thinking, but because "doing" philosophy is wholly unavoidable. We are always, already, doing philosophy—most of the time unwittingly, which often entails doing so poorly.

PHILOSOPHY EVERYWHERE

> *"Why does philosophy matter?" "I don't know, why does science matter?" "Well because scie-" "Annnnnnnd you are doing phi-losophy."* Existential Comics (Twitter: August 4, 2015)

Philosophy (from the Greek, *phileo*: love; *sophia*: wisdom) literally means the love of wisdom. And since only a fool hates wisdom,[3] I guess that means that everyone who isn't a fool is a philosopher—a lover of wisdom! When put that way, I expect more people would be ready to claim their place among the philosophers—among the non-fools. As with most words, however, etymology doesn't quite do justice to a robust understanding of a term. In general, philosophy has emerged in two distinct senses: formal and casual.

In the formal sense, philosophy is limited to an academic discipline. As such, philosophy is sometimes understood as the study of the fundamental nature of knowledge, reality, existence, language, values, reason, etc. This can include the analysis of propositions, using reason to solve practical problems, or attempting to make sense of our experiences. Certainly this description of philosophy is simplistic, as there is an entire discipline called "metaphilosophy," which treats philosophy as a subject for philosophical inquiry. To answer the question, "what is philosophy" is to be doing metaphilosophy. Though one may ask whether or not "doing" metaphilosophy already presupposes an answer to the question. Since metaphilosophy is itself a philosophical project, doing metaphilosophy involves adopting a method which is already presupposed as "philosophical." Consequently, one could ask whether there is a meta-metaphilosophy that treats metaphilosophy as a subject for philosophical inquiry. Following this path could lead to an infinite regress that either takes for granted a notion of philosophy (therefore undermining the project of metaphilosophy), or eternally accomplishes nothing beyond asking the question—"what is philosophy?"

In casual speech, philosophy can simply be a foundational attitude that acts as a guiding principle for behavior. In many cases, philosophy is spoken of as synonymous with rational thinking, or any attempt to answer the "why" questions.

I don't see the two senses as mutually exclusive. The formal use of philosophy as an academic discipline does not mean philosophy cannot also be a foundational attitude or guiding principle for behavior. These two senses of philosophy can be inclusive (even complementary). It is philosophy (in both the formal and casual sense) that needs to be freed from philosophy in the formal sense.

Naomi Klein argues, as noted by Catherine Keller in the previous chapter, that "any attempt to rise to the climate challenge will be fruitless unless it is understood as part of a much broader battle of worldviews: a process of rebuilding and reinventing the very idea of the collective, the communal, the commons, the civil, and the civic after so many decades of attack and neglect."[4] While sociologists, political theorists, economists, and the like will see Klein's challenge as the responsibility of their respective disciplines, it is in fact the very ghettoizing act of disciplinizing that contributes to a destructive fragmentization — a fallacy of misplaced concreteness — that simultaneously contributes to climate change and impedes solutions to the same.

This has been outlined eloquently by people like John Cobb and Catherine Keller. Disciplinization requires setting artificial boundaries to distinguish one "discipline" from another. Disciplinary boundaries are abstractions, but are concretized in the creation of academic departments, societies, and journals. As such, rather than helping organize and arrange complex themes into workable categories, disciplinary boundaries become concrete divisions that fragment the quest for knowledge. This is an example of the *fallacy of misplaced concreteness* (also known as reification — where abstractions are mistaken as actual things). John Cobb puts it this way, "This fallacy flourishes because the disciplinary organization of knowledge requires a high level of abstraction; and the more successfully a discipline fulfills the criteria established for it, the higher is the level of abstraction involved. Inevitably, many practitioners of successful disciplines, socialized to think in these abstractions, apply their conclusion to the real world without recognizing the degree of abstraction involved."[5]

So long as everyone stays in their own discipline, responses to the climate crisis will be fragmented, and progress will be marginal. A powerful and comprehensive solution can only emerge out of integrative cooperation across all fields of specialization. It's not as if expertise is the problem. Not everyone can be an engineer. Not everyone can be a physicist. Not everyone can be a surgeon, a musician, or an educator. We need each of these experts (and more!) if we are to build a sustainable future — an ecological civilization.

But to do this, we must overcome the fallacy of misplaced concreteness in the form of disciplinization. That is, we must all recognize the abstraction involved in the separation of the disciplines and the truly interconnected nature of all fields. It is not as if the phenomena studied in sociology exist in separation from those studied in economics, which exist in separation from those studied in agriculture, which exist in separation from those studied in education. The world itself is not divided in this way. Once practitioners of a discipline are socialized to think in its terms, they expect the theories developed in the discipline to have direct relevance to the actual world. Whether in fact they do depends on factors from which they have abstracted their data. When, in response to this awareness, they try to work in an interdisciplinary way, the improvement is limited. Adding together theories based on different sets of abstractions does not recover the original unity. With this in mind, for me to say that "philosophy" is an essential solution to Klein's concern, I do not mean philosophy—a discipline—to the exclusion of other disciplines. Rather, I mean a "philosophical way" that considers the situation as a whole, employing the work of the disciplines only with full recognition of the consequences of misplaced concreteness. This is a philosophy free from itself.

THE PROCESS-RELATIONAL PHILOSOPHICAL WAY

> *I have endeavoured to outline an alternative cosmological doctrine, which shall be wide enough to include what is fundamental both for science and for its critics. In this alternative scheme, the notion of material, as fundamental, has been replaced by that of organic synthesis.* ~ Alfred North Whitehead, *Science and the Modern World,* 157

The problem of disciplinization represents a deep underlying problem in our dominant educational model (particularly in Higher Ed). So long as we are constrained by disciplines, our knowledge will be fragmented. It is often assumed that simply bringing together each of the separate disciplines (bringing together the parts) will result in a whole, complete picture. This is, in part, the goal of increasingly popular transdisciplinary education. However, this, too, is built on mistaken assumptions. Specifically, this model fails to recognize the importance of internal (as opposed to external) relations. In truth, the whole is much more than the sum of its parts.

> Put simply, external relations treat the self-identity of a thing as the first, analytically given fact, while internal relations treat it as the final, synthetically developed result. . . . On the other hand, the mereological relations of part and whole from which extension is built, are themselves so intrinsically correlative to one another that each only meaningfully expresses its own relational structures to the extent that it completely internalizes the other.[6]

Well, I guess that is "put simply" for an academic philosopher. Put *even more* simply, "internal relations" is a way of talking about how the identity of an "actual entity," (Whitehead's name for the experiences that actually make up the world) is constituted by its relation to other actual entities. "In so far as there are internal relations everything must depend upon everything else."[7] When it comes to disciplines, problems ensue when we treat physics as separate from biology and chemistry, or agriculture as separate from economics, and expect that bringing these separate disciplines together will result in a complete picture. Instead, what must happen is a realization that not only should every field of inquiry recognize that its work always necessarily abstracts from the full reality of what it studies, but also that its theories are interconnected with those of all other fields of inquiry.

The notion of internal relations is not simply an additional category, but an alternative theory about the way the world works. The philosophical term for this sort of discourse is *metaphysics*. The philosopher who has developed the metaphysics and cosmology of internal relations most fully is Alfred North Whitehead. Whitehead's philosophy has been described a "philosophy of organism," and it is part of a family of philosophies known as "process philosophy" or "process-relational philosophy." Process thought provides a unique explanation for how the world works. Most basically, the process perspective argues that many of the problems in our world today (problems in philosophy, science, society, etc.) grow out of a mistaken understanding about the nature of the world—of metaphysics— treating abstractions as if they were the actual reality. Often this is a matter of viewing the things that make up the world as physical substances when in fact events or happenings are more fundamental. This is a problem because it fails to grasp the dynamic and ever-changing nature of the world, as well as the internal relatedness of things. Whitehead proposes a metaphysical shift from "static being" to "dynamic becoming" that understands reality in terms of "actual occasions," rather than objects or substances.

In his short book, "What is Process Thought," Jay McDaniel offers a few key ideas for understanding process thought.

1) No one crosses the same river twice: being is becoming.

2) No person is an island: all things are interconnected.

3) Seeing heaven in a wildflower: all living beings have value.[8]

Because everything is, like a river, constantly moving and changing (becoming), Whitehead needed a way to explain how something that is always changing can be fully actual. He came up with the concept of "concrescence." Concrescence is simply the process of becoming "concrete." As John Cobb explains, "Concrete means fully actual, and that means a completed actual occasion [an entity]. The use of the term "concrescence" places emphasis on the idea that even these momentary flashes of actuality that Whitehead calls actual occasions are processes."[9]

The process of becoming fully actual (becoming "real" or "concrete") also involves something Whitehead calls "prehension." Prehension is the process of becoming what one is, by virtue of one's relation to the past. As Cobb explains, "Prehensions are the way that what is *there* becomes something *here*. A prehension is the bond between two actual occasions. The past occasion shares in the constitution of the new occasion."[10] This is not an external bond, but an internal one, by which the prehending being (entity) internalizes its relatedness to the rest of the world. We become what we become through our prehensions—always (at least partly) constituted by the past.

Together, the process of prehension and concrescence explain what it means for everything to be a process of interrelated becoming. The third notion, that all life has value, is a conclusion that arises from understanding the interconnected process of becoming. The importance of this metaphysical shift—a shift in the way we think about how the world works—is deeply practical. To assume, for example, that deforestation in Indonesia is irrelevant to buying lotion in California is a failure to recognize the interconnectedness of things (a metaphysical mistake with serious practical implications). As such, Whitehead's philosophy—a philosophy or organism that emphasizes becoming, interrelatedness, and the value of all things—can help overcome some of the major obstacles facing a transformation toward ecological civilization.

WHY PHILOSOPHY MATTERS: ECONOMIC GROWTH—ANOTHER FALLACY

Philosophy is often identified with abstraction, and it is not usually a compliment. This is because philosophy is thought to deal in the realm of ideas apart from concrete realities, in contrast to the "concrete" work of the "hard" sciences. Ironically, even this notion of abstraction has been abstracted from—that is, withdrawn from the idea of abstraction in order to consider the general quality of abstraction itself—such that "abstraction" has become synonymous with "unrealistic" or "impractical." Again, we see that when we concretize the abstraction of abstraction it leads to a fallacy of misplaced concreteness—a false separation between ideas and reality, between the practical and the abstract. Certainly, if philosophy is seen as affiliated with abstraction, and abstraction is understood as unrealistic and impractical, then it's easy to see why philosophy is seen (by so many) as irrelevant to practical concerns. What I am suggesting, however, is that philosophy is essential to everyday life and practical matters. This is not to say that philosophy is unrelated to abstraction, but that abstraction is essentially connected to reality.

In *Science and the Modern World*, Whitehead speaks of "the accidental error of mistaking the abstract for the concrete. It is an example of what I will call the 'Fallacy of Misplaced Concreteness.' This fallacy is the occasion of great confusion in philosophy."[11] Put another way, failure to recognize abstractions for what they are—abstractions—is a source of many problems in philosophy. This is not an objection to abstractions as such, but to treating the abstract as if it were concrete. This is an important distinction, since Whitehead isn't rejecting abstractions. After all, specialization is essential to achieving the level of precision necessary to make significant advances in knowledge; while thinking in abstractions is wholly unavoidable—and philosophy can help us to manage this.

All concepts that reflect or represent our physical realities are abstractions. The concept of "cow" is an abstraction from particular animals in the world, categorized together due to apparent shared qualities. As John B. Cobb, Jr. notes, "In concrete experience there are no points. Everything we experience has some extension. The idea of a point is an abstraction . . . it [was] important to develop a definition of a point that showed how it is derived by abstraction from experience."[12] It is not as if the concepts "cow" or "point" are particularly problematic as concepts, but if we confuse "cow" in the abstract with particular animals referred to as cows, we encounter problems. Also, if we suppose that points exist as actual things, we will misunderstand the nature of the actual world.

Societies, social contracts, laws, money—these are all abstractions with incredible significance for our daily lives. When it comes to the possibility of developing an ecological civilization, basic aspects of society must be recognized as inherently abstract. Among the fallacies of misplaced concreteness most clearly problematic for building an ecological civilization are those fallacies related to economics. In their award winning book, *For the Common Good: Redirecting the Economy Toward Community, the Environment, and a Sustainable Future*, Herman Daly and John Cobb demonstrate how many of the problems with our current economic theory and practices are rooted in mistaking an abstract economy for something concrete.

Daly and Cobb refer to "money fetishism" in economics as a "classic instance of the fallacy of misplaced concreteness."[13] They state, "It [money fetishism] consists of taking the characteristics of the abstract symbol and measure of exchange value, money, and applying

 them to the concrete use value, the commodity itself. Thus, if money flows in an isolated circle, then so do commodities; if money balances can grow forever at compound interest, then so can real GNP, and so can pigs and cars and haircuts."[14] What is the relation between a taco and the dollar used to pay for it? Why is it that I can give you a dollar and you will give me a taco (or two tacos if it's Tuesday)? Are tacos and dollars of the same kind? The taco is not a symbol; it is a taco, you eat it. Can you eat the dollar? Perhaps, but it's not recommended. What then is its purpose? Unlike the taco, whose value is found in its physical uses (i.e., food), the value of the dollar is symbolic — social agreements and numbers on computers. Numbers are abstractions. There is an infinity between 1 and 2 (e.g., 1.1, 1.11, 1.111, etc.), as well as from 1, 2, 3, to infinity. So, while it is easy to consider a scenario where, as Cobb and Daly explain, we conceive of money flow in an isolated circle (or perhaps upward spiral) that can continue infinitely, to assume that the production of tacos can follow a similar model of unlimited expansion is a failure to recognize the limits of the physical components that make up a

taco. It is the mistake of applying one's conclusion (developed at the level of abstraction) to the real world without recognizing the degree of abstraction involved.

As Cobb-Daly explain,

> Indeed, money balances do not imply the existence of any real goods at all . . . The concentration on money and the market rather than on physical goods, with the concomitant decision to model itself on the methods (but not the content!) of physics, has been characteristic of the whole of modern economics. This paved the way for the primacy of deduction and the focus on mathematical models and computer simulations that are the hallmark of current practice in the discipline. Such elaborate and beautiful logical structures heighten the tendency to prize theory over fact and to reinterpret fact to fit theory.[15]

The problem of economics is not unrelated to the problem of disciplinization discussed above. For it is within economics *as an academic discipline* that

> the complexities of the impact of economic growth on the economy, are largely ignored. Again, this is not because it has been shown that these relationships are not important. It is because the disciplinary organization of knowledge requires a separate subject matter for economics, for demography, for sociology, and so on.[16]

Economics, when confined as an academic discipline, encourages (if not requires) a set of blinders that allows economists to be economists and think only about economics, which implies keeping economics separate from other concerns. Hence, economists are less likely to consider the impact of a particular economic model on the environment, in so far as environmental concerns are brushed away as "externalities."

In critique of neoclassical economics and the problem of externalities, Daly and Cobb state,

> One of the most important [fallacies] is the abstraction of a circular flow of national product and income regulated by a perfectly competitive market. This is conceived as a mechanical analog, with motive force provided by individualistic maximization of utility and profit, in abstraction from social community and biophysical interdependence. What is emphasized is the optimal allocation of resources that can be shown to result from the mechanical interplay of individual self-interests. What is neglected is the effect of one person's welfare on that of others through bonds of sympathy and human community, and the physical effects of one person's production and consumption activities on others through bonds of biophysical community. Whenever the abstracted-from elements of reality become too insistently evident in our experience, their existence is admitted by the category 'externality.'[17]

Translated generally into ecological concerns, failure to recognize the degree of abstraction present in economic theory (and money fetishism in particular) has led to the rationalization of an unlimited exploitation of natural resources—assuming that the availability of real goods (water, trees, crops, soil, tacos, etc.) will increase in the same way that neoclassical economic theory tells us money can. In this way, the fallacy of misplaced concreteness exemplified in economics is not an irrelevant philosophical obsession, but a philosophical mistake that threatens our very existence.

PUTTING PHILOSOPHY TO WORK

A philosophy for the people and for the sake of the planet means philosophy as a tool for overcoming the deeply rooted and mistaken assumptions that have led our civilization toward catastrophe. The problem is not simply that we have taken our environment for granted, or that the notions of progress and growth have been wrongly applied to a world with limits. The real problem is an attitude of objectification that understands nature as a commodity.

Western philosophy (or more generally, Western intellectual discourse) has been dominated by "thing" language; so much so that it is difficult to talk about any*thing* without using the term. One of the problems inherent in "thing"-dominated discourse is the tendency to emphasize objects over subjects. Such emphases have contributed to an alienation from nature, ignorance of internal relations, and failure to recognize human impacts on the environment.[18]

As Whitehead notes, "To be abstract is to transcend particular concrete occasions of actual happening. But to transcend an actual occasion does not mean being disconnected from it."[19] Abstractions are not the problem. The world of particulars and concrete actuality is not the problem. The problem is confusing the two — conflating the abstract with the concrete, which entails a neglect of both particularity and abstraction. "It is recognized that the man in the street tends to think in naively realistic terms. He tends to think of the reality or the things he experiences as being independent of his experience."[20] A process-relational philosophy can help remind us of the interrelatedness of all things, of the importance of not confusing abstractions with concreteness, and the value of all life. We don't need fewer philosophers, we all just need to do philosophy better — and soon.

ENDNOTES

1 And yes, the stereotype is male.

2 Though I'm sure what Rubio meant was "fewer" philosophers.

3 Proverbs 1:7 (author's paraphrase).

4 Naomi Klein, *This Changes Everything: Capitalism vs. The Climate* (NY: Simon & Schuster, 2014), 460.

5 Herman E. Daly and John B. Cobb, Jr., *For the Common Good: Redirecting the Economy toward Community, the Environment, and a Sustainable Future* (Boston: Beacon Press, 1989), 25.

6 Gary L. Herstein, "Alfred North Whitehead," in *Internet Encyclopedia of Philosophy* (accessed February 16, 2016).

7 Alfred North Whitehead, *Science and the Modern World*, 1925 (New York: Free Press, 1967), 163.

8 Jay McDaniel, *What is Process Thought: Seven Answers to Seven Questions* (Claremont: P&F Press, 2008), 8–11.

9   John B. Cobb, Jr., *Whitehead Word Book: A Glossary with Alpha-betical Index to Technical Terms in* Process and Reality (Claremont, P&F Press, 2008), 59.

10   Cobb, *Whitehead Word Book*, 31.

11   Whitehead, *Science and the Modern World*, 51.

12   Cobb, *Whitehead Word Book*, 16.

13   Daly and Cobb, *For the Common Good*, 37.

14   Daly and Cobb, 37.

15   Daly and Cobb, 38.

16   Daly and Cobb, 33.

17   Daly and Cobb, 37.

18   Even the language "the environment" with a definite article, is **objec**tive. That is, at least, when it is concretized. When left as an abstraction, "the environment" is simply a category for talking about the natural world. Yet again, "the natural world," is an abstraction and linguistically objective. Perhaps the best way to avoid objectifying nature and non-humans is to name them. Not so much because a rose by any other name wouldn't smell as sweet, but because objects are only passive recipients of actions done by subjects. To recognize that we are as much dependent on nature as nature is dependent on us (that we are interdependent and internally related) is to recognize nature as both subject and object. Historically, only subjects yield respect, whereas objects are mere possessions (e.g., slavery).

19   Whitehead, *Science and the Modern World*, 159.

20   John B. Cobb, Jr., *Is It Too Late?: A Theology of Ecology* (CA: Bruce, 1972) 101–02.

> 3 >

HAVE YOU EVER WONDERED WHAT
IT'S LIKE TO BE A CHIMPANZEE?

Nancy R. Howell

EDITORS' INTRODUCTION: *Some of the worst instances of misplaced concreteness are committed when humans talk about what constitutes humanity. People whose ethical sensitivity is shaped by the culture of India will have a leg up on Whitehead. Ethics there has long been sensitive to the intrinsic value of all "sentient beings." Our traditional Western ethical thinking in general deals only with human beings and relationships among us.*

In Western thought, rarely is our treatment of other animals viewed as part of ethical theory or moral teaching. One sometimes has added, as an afterthought, that we should not treat our animals cruelly, but the explanation is likely to be that we may develop habits that carry over to our treatment of humans. The anthropocentric character of ethics was already present in ancient Greek and Hebrew thought and the medieval teachings that took root in these traditions. Descartes only made modern ethics worse by declaring that the physical world, including nonhuman animals, is purely material.

This chapter, in part, was previously published as "Locating Nature and Culture: *Pan-Homo* Culture and Theological Primatology," *Verbum et Ecclesia* 36, no. 3, Art. #1440, 2015: 9 pages. http://dx.doi.org/10.4012/ve.v36i3.1440.

*Presupposed, of course, is that there is some all-important charac-
teristic of human beings that other animals totally lack. One proposal,
stemming from the Greeks, is that human beings are rational whereas
other animals are not. Some Christians proposed that human beings
have immortal souls, whereas other animals do not. Descartes taught us
moderns that human beings have subjective experience, whereas other
animals do not. After the acceptance of evolutionary theory, the distinction has often been made in terms of using tools or language.*

*Whiteheadians do not question that species of animals differ from
one another, and that there are real differences between human beings
and other species. Most Whiteheadians believe that human beings have,
in general and overall, richer and more valuable experiences than any
other species. But for one who follows Whitehead, this does not mean
that every human being has richer and more valuable experiences than
every member of all other species. Not every member of the human
species at all times and places is more rational than every member of
another species. Humans have certainly developed more complex tools,
but they are by no means the only tool users. Language is not unique to
humans. Of course, certain kinds of language may be unique to humans,
but the capacity among animals to communicate meaningfully and
practically, and the capacity of animals to learn human languages, is
well documented.*

*The result of careful study and reflection by no means warrants treating
all members of the human species as worthy of a moral consideration
of which no other creatures are worthy. For us, every actual entity has
some value in itself and also for others. Some conclude, from the moral
considerability of all, the idea that all should be treated as equally worthy.
Whitehead rejects this move. He noted that "Life is robbery." That is,
from unicellular organisms to humans, to live is to use and destroy other
living things. This is the fact of entropy. Whether plants taking nutrients
from the soil, or humans consuming plants, robbery is a basic component
of sustained life. There is no way in which we can avoid doing harm.
Whitehead goes on to say, "The robber requires justification." We cannot,
of course, do exact calculations, but to be morally responsible is to weigh*

the damage that we inflict on others against the gains. In most cultures, there is agreement that killing another person weighs far more heavily in the balance than killing a rabbit for the family dinner. Some judge that those who can live healthy lives without eating the flesh of other animals should consider doing so.

This example of a Whiteheadian consideration is simply one example of the vast range of issues that arise once we give up notions of radical difference between ourselves and other animals. There is no one position on these matters to which all Whiteheadians subscribe. Some emphasize ecosystems as our central concern; some focus on species; some, on individuals. All these interests are well grounded in Whitehead's theory of value. What we can, without hesitation, say is Whiteheadian, is this: that we include in our ethical reflections the other living things with which we share this planet.

It is one thing to accept this idea theoretically; it is another to do so existentially. Nancy Howell has lived into a recognition of other animals as making demands on our moral consideration far more than most of us. Her lecture at the conference was designed to challenge not only the theoretical beliefs of her hearers but also their actual decision-making. If you want to live in our cruel world with equanimity, read this chapter at your own risk.

CONCENTRATION KEEPS ME ATTENTIVE TO DETAILS, but also makes me selective about what is pushed to the margins. Sometimes I regret what I've missed. On a visit to the Iowa Primate Learning Sanctuary a few years ago, I was intensely focused on committee business at hand. My colleague asked me an odd question, 'Did you see a rabbit?' I dismissed the question, knowing that we were indoors and that no rabbits inhabited the premises — only bonobos and dogs. When my meeting ended, two caregivers for the bonobos told me a story. Panbanisha, a female bonobo particularly gifted with lexigrams and language, had asked for M&Ms and ice. She was on a diet and realized that she should not have candy, so she decided (perhaps) that mixing the candy with ice would dilute the calories. The caregivers than asked her, 'Who would you like to bring you the M&Ms and ice?' Panbanisha pointed to two lexigrams: gorilla and rabbit. In response, the caregivers dressed in gorilla and rabbit costumes and brought the requested foods. For all my concentration on the business at hand, I had missed the most interesting event of the day. A rabbit had actually hopped through the lab.

The event with Panbanisha may be anecdotal, but the scenario is not unique. Anderson Cooper visited the bonobos to film for his CNN program 'Anderson 360' (AC360). Panbanisha and Kanzi asked to see his promised surprises in the demonstration of their language ability, and then Cooper found himself dressed in the bunny suit and delivering pine needles, eggs, bread, green beans, and ice. Though embarrassed by his costume, Cooper understood the reason for Panbanisha's request: the video skits used to facilitate learning language when she was young included a character dressed in a bunny costume. Her memory of the skits lingered in her communication and relationships.

Though not rising to the status of reproducible data, these recollections suggest that humans and animals have engaged in cultural exchanges involving memory, communication (perhaps even language), imagination, negotiation, and learning. I wonder whether enough anecdotes of this sort might convince humans that nonhuman animals are not merely social, but cultural beings. Consequently, my claim in this reflection is about the importance of primate studies for overcoming our sense of the nonhuman as quite alien to us. It can start with the specific observation that the bifurcation of nature and culture may be an unsustainable feature of any worldview, which includes extraordinary status for humans (at least, some humans) as a key presupposition.

METHOD AND CHALLENGES

I didn't set out to undertake this research; I think I was goaded into the project by a number of scholarly challenges. The first challenger was Stephen Jay Gould, noted Harvard University naturalist, whose book *Ever Since Darwin: Reflections in Natural History* (1977) posed a serious question for philosophers:

> Chimps and gorillas have long been the battleground for our search for uniqueness; for if we could establish an unambiguous distinction — of kind rather than of degree — between ourselves and our closest relatives, we might gain the justification long sought for our cosmic arrogance. The battle shifted long ago from a simple debate about evolution: educated people now accept the evolutionary continuity between humans and apes. . . . But we are so tied to our philosophical and religious heritage that we seek a criterion for strict division between our abilities and those of chimpanzees. . . . Many criteria have been tried, but one by one they have failed. The only honest alternative is to admit the strict continuity in kind between ourselves and chimpanzees. And what do we lose thereby? Only an antiquated concept of the soul to gain a more humble, even exalting vision of our oneness with nature. (50-51)

'What do we have to lose?' is the question that sticks with me. What real difference does it make that humans and animals might be admitted to be very, very near kin? Shall we humans simply wait until apes have crossed the nature/culture line, which has functioned as one criterion used, not just to separate humans and apes in kind, but sometimes also used to be sure that the distinction in degree is sufficient to keep a safe distance?

The next challengers appeared casually on the front cover of *Science* magazine in 1999. The cover announced the report of "Cultures in Chimpanzees" (Whiten *et al.* 1999), first published in *Nature* and collaboratively authored by a number of scientists noted for their field work in Africa (including, of course, Jane Goodall).[1] The metastudy systematically compiles observational data from seven regions of Africa with interesting notations of the variations in behaviors among diverse groups of chimpanzees. The kinds of differences range from distinctive forms of tool use to access food to different styles of vocalizations and grooming. The scientists propose that the distinct behavioral differences point to cultural variation among the chimpanzees, and they define culture as "any behaviors common to a population that are learned from fellow group members rather than inherited through genes" (Whiten et al. 1999:682).

Obviously the primatologists' definition is not without controversy, and anthropologists are likely critics because cultural anthropology typically reserves the term *culture* for humans and understands culture to be mediated linguistically. On the other hand, biologists suggest that behavior moves from generation to generation by means of genetics and social learning—and both have an effect on evolutionary change. As the article in *Science* (Whiten et al. 1999) explained:

> From this perspective, a cultural behavior is one that is transmitted repeatedly through social or observational learning to become a population-level characteristic. By this definition, cultural differences (often known as 'tradition' in ethology) are well-established phenomena in the animal kingdom and are maintained through a variety of social transmission mechanisms. (682)

As if the collaborative article is not bold enough in its claims about chimpanzees, note that the quoted statement indicates that the phenomenon of animal culture or tradition is well established broadly.

The third influence and goad for my research is attention epistemology, a methodological concept described in Sallie McFague's book, *The Body of God: An Ecological Theology.* Attention epistemology pays attention to concrete, particular being outside oneself and setting aside oneself: "Attention epistemology is listening, paying attention to another, the other, in itself, for itself." (1993:49). Attention epistemology is knowing that requires setting aside vested interest in the instrumental or utilitarian value of the other while engaging in wonder at the intrinsic value of the nonhuman other. McFague writes:

An attention epistemology is central to embodied knowing and doing, for it takes with utmost seriousness the differences that separate all beings: the individual, unique site from which each is in itself and for itself. Embodiment means paying attention to differences, and we can learn this lesson best perhaps when we gauge our response to a being very unlike ourselves, not only to another human being (who may have a different skin color or sex or economic status), but to a being who is *in*different to us and whose existence we cannot absorb into our own—such as a kestrel (or turtle or tree). If we were to give such a being our attention, we would most probably act differently than we presently do toward it—for from this kind of knowing—attention to the other in its own other, different embodiment—follows a doing appropriate to what and who that being is. (50–51)

The embodied knowing expressed in attention epistemology requires a decentering of human self for the sake of centering another creature as the focus of observation, wonder, and regard. Such knowing negotiates and interprets embodied difference without diminishing the value of the newly known other and with astonishment at the detail and elegance of its being.

Attention epistemology encourages two directions in my work. First, attention epistemology has challenged me not only to be precise about which species are my focus, but also to understand complex intra-species differences and to remember the names (e.g., Kanzi) of individual nonhuman animals.[2] Second, I have become aware of how tempting discovery of behavioral data supporting preconceived notions can be. If one species' behavior presents an anomaly, we can easily move to another species to support an argument. Rather than cede my argument to biological convenience then, I have chosen to focus on chimpanzee and bonobo ethology, learning, and cognition— regardless of whether their behavior supports my case. The Great Apes are an empirical test of the comprehensiveness, coherence, and integrity of my proposals.

APE CULTURE AND NATURE

Recently my reflection has been inspired by Kanzi, a bonobo, who is the undisputed celebrity in the *Pan-Homo* culture shaped by multiple forms of language and communication. Terrence Deacon, author of *The Symbolic Species,* has declared Kanzi to have "the most advanced symbolic capabilities demonstrated by any nonhuman species" (1997:124), and Deacon's understanding of the term *symbol* follows Charles Sanders Peirce and connotes "some social convention, tacit agreement, or explicit code which establishes the relationship that links one thing to another" (124). The bonobo-human culture, most recently located in Des Moines, Iowa, in the United States, is a generational and longitudinal experiment in language culture, especially involving the use of lexigrams for communication.

Language studies with apes are not new, but the early successful work involved teaching American Sign Language to apes who were cross-fostered with humans. Washoe is a noted chimpanzee who was born circa 1965 and died in 2007. She was part of Allen and Beatrix Gardner's study, which suggested that teaching vocalizations of English to apes made less sense than teaching a gestural language to animals who already communicate with gestures. Roger Fouts' book, *Next of Kin* (1997) is an account of his long-standing project with Washoe and a small group of chimpanzees, which continues at the Central Washington University Chimpanzee and Human Communication Institute. Nim Chimpsky, recently remembered in the film *Project Nim,* was born in 1973 and died in 2000. Herbert S. Terrace of Columbia University led a rather large group of students in the effort to teach Nim American Sign Language (Hess 2008). The gorilla Koko (born 1971 and still living) is famous for her empathetic connection with a pet kitten, and Koko's language learning occurred with Francine Patterson (Patterson and Linden 1981). Critics of the American Sign Language studies are suspicious of the claims that the animals actually understand grammar and syntax and allege that the human participants must be signaling or over-interpreting the ape signs. At best, the critics are willing to acknowledge that some apes can name objects, but naming is not the same as language ability. Some of the dispute may be related to different levels of understanding of the structure of ASL and to different interpretations of the nature of language and communication.

Not all language studies involve sign language; some studies have used lexigrams as symbolic representations of words. Lana, who was born in 1970, was the first chimpanzee to be part of the language analogue (LANA) project, which investigated language ability in apes. Rather than using gestural language, the project required Lana to use a computer keyboard to select symbols or lexigrams representing English words. She was able to sequence words grammatically and create novel expressions. Important in this work was Duane Rumbaugh's invention of random symbols representing words and the lexigram keyboard, which made communication possible. Lana gained some facility with the keyboard, but her language abilities were limited (primarily to food requests) (Savage-Rumbaugh and Lewin, 1994:48, 183).

The next phase of the research involved Sherman (born 1973) and Austin (born 1974), both of whom also used the LANA keyboard. With Sherman and Austin the focus was peer communication because language is related to sociality. While Lana, the chimpanzee, achieved the ability to make requests, she did not comprehend language, especially when asked to respond to communication from others. Consequently the work with Sherman and Austin concentrated on placing language usage in contexts that facilitated understanding (Savage-Rumbaugh and Lewin, 1994: 126). Savage-Rumbaugh writes that the work with Sherman and Austin involved a new approach to ape-language research:

> Consequently, by focusing on the ability of Sherman and Austin to comprehend symbols, we were forced to develop paradigms in which the execution of the symbol and the ape's receipt of some object or activity associated with that symbol became completely detached. This marked a dramatic break with all other ape-language efforts, and it led to the

apes recognizing that symbols can be used to communicate information about a specific object, event, or whatever without being tied to the occurrence of that event. (126-27)

Ape language studies then advanced to verifiable communication expressing future intentions (127). Sherman and Austin did not learn to understand spoken English (63, 177). However, they spontaneously developed important aspects of communication—chimp-to-chimp peer communication—using the lexigrams: attending to each other's communications, engaging each other before communicating, gesturing to clarify messages, and taking turns at communication (84). The sociality and cooperation of the chimps increased with more complex usage of language.

The project entered a different phase when bonobos became the center of attention. Kanzi was born to Lorel, a female bonobo from the San Diego Zoo, on October 28, 1980 (Savage-Rumbaugh and Lewin 1994:121). Matata, an African-born female bonobo, adopted Kanzi on the day he was born (with some plaintive resistance from Lorel) (122).

Matata was part of the language study at the Language Research Center, but initial work with her was not proving very successful (Savage-Rumbaugh and Lewin 1994:127). Matata was able to distinguish one lexigram symbol from another, and she could make requests for food, but she could not respond to lexigram communication from others (129).

Kanzi was an active and playful infant around Matata and was interested in the lexigrams, trying to grab them as they flashed on the keyboard (Savage-Rumbaugh and Lewin 1994:129). Matata was an indulgent mother with Kanzi (130) and was a patient and interested student, but she did not progress in the systematic training program (as well as Sherman and Austin had) (130). Yerkes made the decision to separate Kanzi from Matata for a few months while she was sent to breed with Kanzi's father, Bosondjo (132)—and Kanzi was introduced to the language learning program.

Something remarkable happened next:

The day after Matata's departure, we set up the keyboard in the expectation that Kanzi would begin his language instruction — if he could learn to sit in one place long enough. Kanzi, however, had his own opinion about the keyboard and he began at once to make it evident by using it on more than 120 occasions that first day. I was hesitant to believe what I was seeing. Not only was Kanzi using the keyboard as a means of communicating, but he also knew what the symbols meant — in spite of the fact that his mother had never learned them. For example, one of the first things he did that morning was to activate 'apple,' then 'chase.' He then picked up an apple, looked at me, and ran away with a play grin on his face. Several times he hit food keys, and when I took him to the refrigerator, he selected those foods he'd indicated on the keyboard. Kanzi was using specific lexigrams to request and name items, *and* to announce his intention—all important symbol skills that we had not recognized Kanzi possessed. (135)

Kanzi demonstrated for the researchers that enculturation in a language community is key to learning language, which suggests that language training of older chimpanzees and bonobos should be expected to produce less successful language usage and comprehension in apes. Kanzi's language enculturation within the *Pan-Homo* family resulted in his ability to communicate using lexigrams, but also to comprehend spoken English.

The lexigrams are central to the language learning studies with Lana, Sherman, Austin, Matata, and Kanzi. The lexigrams are not pictures of the objects or actions, but are random geometric symbols. They include nouns, verbs, prepositions, and interrogatives — which are significant grammatical parts of speech for constructing sentences that describe observations, name objects, and make requests. Two interesting aspects of the lexigrams are rather surprising. First, the lexigram keyboard includes written words below the symbols, so that more human persons in the lab may use them to communicate. Second, the bonobos have developed ability to recognize the written words, too, and now some words are written rather than having a geometric symbol.

Not all primatologists agree that the best approach to studying language learning and comprehension in apes begins with training apes to use existing or created human language models. Andrew R. Halloran, author of *The Song of the Ape: Understanding the Languages of Chimpanzees* (2012) is actually a skeptic about ape capacity for human language. Following Herbert Terrace (who attempted language studies with Nim Chimpsky in Project Nim), Halloran claims that gorillas (e.g., Koko) and chimpanzees (e.g., Nim and Washoe) can be *trained*, but not taught American Sign Language. Unfortunately the apes fall far short of being able to arrange the signs in any appropriate or understandable order (even though they choose appropriate signs) (2012:59).

In spite of Halloran's skepticism about "training" apes to use human language, he advocates for study of ape language itself—and offers his "conversion" experience in an anecdote about ape communication and collaboration. Halloran worked at a Florida animal park and one day rowed his boat to the chimpanzee island for the purpose of routine cleaning of a building. A small group of chimpanzees who were loyal to Higgy (a deposed alpha male) opportunistically commandeered the boat, which was not secured to the shore. Halloran heard his coworker yelling, threw down his broom, and walked outside to see Higgy driving the boat with a gondola pole. In the boat were Higgy's last allies: "the neurologically impaired male named Elgin; an unpredictable and vicious female named Gin; Hank's oversized mother, Cindy; and a very small sixty-eight-year-old female named Little Mama" (Halloran 2014:4). Halloran was/is convinced that the boating excursion was no accident, but a "planned and orchestrated escape" from the competing new alpha male Hank and his allies.[29] But, how was the escape plan communicated? Halloran writes, "The five chimps in Higgy's alliance somehow knew to get on that boat with Higgy at the instant the situation presented itself. The chimps aligned with

Hank knew *not* to get on the boat." (2012:7) Halloran further recalls his response to the incident:

> The incident had a profound effect on me. I kept thinking of how planned and orchestrated the escape seemed to be. I began to wonder how this orchestration was communicated. . . . I was preoccupied with the notion that, perhaps, chimpanzees communicated on a deeper and more complex level than I had ever imagined. Perhaps chimpanzees had their own language; a language which, unlike other forms of animal communication, was learned, differed from population to population, had definitions, had a structure, and conveyed information that didn't necessarily relate to a present time or place. (2012:7-8)

As a consequence of this experience and observation, Halloran developed a new approach, which eliminated "training" apes to use human languages and instead examined the vocalization and communication already present in the apes. Instead of teaching chimpanzees a human language and assessing whether apes can be proficient in the language of another species, Halloran believed the project of ape language studies might best be conducted by looking at how apes already communicate. In other words, human researchers should be learning ape language.

Hence, Halloran's research involves detailed recordings of chimpanzee vocalizations, with an ear to the context and meanings of their communications. His statistical study of calls and their correlation with specific meanings includes also the cultural divergence of calls (between Higgy's group which remained in Florida and Hank's group which moved to Lincoln Park Zoo in Chicago). Halloran's hypothesis is that if "chimpanzees learned their own vocalizations, like human language, then it stands to reason that these vocalizations would evolve (like human languages do). The evolution would begin as a slightly different dialect then, eventually, become its own system of vocalizations—a separate chimpanzee language" (Halloran 2012:186). Halloran's assumption is based, in part, on earlier research about culture in wild chimpanzees, which demonstrated that chimpanzee communication is not genetically determined, but is a matter of learned group-specific vocalization (186).

Central to debates about what differentiates humans and apes is the discussion of language, so I will take the language issue as an important case that obfuscates the discussion of human uniqueness in evolutionary perspective. The rhetorical character of the discussion lends to the confusions and imprecision of the debate because scholars can sometimes become casual about what constitutes uniqueness, which I understand to be something unparalleled (one of a kind). Clarification of language capacity in humans and apes rests in deciphering what is meant or intended by *language*—and the discussions range from grammar and syntax to symbolic representation and a wider concept of communication.

Barbara King, author of *The Dynamic Dance: Nonvocal Communication in African Great Apes* (2004), pushes a broader understanding of communication in African Great Apes in the wild. Using the metaphor of "dynamic dance," King refers to long-term data on African apes to say that gorilla, chimpanzee, and bonobo communication occurs within a socioemotional context—not only social, but more emotionally grounded and related—that facilitates strategic planning for the future, as well as attachment to social partners (22). The complexity of communication is that meaning is not merely signaled or symbolized by one individual and then interpreted by another. As King understands communication, meaning emerges by co-regulation rather than in linear transfer of information (52). King describes co-regulation:

> Co-regulation implies, by its very definition, internally related, nonindependent elements—nonlinearity. When co-regulation is taken into account, we can see that information is not transferred by facial expressions, body movements, gestures, and vocalizations, nor by bits of information that they supposedly carry. These movements (of the face, body, limbs, or vocal tracts) *become communicative*

when the social partners enter into interaction. The social partners are anything but autonomous, because they may transform each other as they act. (52)

Further, King explains, "The relevant process in social communication is not transfer, but emergence. . . . Rather, mutual understanding is something that *emerges* as both partners converge on some shared feeling, thought, action, intention, etc. Far from following some predetermined format, such a process is intrinsically creative" (King 2004:52).

As King broadens an interpretation of communication, her "main goal in pursuing qualitative research on African Great Apes is to assess whether and when co-regulated social interactions mediated by gesture and body movement result in coordinated social behavior within dyads, families, or social groups" (King 2004:74).

The central point, for my purposes, is to emphasize that communication (even among humans) is not merely the translation of words and their relationships into meaning, but is a much more complex process that involves vocalizations, gestures, facial expressions, body position, and nonverbal sounds.

Given Halloran's and King's additions to the discussion of ape language, I return to Kanzi and Panbanisha (his half-sister). Kanzi and Panbanisha are best known for their work with Sue Savage-Rumbaugh, who insightfully discovered that "training" or teaching apes language using lexigrams is far less successful than enculturating bonobos in a *Pan-Homo* family fluent in both spoken English and lexigrams (which now include representational geometric symbols for words, as well as spelled words alone or with lexigrams). A less well-known publication authored by Sue Savage-Rumbaugh and others (2004) includes an interesting communication experiment to surface non-stereotyped vocalizations.

The protocol began with information communicated by the

speaker using a silent keyboard to one of the bonobos or visually by presenting some object. (The silent keyboard is simply a handheld panel containing 348 printed lexical images, and the speaker communicates by pointing at the desired symbol.) The bonobos were located in various separated caging areas, which prevented the receiver of the information from having access to the visual information transmitted to the first bonobo. Once the information was communicated, if the first bonobo did not vocally communicate it to the second bonobo, the first bonobo was asked to do so. A second experimenter, blind to the information, requested the second bonobo to use the keyboard, or in some cases photographs, to translate the vocal information, except in cases when the translation occurred spontaneously. (Savage-Rumbaugh et al. 2014:567)

One simple example of the method: "The caretaker told Kanzi (who was in the first sleeping room) that we're going to have yogurt, by using only the silent keyboard. Kanzi was asked if he would like to announce this to Panbanisha. Kanzi vocalized, then Panbanisha vocalized in return and selected 'yogurt' on the keyboard for the caretaker in front of her cage" (Savage-Rumbaugh et al. 2014:567).

Kanzi and Panbanisha, therefore, have multiple modes of communication because of their enculturation. In addition to typical bonobo vocalizations, the bonobos use lexigrams and spelled words, understand spoken English, and utter unique non-stereotyped vocalization to communicate what the English and lexigram equivalents say. The experiment shows that "*they can be asked to vocalize to another, as well as the other bonobos at the center and to tell one another specific things— and they respond by so doing, making it quite clear that their vocalizations are under voluntary control*" (Savage-Rumbaugh et al. 2014:567). Because Kanzi and Panbanisha understand "human symbolic exchanges" and because they have the "capacity for modulating their speech to produce human-like words, one would also expect them to utilize their vocal abilities to convey semantic information to one another"(567). The significance of the vocal translation of English and lexigrams to communicate between bonobos is not a matter of genetic programming (not even of gestures), but is a combination of imitation, learning, and creating novel language attributable to the *Pan-Homo* culture within which they were reared.

Western thinkers from the Greeks to the present age have tended to depict human beings as fundamentally superior to other animals. As a result, the word "animal" does not usually include human beings. We ask how we are related to animals, or even more broadly, to nature. Even after Darwin showed that we are one species alongside others, most thinkers have not changed the dualism of their thought about human beings and animals, or nature, or the environment.

The dualism rarely expresses simply difference. It typically justifies dualism and an exploitative attitude toward what is not human. Nature remains an "other" sometimes to be feared, mainly to be reshaped for our short-term gains. This alienation from nature, we now recognize, hinders our efforts to change our way of being in the way toward sustainability. But most of our philosophy and culture and language work against overcoming this alienation.

Learning of the similarities with other animals works against thinking of ourselves as fundamentally separate from them. Sadly, the disciplinary compartmentalization of the university tends to limit the learning to specialists in a few fields. We also need systematized ways of comprehensive thinking that reshape our thinking so as to see the world as a vast plurality of interrelated entities. All are similar in some respects. All are different in other respects. Difference gives us the richness of diversity. Each species and each individual makes a distinctive contribution.

One can derive this vision from a number of sources today. But the one that is most fully developed is that of Alfred North Whitehead. For him, everything is, or is composed of, actual occasions of experience. Every occasion is unique. Every occasion is a value for itself and in itself. Every occasion depends on the earlier occasions that make up its actual world and affects all those in its future. In all these respects the occasions of experience that constitute a human person are no different from those that collectively make up a stone.

The world needs stones, and human persons add immensely. What human beings add is much the same as what chimpanzees and bonobos add, yet it is also different. Each bonobo makes a different contribution and so does each human being. When we see ourselves and others in this radically pluralistic and Whiteheadian way we are both humbled and given pride. We are not alienated.[3]

ENDNOTES

1   The issue of *Science* reported the study in an article by Gretchen Vogel (1999).

2   See my essay "Relations between *Homo sapiens* and Other Animals: Scientific and Religious Arguments" in *The Oxford Handbook of Religion and Science* (Howell 2006). In the essay, I describe the complexity of concepts of similarity and difference between humans and nonhuman animals.

3   I am indebted to John B. Cobb, Jr., for his contribution to these concluding paragraphs.

BIBLIOGRAPHY

"AC360—Anderson Cooper Entertains Bonobo Apes in Bunny Suit." https://www.youtube.com/watch?v=qsUHuurFLXM/.

"Chimp Memory Beats Humans'" https://www.youtube.com/watch?v=C18jtrWYQio.

Deacon, Terrence W. 1997. *The Symbolic Species: The Co-Evolution of Language and the Brain.* New York and London: W. W. Norton & Company.

Fouts, Roger, with Stephen Tukel Mills. 1997. *Next of Kin: My Conversations with Chimpanzees.* New York: Avon Books Inc.

Goodall, Jane, 1986, *The Chimpanzees at Gombe: Patterns of Behavior,* Cambridge, MA: Harvard University Press.

Goodall, Jane,, with Phillip Berman. 1999. *Reason for Hope: A Spiritual Journey.* New York: Warner Books.

Gould, Stephen Jay. 1977. *Ever Since Darwin: Reflections in Natural History.* New York: W. W. Norton & Company.

Halloran, Andrew R. 2012. *The Song of the Ape: Understanding the*

Languages of Chimpanzees. New York: St. Martin's Press.

Hess, Elizabeth. 2008. *Nim Chimpsky: The Chimp Who Would Be Human.* New York: Bantam Books.

Howell, Nancy R. 2006. "Relations Between *Homo Sapiens* and Other Animals: Scientific and Religious Arguments." In *The Oxford Handbook of Religion and Science,* edited by Philip Clayton and Zachary Simpson, 945–61. Oxford: Oxford University Press.

Howell, Nancy R. 2015. "Locating Nature and Culture: *Pan-Homo* Culture and Theological Primatology." *Verbum et Ecclesia* 36, no. 3, Art. #1440 (9 pages). http://dx.doi.org/ao.4102/ve.v36i3.1440.

"Kanzi the Toolmaker." http://www.youtube.com/watch?v=1zsSH9 UUQtQ&feature=share&list=PL39720F7F0DAC9257&index=1.

Keller, Catherine. 2008. *On the Mystery: Discerning Divinity in Process* Minneapolis: Fortress.

King, Barbara J. 2004. *The Dynamic Dance: Nonvocal Communication in African Great Apes.* Cambridge: Harvard University Press.

McFague, Sallie. 1993. *The Body of God: An Ecological Theology.* Minneapolis: Fortress Press.

New Scientist TV. "Best videos of 2012: Bonobo Genius Makes Stone Tools." http://www.newscientist.com/blogs/nstv/2012/12/best-of-2012-bonobo-genius-makes-primitive-tools.html.

Patterson, Francine, and Eugene Linden. 1981. *The Education of Koko.* Austin, TX: Holt, Rinehart, & Winston.

Savage-Rumbaugh, Sue, and Roger Lewin. 1994. *Kanzi: The Ape at the Brink of the Human Mind.* New York: John Wiley & Sons.

Savage-Rumbaugh, Sue, William M. Fields, and Tiberu Spircu. 2004. "The Emergence of Knapping and Vocal Expression Embedded in a Pan/Homo Culture." *Biology and Philosophy* 19, 541–75. https://doi.org/10.1007/sBIPH-004-0528-0.

Vogel, Gretchen. 1999. "Chimps in the Wild Show Stirrings of Culture." *Science* 284, 2070.

Whiten, A., J. Goodall, W. C. McGrew, T. Nishida, V. Reynolds, Y. Sugiyama, C. E. G. Tutin, R. W. Wrangham, and C. Boesch. 1999. "Cultures in Chimpanzees." *Nature* 399, 682–85.

꒰ 4 ꒱

MIND VS MATTER

Philip Clayton

EDITORS' INTRODUCTION: *Chapter 3 was designed to temper the anthropocentrism that has, for so many modern people, reduced the rest of nature to means to our human ends. Many who intellectually recognize that we all belong to one world still, day by day, think and act as if human needs and desires trump all other considerations. After reading about our chimpanzee and bonobo relatives, it will be harder to ignore our kinship and moral responsibilities to them. Perhaps it will be harder to ignore our kinship and moral responsibilities to cows and pigs as well.*

But these changes in our sensibility, changes we need to make if we are to pioneer the way toward an ecological civilization, will not occur unless we free ourselves from a more foundational challenge built into modern intellectual life. Our education encourages adoption of a worldview in which not only chimpanzees but humans, too, are seen as part of a world machine. In such a worldview, all talk of values, purposes, and even meaning is trivialized, and the moral indifference we now extend to other animals becomes the way we treat other human beings, as well, and even ourselves. Accordingly, we turn now to a consideration of what may be the central metaphysical question of modernity: "Mind vs Nature." Whiteheadians believe that discussion of the issues suggested by this pair of ideas has generally been carried on in misleading terms.

Some people believe that only mind as such exists (nonphysical or nonmaterial realities). Others believe that only matter as such exists, or that there are only purely material entities. From Whitehead's point of view, they are both victims of the fallacy of misplaced concreteness. Descartes imposed this fallacy on modern philosophy, and from there it seeped into common language and thereby into popular imagination. To this day it profoundly shapes most scientific thinking. Many scientists are quick to say they have no interest in metaphysics, and this makes it difficult to consider a change in metaphysics that would actually allow scientists greater freedom to consider all the evidence.

The reification of matter and mind inevitably puts an emphasis on static substances. The evidence, however, favors a focus on events; ultimately, momentary ones. Whitehead's prioritizing of events leads to viewing the world in processive ways, and his philosophy thus joins the ranks of "process philosophies." From a Whiteheadian perspective, process philosophies in general are preferable to substance philosophies.

Among followers of Kant, for whom bifurcation between Natur *and* Geist *was taken for granted, some, especially Hegel, nevertheless developed a thoroughly processive view of Geist. But not all process philosophers overcome the bifurcation of mind and matter, and even among those who understand that the actual process of the world includes both objective "nature" and subjective "experience," some do not engage seriously with scientific thought. The separation of philosophy and science has gone so far that disconnection is now common.*

For Whiteheadians this kind of compartmentalization of thought is unhealthy. Whitehead is among those who have given us a way of thinking that is illuminating of both human history and quantum theory. We think he has offered us the most inclusive system available. We consider it a remarkable contribution at a time when more and more people are concerned to overcome the fragmentation so characteristic of modernity, its universities, and its research projects.

We recognize that this holistic thinking has barely found a foothold in our universities, but we celebrate the fact that there are signs of change. Because of the enormous and deserved prestige of the "hard" sciences, we are particularly interested in developments there. Currently they are in disarray. The assumptions that have long guided them do not work in the emerging frontiers. Quantum theory is glaringly "anomalous." But what scientists are learning about life and about conscious experience also calls for deep changes. The scientific evidence fits Whitehead much better than Descartes. This does not seem important to most scientists, but it does to a few.

Of all the limitations of the modern worldview with which the natural sciences have so strongly allied themselves, the one with the most immediate relevance to the pursuit of an ecological civilization is the exclusion from scientific explanation of the distinctive characteristics of life. This has bothered many people throughout the modern period. The Romantic protest was directed especially at this feature of scientific thinking. We chose to feature it in this section of the conference.

THE SEVEN WORKING GROUPS IN SECTION IV of the conference all worked under one common heading, "Re-envisioning Nature; Re-envisioning Science." It was our shared conviction that the major themes of this conference—"seizing an alternative" and moving "toward an ecological civilization"—will require humanity to overturn the mechanistic view of nature that dominated science in the modern period. Through the powerful influence of science, a mechanistic worldview came to dominate the minds, thoughts, and actions of modern men and women.

We propose instead that nature is best conceived as complex and emergent, as filled with organisms and agents. To "seize this alternative" is to call into question the reigning paradigm within which science today is being interpreted.

Activists may at first worry that the topics of our seven tracks are too abstract and divert attention from more urgent matters.[1] After all, are we not living on the brink of planetary disaster? Didn't the other conference sections offer more sexy sounding topics?

I suggest, however, that "Re-envisioning Nature; Re-envisioning Science" may represent the most foundational rethinking of the entire conference — the most comprehensive alternative to modern mechanism. The work of our tracks is urgent because the consequences of this re-envisioning are far-reaching, even revolutionary. Reductive science offers us a world devoid of agents, value, and meaning. Sadly, reductive science has become *the* dominant epistemic authority, the major ideology to justify the modern way of living in and with nature. Reductionism and mechanism are deeply myopic, and ultimately inconsistent. How can one be satisfied with science as a tool if it lacks the ability to conceive scientists — the researchers themselves — as agents carrying out intentions and purposes in the world? How can one *value* science and *be conscious of* scientific insights, if one accepts a worldview in which values and minds are illusions? Maria Teresa Teixeira notes the tragedy of this view "We are not to be included in what we perceive. For we are the perceivers and our minds have come into play."[2]

Let us then explore the three most important reasons to view nature as a world of interacting agents. I organize the case under the headings: how we know; what we know; and what we should do — or, to use the classical terms: knowledge, metaphysics, and ethics.

As a framework for this exploration, the conference organizers have chosen to highlight two pivotal lectures by Alfred North Whitehead, "Nature Lifeless" and "Nature Alive," published in his final work *Modes of Thought*. In the end, we will see, these two lectures have everything to do with ecological civilization. But we mustn't jump too quickly to the punch line. The standard approach is to hang out at the ecological finish line and congratulate folks as they come across. But the purpose of our working groups was more foundational. Our goal was to understand how one gets to an ecological worldview.

For that, we need to ask deeper questions and think deeper thoughts. So fasten your seatbelts and get ready to do some intense philosophy. Once you've understood Whitehead's argument, you will never be tempted by the Siren song of mechanism again.

HOW WE KNOW: THE GREAT DIVORCE

Whitehead formulates the central question: "What are those primary types of things in terms of which the process of the universe is to be understood?"[3] That question — what is really out there?— leads quickly to the question, *and by what methods will it be known?*

Philosophers have long held that the method must be appropriate to the subject matter. Thus Aristotle argued in the *Nichomachean Ethics* that we should expect from no method more precision than the subject matter itself offers. The medieval philosophers also spoke of the fit or correspondence between the "thing" to be known and the ways of thinking of the human intellect (the *adequatio rei et intellectus*). *Scientia,* or organized knowledge, the medievals said, had to possess methods appropriate to the subject matter under consideration. In short, *what science is* will be determined by *what nature is*. Nature first, science second.

The early modern scientific empiricists argued in a similar manner. As Richard Rorty notes in his famous book, *Philosophy and the Mirror of Nature,* the early modern thinkers relied on the model of perception to say what the world "really is." On this view, light waves move outward from the things themselves and impact the eye; nerve impulses then carry the information into the brain, where an internal image is formed of "the thing out there." The image is not the thing, of course; but as long as the image "corresponds" to what's really out there, knowledge is obtained.

Interestingly, even modern theologians availed themselves of the same picture. Karl Barth famously argued in the opening of his *Church Dogmatics* that there is just one necessary and sufficient condition if some area of inquiry is to qualify as science: it must possess methods of knowing that are appropriate to the thing that is to be known. Barth believed that Christian theology possesses the ideal method for knowing God: receptive openness to God's self-revelation in Christ. Theology is therefore *die Wissenschaft Gottes,* the science of God — just as physics is the science for the physical world.

This was the *one* modern answer to how we know: *the world constructs our knowledge of it.* The second answer reversed the two poles, claiming instead that *we construct the world.* Recall the work of René Descartes. At the dawn of the modern age, Descartes famously proclaimed that he could distinguish between illusion and reality by the "clearness and distinctness" of his own ideas. The inner certainty of the knower became the sole authority for what could count as knowledge. (Consider the parallels with the Reformation theologian Martin Luther: hearing the voice of God within, or hearing it in the scriptures, was for him a higher authority than any human institution, such as the church.)

Immanuel Kant deepened this "Copernican Revolution" in epistemology. Knowledge, he said, is the result of the constructive activity of the human mind. The mind takes raw or unformed sense data (phenomena) and imposes "the categories of the understanding" upon them. At first this did not sound like relativism, since Kant believed that *all* sentient beings impose the same 12 identical categories whenever they construct "the world of our experience." But Kant's insistence on universality lasted only a few decades after his death. Before the middle of the nineteenth century, Riemann made the case for non-Euclidean geometries. That is, a variety of different geometries can be useful for science, opening the door to effectively random systems of categories. Suddenly, the order of the medieval world began to collapse. Now, it appeared, agents can impose methods of their own choice upon raw sense data, and *whatever results* may pass as knowledge.

Modern philosophers found themselves confronted with a dichotomy that they were never able to overcome — the dichotomy between objectivism and relativism. Successful predictions and the replication of experiments convinced scientists that their methods really did provide accurate knowledge of reality. By contrast, the rapidly expanding circles of interpretation in literature, philosophy, and religion convinced students of the humanities that each new method, each new way of seeing or reading a text, produces its own world. W. V. O. Quine described these multiple ways of seeing as "webs," Thomas S. Kuhn called them "paradigms," and Nelson Goodman called them "ways of world making." The feminist philosopher Donna Haraway expresses a similar viewpoint when she declares that "all knowledge is situated knowledge." Marshall McLuhan expresses the same judgment more dramatically: "the medium *is* the message."

By the end of the modern period, the modern worldview was rent asunder by the fatal divergence of its two great "cultures," science and the humanities. Most of the damaging dichotomies that define modern existence are symptoms of this great divergence: objective versus subjective, fact versus value, body versus mind, materialism versus idealism, the physical versus the spiritual, science versus religion.

Each one of these dichotomies expresses the same dual tug. If the ways of knowing must (and can) bend to nature-as-it-really-is, then you get objectivism. If the multitude of interpretations come first, such that what you "know" depends on what method you happen to choose, then you get relativism. Modern thought never resolved this conundrum. Instead, it remained forever caught in the pincer movement between the two. Or, to change the metaphor, modern thought vacillated perpetually between absolutism and relativism like the alternating current that powers the lights in your house.

Much of 20th-century philosophy was dithered away in the fruitless struggle to defend one pole of the opposition against the other. But I ask you: when a battle between conflicting concepts appears unwinnable — when the decision between them seems impossible — what do you do? At some point, don't you pause to wonder whether, perhaps, the mistake lies in how you are formulating the question?

When you suddenly begin to see the two sides as complementary pieces of a single whole, you have made the transition from a modern to a postmodern worldview. Alfred North Whitehead is one of the central advocates of this constructive postmodern view. I have chosen the title "Mind vs. Matter" in order to suggest that the problem is not the two terms but the "versus" in the middle. If our seven working groups were to make progress over the three days, it would be because they were willing to leave the modern dichotomy behind.

WHAT WE KNOW: MANY METHODS, MANY REGIONS

We are looking, then, for a whole to which so-called mind and so-called matter both contribute. Unlike the moderns, we begin with the complementary interactions of nature and method—of what is and how we know.

The advantages of this Gestalt-switch immediately begin to make themselves felt. The new approach allows us, first, to subdivide the sum total of nature into regions. "Regional thinking" expresses the both/and nature of the postmodern commitment: The different regions are defined by the specific methods that we use to understand in each case; but it is *the one world* that we seek to understand. Consider some examples: the methods of physical chemistry are appropriate for the region of medium-sized molecules, as the region of organic chemistry is appropriate for large biomolecules. The region of inquiry called genetics helps us to understand the part of nature in which genomes evolve based on selection pressures that operate on the phenotypes that genes code for. The region called primatology includes all methods that help to explain a specific group within nature's animal kingdom. The inquiries that fall under the heading ecology study systems of interacting organisms within nature, including both the living and the nonliving components of these systems.

I deeply support the pluralism of postmodern science. Too often the history of science has looked like the history of philosophy. We philosophers are famous for "totalizing," for placing "all things" or "all reality" under the control of a single theory. Philosophers are hyperactive when it comes to theorizing; we tend not to worry very much about the data. But what may be a virtue among philosophers is the cardinal sin among scientists. Science errs when it hands over control of all reality to a single method. Just one scientific field ought never to serve as the knowledge standard for *all* parts of nature — not particle physics, not quantum physics, not string theory. A variegated world requires a plurality of explanations and explanatory methods.

Something beautiful happens, I suggest, when we start to see nature through the many lenses of these many different methods. I call it a "natural piety" . . . the piety of a naturalist. The different methods of knowing, applied to the different regions of the world, produce a complex collage of insights. You learn different things from chemistry, cell biology, morphology, population genetics, eco-systems theory. You learn different things from studying a person as a psychological entity, as a member of a social group, in terms of her culture, as a product of biological evolution . . . and the list goes on. Re-envisioning science and nature in an adequate way requires rethinking a multitude of different regions of scientific practice.

I've just made a strong claim about science, and I don't want you to miss it. I dispute that science, as science, justifies the claim that all regions of nature are best explained by the laws and methods of *just one region* of nature. It may well be that the laws of physics constrain all behaviors in biology, and that biochemistry constrains how our brains work. But it doesn't follow that physics best explains all biological phenomena, or that the biochemistry of the brain best explains your acts of charity and compassion. Scientists *qua* scientists cannot stand above, or outside of, the many methods of the many regions of the world.

WHY "NATURE LIFELESS" CAN'T BE THE BEST PHILOSOPHY

We can't determine the best science; but can we determine the best philosophy? Notice the difference between the two. Scientists can, and should, limit their methods to the appropriate regions. Philosophers, by contrast, offer general theories that help people recognize similarities across the regions. Years ago, Stephen Pepper called these "world hypotheses."

There are very many different world hypotheses that we could consider—uncountably many. To waste no time, let's focus right in on the two world hypotheses that Whitehead considers: *nature lifeless* and *nature alive*. These also happen to be the two options that have most dominated the debate about nature for centuries now.

"Nature lifeless" takes its model from the pre-biological sciences, physics and chemistry. That means that, on this view, *living agents* are not explanatory units. Nature lifeless can point to rabbits and squids and other living agents; it can recognize them as things to be explained. The behaviors of living agents are then explained in terms of non-living factors: underlying physical laws, catalytic systems of chemicals, the way that genes code for proteins, osmosis through a cell wall. In each case, the reductive scientist *models* the behavior of what ordinary language calls agents, using non-agential explanations.

Think of the parallel with calculus. The calculus considers quantities that come very close to a whole number. We thus say that (for example) we will treat 0.999 continuous *as if it were exactly 1*. Similarly, "nature lifeless" jumps from *agent-like* processes to agents, acting *as if* the two were identical. Thus nature lifeless treats a genetic algorithm *as if* it were describing the formation of an agent; in neuroscience, it treats brain biochemistry *as if* this were sufficient to describe the decision-making of a person; in an ecosystem, it treats quantitative changes in the system *as if* they were the results of animal agents and their intentions and actions.

Of course, in the end *as if* means *isn't really*. On this approach, *agents* don't really explain agent-like behavior; the lower-level, lifeless regularities do the explaining. Whitehead argues that the result is "merely a bloodless dance of categories."[4] Nature, on this view, "is described as made up of vacuous bits of matter with no internal values, and merely hurrying through space."[5] Again, as Maria Teresa Teixeira notes, on this view "*We* are not to be included in what we perceive. For we are the perceivers and our minds have come into play."[6]

Much follows once you have adopted "nature lifeless" as your worldview. Indeed, a whole worldview follows . . . a worldview that has birthed a disastrous way of living in nature and with other agents. It's the task of Whiteheadians to identify what has been wrought by the "nature lifeless" view, including how it has defined the modern world and determined its treatment of the planet and its inhabitants.

Let's summarize this "nature lifeless" view before we leave it behind. On this view, scientific explanations don't appeal to agents and their intentions. Once you've explained agents in terms of non-living forces and laws, you don't really need the language of agency anymore. Agency language has been explained away.

As agent-language is evacuated of its force, so too are all the characteristics of agents: values, purposes, goals, intentions — and with them, all the features of personhood and of human life that we, as human agents, value the most. Gone also, by the way, are the values pertaining to broader groups of agents: families, societies, communities, religious traditions. Of course, these *words* may still survive in the resulting sciences; but they no longer express the values and existential realities that they once expressed. As Whitehead notes bitingly, "all reference to life was suppressed."[7] Not only human agents are placed under erasure; the study of *all* living agents suffers. The entire biosphere becomes harder to understand . . . and harder to value.

HOW WE LIVE: "NATURE ALIVE" AND THE ECOLOGICAL MINDSET

And that, in short, is the philosophical dilemma bequeathed to us by modernity. Modern physics gives us process, activity, and change. It gives us "rules of succession," but not the meaning, value, or purpose of that succession. Whitehead asks, "How do we add content to the notion of bare activity? Activity for what, producing what, activity involving what?"[8]

Hence our turn to the other option that Whitehead identifies: *nature alive.* Remember the postmodern both/and that I identified above: nature presents as multiple regions, and differing regions are comprehended using differing methods. The "nature lifeless" view draws its methods from the pre-agential world, from physics and chemistry, and extends them upward and outward to all of nature. The "nature alive" view, by contrast, begins with the opposite assumption. There are regions of nature that are best explained in terms of the behaviors of agents. These regions require scientific and explanatory methods that capable of parsing what agents do and why.

Just as everything changed when "nature lifeless" became the overarching framework for living in the world, so everything changes when you understand yourself as one real agent in a world teeming with other agents. Now the various features of personhood and of human life become real constituents of the world: values, purposes, goals, and intentions. Whitehead's analogy is intriguing, "The energetic activity considered in physics is the emotional intensity entertained in life."[9] Seen in this way, we are "implicat[ed] in the creative advance."[10]

AGENTS AND THE COMMUNITY OF LIFE

How far we have come from "Mind vs. Matter"! We now recognize those terms as shorthand for a false dichotomy. Leaving it behind opens doors to a more adequate science of life. The forms of life, as Whitehead says, "touch upon human mentality at their highest, and upon inorganic nature at their lowest."[11] Measured against the continuities, the deeper unity, the differences among agents now make more sense.

Under the new paradigm, beyond mechanism, life is permeated by goals, purposes, and directions. What we call "mind" and "matter" have become deeply interconnected, and both are transformed as they become Siamese twins. Among our fundamental experiences, Whitehead insists, is the "direct feeling of the derivation of emotion from the body."[12] Yet we are also aware of "our own state of mind directly preceding the immediate present of our conscious experience."[13] "Bottom-up" and "top-down" factors intermingle in our experience. And indeed, biologists are now discovering that the biosphere is permeated by both bottom-up and top-down causality, as systems biology and ecosystem studies are now revealing.

"Nature alive" also allows us to view ourselves differently. Whitehead recognizes that "The one individual is that coordinated stream of personal experiences, which is my thread of life or your thread of life. It is that succession of self-realization, each occasion with its direct memory of its past and with its anticipation of the future. That claim to enduring self-identity is our self-assertion of personal identity."[14]

Gone is the anthropomorphism of old; we now see that human agents share their essential features with *all* living agents. Whitehead's focus on "occasions of experience" leads him to recognize that "creative activity belong[s] to the very essence of *each* occasion."[15] For all living agents, "the process of self-creation is the transformation of the potential into the actual."[16] Each occasion of experience has its own aim,[17] and no living agent can be comprehended apart from its aims. We seek not a biology without teleology, but rather a biology capable of enunciating the "immanent teleology" that undergirds all life . . . the goal-driven drives manifested by every living agent.

At the end of the day, where all of this points, at least for Whitehead, is the affirmation of "mutual immanence"[18] or, as he beautifully puts it, "We are in the world and the world is in us."[19] Using the word "soul" as shorthand for the experience of all living things, Whitehead writes that "the world is in the soul" and "the soul itself [is] one of the components within the world"[20]—a view that has come to be known as panpsychism or panexperientialism.

CONCLUSION: ALL ARE INTERRELATED; WE ARE
CONNECTED TO ALL; WE ARE RESPONSIBLE FOR ALL

The title of this chapter, "Mind vs Matter," alludes to a core theme that runs across the philosophy of science. Questions of consciousness arise in quantum physics; questions of agency, meaning, and value arise across the biological sciences; and the most fundamental questions of who we are as embodied beings are raised in contemporary neuroscientific studies of the relationship between brains, thoughts, emotions, and consciousness.

> A philosophy of processes and events explores manners of being rather than states of being, "modes of thought" rather than any supposed essence of thought, and contingent inter-actions rather than unchanging substances. It focuses, you might say, on adverbs instead of nouns.[21]

We have made seven discoveries over the course of these reflections:

(1) *It is time to free ourselves from the modern dichotomy between objectivism and relativism.* We are not forced to choose between methods that perfectly reveal the objective world on the one hand, and interpretations that randomly create subjective worlds on the other.

(2) *Instead, science qua science requires a plurality of methods, depending on which regions of nature one is studying.*

(3) *The choice* against *agents*—*"nature lifeless," as we called it*—*is not only damaging for science; it is devastating for our understanding of ourselves and our relationships with livings things around us.*

(4) *Everything changes when we move to the paradigm of "nature alive."* Now we study, and belong to, a world where agents are central. On this view, the features that are fundamental to our own experience of the world are actually embedded in the world. Aims and purposes are manifested by agents all around us (and within us). It follows that *we* are embedded in the world as well. Rather than being a lone island of meaning in a sea of cosmic meaninglessness, each of us is a center of awareness and value, inhabiting a world permeated by similar centers.

(5) *The key feature of agent-centered existence is community.* We know ourselves as members of communities—vast networks of interdependent communities of living agents. No longer can humanity be singled out as the "thinking animal" (*zoon logikon*) stranded within a world of machines. Sensations, perceptions, feelings, emotions, thoughts, awareness—the various attributes of agents emerge

across the biosphere, manifesting in different forms and functions in different environments and different stages of evolutionary time.

(6) *A community of agents is a community of value.* The things that we value are valued by other agents. All agents seek pleasure and aim to avoid pain; all perceive and respond to their environment; all seek to actualize the potential of the greatest thriving appropriate to their nature. Kant's famous dictum applies to all: *treat others never merely as a means to an end, but always at the same time as ends in themselves.* The implications of this insight for the global environmental movement are monumental.

(7) *We are simultaneously responsible for all the communities of value-laden agents with whom we interact.* Obligations emerge as we recognize that other living agents are far more like us than we had hitherto acknowledged. If we are one step in a chain of development of similar agents — or better: if we are one center of experience in a vast community of "experiencers" — then we share a responsibility for others, as they do for us (to the extent that they are able). We have discovered that the others are ontologically like us; they suffer in every way as we do. As Whitehead puts it, each occasion [of experience, i.e., each living thing] "is an activity of concern, in the Quaker sense of that term. It is the conjunction of transcendence and immanence. [Each] is concerned, in the way of feeling and aim, with things that . . . lie beyond it."[22] Communities of interdependence are simultaneously communities of responsibility, as David Griffin writes:

> A reenchanted, liberating science will be fully developed only by people with a postmodern spirituality, in which the dualisms that have made modern science such an ambiguous phenomenon have been transcended, and only in a society organized for the good of the planet as a whole.[23]

The global climate crisis can be addressed only through an intimate working partnership between the natural sciences, the humanities, and the world's religious and spiritual traditions. Any view of science, or of religion, that forecloses the possibility of these collaborations entails a *de facto* suicide for our species. The synthetic vision sketched by Whitehead and defended in this chapter is meant to inspire a different mode of living in the world. The details of the vision will be worked out in the more concrete (and thus more important) discussions that are taking place in conferences and working groups and publications around the planet. Ever more concrete agendas for action are being developed and implemented in experimental communities or what we call "ecological laboratories."[24] But without rethinking the fundamental vision of Nature, as humanity must do, all activist efforts will eventually sputter out, like a fire with inadequate fuel.

I close with a final quote from Whitehead:

> Philosophy begins in wonder. And, at the end, when philosophic thought has done its best, the wonder remains. There have been added, however, some grasp of the immensity of things, some purification of the emotion by understanding . . . The aim at philosophic understanding is the aim at piercing the blindness of activity [in order to discover its purposes and goals].[25]

So: let's welcome each other to this world filled with cousins, with agents like ourselves. We are images of them, as they are of us. If we did not stand on the shoulders of giants, we would not be here now, breathing and interacting and thinking.

Honor and value these cousins who exist around you. Not as a mere projection of yourself, not in an anthropomorphic way. Rather, honor them as part of the interdependent web of life, whose value manifests both in the whole *and* in the parts — and not just in the parts that are us. This is not anthropomorphism; it is *biophilia*. We know ourselves because we belong to a vast community, without which we would cease to exist. We find relatives wherever we turn in the biosphere. We are coming to understand ourselves as a community of communities. Let's join in sharing this responsibility for all, to the extent that the power within us lies.

ENDNOTES

1   The seven tracks of this section included: 1. Telling the Story: Systems, Processes, and the Present (Zach Simpson, chair); 2. Intuition in Mathematics and Physics (Ronny Desmet, chair); 3. Systems Theory, Complexity Theory, and Radical Emergence (Michael Dowd, Dongping Fan, and Stuart Kauffman, chairs); 4. Beyond Mechanism: The Emergence and Evolution of Living Agents (Adam Scarfe, chair); 5. Ecologies, Becoming, Networks, and Value (Robert Ulanowitz and Elizabeth McDuffie, chairs); 6. Unprecedented Evolution: Human Continuities and Discontinuities with Animal Life (Spyridon Koutroufinis and René Pikarski, chairs); 7. Neuroscience and Consciousness: Toward an Integral Paradigm (Alex Gomez-Marin and Rod Hemsell, chairs).

2   Maria Teresa Teixeira, "Purpose and Value in Whitehead's Ontology of Science," http://www.philosophyatlisbon.com/userfiles/file /Philosophy01.pdf#page=64

3   Alfred North Whitehead, *Modes of Thought* (Toronto: Macmillan, 1938; New York: Free Press, 1968), 144. All subsequent parenthetical references are to this edition.

4   Alfred North Whitehead, *Modes of Thought,* 1938 (NY: Free Press, 1968), 144.

5   Ibid., 158.

6   Maria Teresa Teixeira, "Purpose and Value in Whitehead's Ontology of Science," http://www.philosophyatlisbon.com/userfiles/file /Philosophy01.pdf#page=64, emphasis added.

7   Whitehead, *Modes of Thought,* 144.

8   Ibid., 147.

9   Ibid., 232.

10 Whitehead, *Modes of Thought,* 146.

11 Ibid., 150.

12 Ibid., 159–60.

13 Ibid., 160.

14 Ibid., 161

15 Ibid., 151 (emphasis added).

16   Ibid., 151.

17   Ibid., 152–53.

18   Ibid., 164.

19   Ibid., 165.

20   Ibid., 163.

21   Steven Shaviro, "Self-Enjoyment and Concern: On Whitehead And Levinas," http://www.shaviro.com/Othertexts/Modes.pdf.

22   Whitehead, *Modes of Thought*, 167.

23   Griffin, "Preface," in *The Reenchantment of Science,* xiii.

24   See the new organization, Toward Ecological Civilization, at EcoCiv. org.

25   Whitehead, *Modes of Thought,* 168–69.

＊ 5 ＊

WHAT CAN WE HOPE FOR?

Sandra Lubarsky

EDITORS' INTRODUCTION: *The title of the conference was "Seizing an Alternative: Toward an Ecological Civilization." But thus far we have hardly considered "ecological civilization." Chapter 1 introduced the most urgent crises, those with which we must deal even without the deep changes required for an ecological civilization. We appealed for only one change at the level of thought and sensibility, a recognition of how often we go astray because we reify what does not in fact exist. Whitehead calls this the "fallacy of misplaced concreteness," and we hope that people understand this and learn to avoid it even with very little philosophical reflection. We need to define our problems without abstracting from the interconnectedness of things or being tangled up in our linguistic formulations.*

The remainder of the conference looked ahead, beyond the immediate crises we can no longer hope to evade, to what may yet be possible constructively, provided we do not wipe ourselves out in bad responses to immediate threats. We think the clearer the long-term goals are, the better the chance that we will respond well; so we do not consider the proposals made in the conference as a whole irrelevant to the immediate challenges. Still, to a large extent, people who have not thought deeply about these challenges, or who remain committed to established thinking

81

in philosophy, science, politics, and economics, will have to share in slowing climate change and avoiding starvation and nuclear war. Perhaps even as we work together to keep alive, setting our differences aside, we can also gain allies in making deeper changes.

We believe that the changes involved in moving toward an ecological civilization involve our basic worldview. Modernity has achieved huge advances in science and technology, but it has not prized wisdom, and its very advances now threaten to destroy us. Given our technological prowess, wisdom is more important than ever. We need to renew the love of wisdom, that is philosophy, recognizing that it has been too little sought by moderns who call themselves philosophers. Their failure has led to people looking elsewhere for guidance, but they should instead be seeking real philosophy. Chapter 2 indicates that if they seek, they can find. Whitehead is among the world's great lovers of wisdom.

Fundamental to the worldview that we need is a decisive break from the alienation of human beings from nature that began with the rise of civilization; that is, with the shift of leadership to the cities. City dwellers surround themselves with an artificial environment. They separate themselves from the soil. They protect themselves from the weather. In many cases they enslave other people to produce their food. Other species of animals are to be hunted or domesticated. Modernity and subsequent industrialization furthered this alienation. Chapter 3 was designed to introduce readers to their relatives in other animal species in a way that touches us more deeply than theoretical statements. We hope that we can all come to feel the connection.

Chapter 4 puts the choice of worldview before us in stark and simple terms. We can continue to view nature in mechanical terms, restricting agency to humans, or we can recognize that nature is alive and composed of agents like us. When we realize that there are, in fact, no good reasons for adopting the first position, and that it is damaging in multiple ways, many of us will seek to liberate ourselves from our academic socialization into mechanical thinking. That is not easy, but it is urgent.

If we choose to recognize that the mechanical vision is wrong, that there are real alternatives before us, that we are agents whose decisions matter, then we can "hope" in a meaningful way. In this conference, and thus in this book, we named what we hope for: "ecological civilization." Now we are at last prepared to turn to this topic. "Ecological" certainly includes "sustainable," and most people think that we should try to keep civilization going. However, most people want to support sustainable civilization without changing the basic way they think and behave. Fortunately, the number who at least see that this is not possible is growing. A civilization that can be sustained will be profoundly different from any civilization that now exists or has existed in the past. It will be "ecological." That is, human activities will be related to the patterns of the nonhuman world in a way that enables the whole to flourish.

Before the rise of civilization (city culture), a much smaller population lived in a relatively sustainable way with other animals and the rest of the natural world. We have much to learn from them. Some think that "ecological civilization" is an oxymoron, since they suppose that the only way to live ecologically is to undo civilization. It is indeed possible that civilization will self-destruct and that the few survivors will reorganize in tribal ways similar to our ancient ancestors. But this conference was organized by people who have not given up on the survival of civilization. That there has never been an ecological civilization does not mean that there cannot be one in the future.

Subsequent chapters will ask what that would mean for particular communities; this chapter wrestles with how hope, as such, can occur and be supported, while suggesting in broad strokes what ecological civilization as a whole would look like. It is definitely "utopian" in the sense that what we hope for does not exist and cannot in any simple or rapid way be called into existence. But we are not interested in mere fantasy. We need a sense of what might be and should be, and what is worth striving for.

THE TOPIC OF THIS CHAPTER IS "What can we hope for?" It is another way of framing the theme of this conference, which is dedicated to finding—and seizing—strategies that give reason for hope. But it is also about generating hope, as well.

I am, however, compelled to begin this presentation on hope by situating my thoughts within the sober context of our climate crisis. There are now more than 400 parts per million of CO_2 in the atmosphere. Though we've seen this measure appear before, it was for a few hours or days. But for the whole month of March of this year, the average global concentration of CO_2 has been 400 ppm for a month. The head scientist of NOAA, is quoted as saying, "Reaching 400 parts per million as a global average is a significant milestone."[1]

That milestone is part of what has been described as a "planetary-scale critical transition," never before witnessed by human civilization.[2] In the face of this kind of terrifying projection, anticipating the crossing of biophysical boundaries not meant to be crossed, what are we to hope for? We are headed into a territory we have never known, with little knowledge and no GPS. The more appropriate question seems to be: "What should we fear?" The question that comes more easily to mind is: "What can we despair about?"

So let us start with some gallows humor, in the form of the advice of a Jew during the Holocaust: **"Save your despair for when you really need it."** Gallows humor is by definition grim and ironic, mocking the immediate facts of a dire reality. You think THIS is bad? But it's not merely ironic. It's also a cheeky, insolent reminder of *the tendency to despair too soon.* The immediate situation is bad, even terrible, but the world might yet be different. To despair too soon is counterproductive. When do you really need despair? The implicit answer is not as long as there is a flicker of hope. "Save your despair for when you really need it."

Still, it's hard to know what we know about the state of the world and be hopeful. I awoke the other day to two messages in my email: one was an article reporting that 93% of seed varieties have been lost in the last 80 years; the other was from The Greater Good Science Center with advice on "How to Learn to Love Your Stress." To know what we know is to live between hope and despair, trying not to be immobilized by either.

The literary critic Raymond Williams wrote, "to be truly radical is to make hope possible, rather than despair convincing." In her important new book, *This Changes Everything: Capitalism vs. The Climate*, Naomi Klein makes the case that the climate crisis *can become* a catalyst for social and economic transformation. If treated as a "true planetary emergency," she believes that climate change could "become a galvanizing force for humanity, leaving us all not just safer from extreme weather, but with societies that are safer and fairer in all kinds of other ways as well." Klein devotes the last part of her book to examples of hope-in-action, to what she calls "Blockadia"— efforts of people across the world to preserve the integrity of their land communities by blocking the work of extractive industries. While I was writing this presentation, the "sHell No!" Paddle in Seattle protest, a Blockadia action, was underway in the Port of Seattle. The image was iconic: thousands of small boats, kayaks, and tribal canoes filling the waterway, blocking massive drilling rigs from entering the port in order to ultimately block Arctic drilling further north.

Klein distinguishes between "optimism" and hope—and it's an important distinction; one that I'm sure you've heard before. She's not at all optimistic that we'll be able to keep the earth's temperature from rising more than 2-degrees Celsius. Nor is she confident that there is wisdom or will enough to prevent technophiles from dangerously toying with natural systems, or politicians from crafting supercharged neoliberal policies on behalf of their campaign funders.

And yet, even so, she's been accused of being "maddeningly" optimistic by no less a personage than the environmental journalist, Elizabeth Kolbert, author of (among other things) *The Sixth Extinction: An Unnatural History*. Kolbert accuses Klein of "telling a fable she hopes will do some good."[3] And Kolbert's cynicism cannot be dismissed out of hand. There is simply no cause to be confident about the future when the last northern white rhino male has to be guarded 24 hours a day or he and his entire species will be murdered for the price of his horn. There is no cause for confidence in the capacity of humans to respond effectively and compassionately to the 52 island nations now at risk of being swept away by rising sea levels. John Oliver, the satirist and social critic, says—and I've toned down his comment a bit—"We've proven that we cannot be trusted with the future tense; we've been repeatedly asked, 'Don't you want to leave a better earth to your grandchildren?—and we've all collectively responded, 'eh . . . screw 'em.'"[4]

But Klein's response is equally deserving of attention. She says, "I have yet to meet anyone professionally focused on the science of our warming planet who does not wrestle with despair, myself included. *Yet surely the decision about whether to maintain some hope in the face of an existential crisis that is still technically preventable is not just a matter of cold calculation. It's also a question of ethics.* If there is any chance of turning the tide, and if taking action could actually lead to all kinds of ancillary benefits, then it seems to me that those of us with public platforms have a responsibility to share that good news, alongside all the painful truths."[5]

So let us consider hope.

My colleague's aunt lives on the 26th floor of a building in Calcutta. Her aunt has a bad hip and there's only one lift in the building. The earthquake that hit Nepal so hard also made buildings in Calcutta sway and left large cracks in the concrete. "So what will your aunt do?" I asked my friend. "Will she move?" "No, no," she answered. "Definitely not. There is nothing to be done. That is Calcutta." Her aunt is resigned to dying in the building, should a strong enough quake hit her neighborhood again. **Her hope** is that despite the terrestrial geography, despite nonexistent zoning codes, and despite the limitations of her own body, she will *not* meet her death on the 26th floor of her apartment building. She *is* fatalistic about the future. Hers is a wistful hope, a yearning restrained by the graceful acceptance that "this is Calcutta." If wishes were horses, beggars would ride.

In reaction to **passive** forms of hope, Derrick Jensen, a leading environmental activist and writer, urges us to move "beyond hope." He writes, "Many people say they **hope** the dominant culture stops destroying the world. By saying that, they've assumed that the destruction will continue . . . and they've stepped away from their own ability to participate in stopping it. . . . When we realize the degree of agency we actually do have, we no longer have to 'hope' at all. We simply do the work. We make sure salmon survive. We make sure prairie dogs survive. . . . We do whatever it takes."[6] For Jensen, hope immobilizes action; to be hopeful is to be helpless.

Jensen's reaction to hope as an excuse for irresponsibility is warranted. There *is* a kind of hope that leads to passivity. But it's not just hope that can cripple initiative. Pessimism and despair are equally liable to constrain action. And so are extreme forms of optimism.

There is nothing simple about hope. Take, for example, the radical and alarming hope of those who propose geoengineering as a solution to climate change. Theirs is a brew of total pessimism about human nature and our ability to overcome our carbon addiction, and total optimism in technology and our ability to manage entire earth systems.

Hope and its varieties are based on assumptions about what we're capable of doing and about what is important and possible. Those assumptions are the outcome of often-unstated philosophical assumptions.

I think it's telling that when John Cobb formulated this plenary session, he didn't ask the question, "Is hope possible?" Instead, he asked us to consider, "What can we hope for?" That question assumes that hope *is* possible, *is* feasible, despite the very grave circumstances that are the reason for this conference. As John wrote in a preconference essay, "Our inaugural conference is based on the hope that hope will help."[7]

The reason why hope is feasible for someone like John Cobb is because it is part of a metaphysics that makes it so. That metaphysics is process thought. Process thought offers a way of understanding reality that makes radical hope possible. By "radical hope," I mean hope that is sustained not simply by sheer force of personal conviction or by willful ignorance of reality or because of a privileged immunity from reality's worst contingencies. Radical hope is secured—in its roots—by a metaphysics that affirms change and possibility, agency and power, novelty and creativity, and value and importance. These are philosophical concepts that secure hope as something real, not to be dismissed, in spite of what we know about the depletion of topsoil, the death of coral reefs, the oil spill in Santa Barbara, and on and on. Amidst this proliferation of tragedies, it is not naïve to ask the question, "What can we hope for?" because there is a process-relational metaphysics in which certain things are possible —including hope—even in a time of mass extinctions, even in a time of ecocide.

So let me spend a few minutes sketching the metaphysics of hope provided by process philosophy (and forgive me, all of you who are already familiar with this).

First, the word "process" in process philosophy. "Process" describes the fundamental activity of the world. Everything is always in process, always undergoing some degree of change. Often this change is hardly perceptible and so we experience a general stability of conditions. But change is the rule, and in this case, there are no exceptions. Change is, as Whitehead says, "in the essence of the universe." Reality is a process of dynamic "becoming," not static "being."

But though *change* is guaranteed, positive change is not. Unlike campaign rhetoric of recent years, change does not presuppose progress. Positive change is a possibility but change can also be detrimental. **Still**, the fact that the world is in a constant state of change provides a foothold for hope because it means that the status quo is ephemeral.

Whitehead's explanation for the process of change is brilliant and complex. I am going to reduce that brilliance and complexity to a very quick look at three principle reasons why change happens: **possibility, agency, and value**.

First, *possibility*: The idea of process requires the notion of potentiality.[8] In a world that is in process—that is characterized by change—possibilities must abound; otherwise, there is only repetition. But **we know** that novel ideas and new sensibilities do come into the world. Whitehead offers the example of the idea of freedom and individual self-determination, tracing the history of slavery as an unchallenged, taken-for-granted practice in Plato's time to a deplorable practice when he was writing in the 20th century. Change happens—often slowly, often in unplanned cooperation with chance—it took millennia before human servitude was broadly recognized as an atrocity—but novelty builds on novelty, new insights replace old ways, and new patterns of behavior reinforce change. The future is conditioned by the past but it is not determined by it. Though there are strong patterns of repetition, there is not sheer repetition. This is because the facts of the world are supplemented by possibilities that are inherent in the world, waiting to be actualized. As Whitehead writes, "a great idea in the background of dim consciousness is like a phantom ocean beating upon the shores of human life in successive waves of specialization. A whole succession of such waves are as dreams slowly doing their work of sapping the base of some cliff of habit: but the seventh wave is a revolution."[9]

Second, *agency*: To be realized, possibilities must be incorporated into the lives of experiencing beings. Whitehead affirms Plato's claim that to be is to have active agency. "The definition of being is simply power."[10] Here "power" means dynamism—the ability to actively participate in the fundamental process that shapes reality. Rather than being an inanimate cog in a machine, each entity shapes its own existence to some degree, determining what weight will be given to the past and introducing its own, unique aim into its final form. Each entity is an original event, a novel coalescence of factors. Human life is our most familiar illustration of what this means, but all entities are, to some degree, self-directed. Each of us has the capacity to reject destructive patterns and construct life-affirming ones. Each of us has some degree of freedom, some degree of creativity—and that's why, in its denial of this truth, slavery is so horrendous. To exercise our creativity is not always easy, and success is not guaranteed. The given-ness of the world *is* formidable. The past has a strong grip on the present, and often it seems that meaningful change is not possible. But the capacity is there. And that capacity is immanent in the natural order, as much a part of the metaphysical landscape as transpiration is a part of the water cycle. This agency, this power to participate in life actively and creatively, and not simply to replicate fixed behaviors and beliefs, is a pivot for hope, the kind of hope that David Orr, a leading environmentalist, describes as "a verb with its sleeves rolled up."

Third, *value*: When we say that we hope things will be different, we imply that they *ought to be different* and we reveal hope's ethical dimension. Hope's deepest grounding is in a metaphysics that affirms value as inherent in the structure of reality. Process philosophy provides such a metaphysical system. Indeed, according to process philosophy, value is "inherent in actuality itself."[11] Whitehead writes, "Our enjoyment of actuality is a realization of worth, good or bad. It is a value experience."[12] The whole process of becoming is directed toward the grasping of value in others, the incorporation of it within oneself, and the furtherance of value in creative ways. And the process of each actuality and of life in general is directed toward attaining value, increasing value, and enjoying value. Above all, what is valued is "the simple craving to enjoy freely the vividness of life."[13] I love that phrase: "to enjoy freely the vividness of life." Surely, this is what we hope for, in the most general sense: to freely and fully engage with life.

There is much more that can be said about how a process metaphysics gives grounds for hope. Truth, goodness, and beauty, for example, lend their support to the experience of life's vividness. How worth is secured in each actuality occupies most of Whitehead's magnum opus, *Process and Reality*. But for now, I hope my point is clear: that process philosophy secures the idea of hope metaphysically. Without this kind of mooring, hope floats like driftwood, lightweight and eroding. Instead of being a stimulus for engagement, it becomes nothing more than wishful thinking. With metaphysical support, hope is possible not only as the consequence of individual passion, not solely dependent on whether people have the capacity to beckon and sustain it, but as the outcome of a worldview, illuminated by possibility, agency, novelty, and worth.

And so, at last, some reflections on **what** we can hope for. Years ago, Donella Meadows, author of the now-classic book, *The Limits to Growth*, led a series of workshops focused on how to end hunger. Expert agronomists, economists, ecologists, and development specialists came to the workshops. Meadows began the first workshop by asking the question, "What is your vision of a world without hunger?" She asked people to describe, "not the world they thought they could achieve, or the world they were willing to settle for, but the world they truly wanted."

People refused to answer her question. Some called it "stupid and dangerous." Someone said, "We don't need to talk about what the end of hunger will be like, we need to talk about how to get there." Someone else told her to "stop being unrealistic." She pressed them anyway. Eventually, people began to let their defenses down. She writes, "One person said, with emotion, that he couldn't stand the *pain* of thinking about the world he really wanted, when he was so aware of the world's present state." And finally one person voiced what Meadows describes as coming "closer to the truth than any of our other rationalizations." "'I have a vision,' this person said, 'but it would make me feel childish and vulnerable to say it out loud.'"

"Why is it," asked Meadows, "that we can share our cynicism, complaints, and frustrations without hesitation with perfect strangers, but we can't share our dreams? How did we arrive at a culture that constantly, almost automatically, ridicules visionaries? . . . When were we taught, and by whom, to suppress our visions?"[14]

I think it's fair to say that modern education is partly to blame, having promoted objectivity as its primary value, critical thinking as its primary method, and career placement as its primary aim. But visions and hopes are fueled by values, by what we judge to be important and hold to be of worth. If we don't have a vision, if we aren't honest about our real desires, and if we aren't willing to share them publicly, we end up with half-baked policies and strategies for implementation. As British environmental writer George Monbiot said, we need a vision "that proposes a better world, rather than (if we work really hard for it), just a slightly-less-shitty-one-than-there-would-otherwise-have-been."[15]

In answer to John Cobb's 1971 question (*Is It too Late?*), it may be too late to avoid ecological and social catastrophe. After all, the Club of Rome was right—there *are* ecological limits to economic and population growth. On the other hand, "What can we hope for?" is a question about vision, about what we value and how we will direct our energies. Meadows wrote her essay, "Envisioning a Sustainable World," in 1994, slightly more than 20 years after her report to the Club of Rome. To call for vision is to call for possibility and agency within a framework of values. It is, in other words, a practice of hope.

Reading of hard landings that will be the end of civilization and soft landings that are nonetheless sobering, I find myself in a kind of intoxicated dialectic, reeling between hope and despair. The Palestinian peace activist Ali Abu Awwad speaks of "painful hope," and I think that's a good term for describing the kind of hope that combines vision with activism—and his is a vision I deeply support.

My vision is informed by Whitehead's insight that all beings aim toward "the simple craving to enjoy freely the vividness of life."[16] Most of us, rich and poor, in fat world countries and lean ones,[17] don't enjoy the vividness of life to the degree that we might, burdened in the one case with too many material goods and too little time, and, in the other case, with too few of life's necessities and too much insecurity.

To speak of the "vividness of life" is to speak in aesthetic terms, and I would be remiss if I didn't speak about beauty as vision and hope. To do so—to speak about beauty—in our modern world is to court dismissal. It is to hear the voice of that participant in Donella Meadows' workshop who said, "Stop being ridiculous." But our continued trivialization of the value of beauty is evidence of the unremitting grip of the modern worldview on us. Philosophical and economic materialism required the marginalizing of beauty. Just so, a reintroduction of beauty as a public value will serve to break the exclusive control of economics as the determiner of worth. If we are to move toward a paradigm that supports life and that is ecologically sound, I believe we must commit to beauty as a central value and organizing principle.

For Whitehead, "the simple craving to enjoy freely the vividness of life" is an aesthetic aim and involves an aesthetic process. The production of art is one expression of this drive but Whitehead is talking about the production of LIFE. To hope for beauty is to hope for a world alive with a great diversity of life—both biologically diverse and culturally diverse—the consequence of endless creativity. And it is to hope for the coordination of life form to life form so that each individual life is able to enjoy the details of its life and to be supported by and contribute to larger and larger structures of relations.

Right now, we have made many parts of the world ugly—dreadful places (the etymological root of the word, "ugly.") On the one hand, we have outsized corporations in which the whole does not support the parts—depriving them of their individual intensities. And, in regard to our human relations with the natural world, we have a part—human civilization, especially capitalist civilization—asserting itself as the whole and destroying both the many parts and the processes on which it depends. In our drive to promote human life, we have denied the worth of other life forms. Beauty—understood as the name for the value associated with aliveness—calls us to a different relation with the natural world and with each other. It is this different relation on which we need to build our hope.

Naomi Klein and writer-activist Rebecca Solnit are vocal about the need for a coalescence of activist movements. It's all the same conversation, says Klein. That's why her book on climate change is also a book about capitalism. Climate activism **is** transition activism and both are **justice** activism. To create a movement of movements is an aesthetic project: the value and vitality of each individual effort—each mobilization for justice, each boycott or occupation, each legal objection—is affirmed both in its singularity and in its importance for the whole effort to shape the common good. Each effort is one exquisite detail in the emergence of a larger composition whose significance and worth reinforces the value of the individual efforts on which it depends. Whitehead's primary example of beauty is the Cathedral at Chartres with its nine portals, lined with statues. "There are those statues, each with its individual beauty, and all lending themselves to the beauty of the whole."[18] So it might be with a movement of movements, achieving a dynamic mutuality between individual efforts and the great restructuring to which they contribute.

The contributions of individuality to the whole—and of the whole to the constitutions of each individual—this is the dynamic at the core of Whitehead's philosophy. How it might best be achieved involves, I think, localism and local scale, the rebuilding of community life where individuals understand themselves as individuals-in-community and regard themselves as members of a place, in relationship with the land community. In short, it involves restructuring our social lives in ways that strengthen our sense of belonging and our obligations to those with whom we live and to the places where we live. These are the possibilities that I believe will renew our individual agency and restore a sense of worth to our relations with each other.

Let me close with this anecdote,[19] recounted by Rebecca Solnit. It is the story of a woman who was involved in the anti-nuclear movement of the 1960s, Women Strike for Peace. This movement actually succeeded in ending aboveground nuclear testing. In her reflections, the woman spoke about "how—foolish—and futile—she felt standing in the rain one morning protesting at the Kennedy White House." But years later, she learned that Dr. Benjamin Spock—the well-known antiwar activist who became a leader in the nuclear disarmament movement—became active in the anti-nuclear movement **because** he had seen "a small group of women standing in the rain, protesting at the White House." That, he said, was **his** turning point.

Solnit writes, "It's always too soon to calculate effect." This story, this lesson, is, for us, gathered at this conference. Perhaps, five years—or ten or twenty years—from now, people will remember our gathering in Claremont, in the middle of a drought in California, just after an oil spill north of Santa Barbara, and they will think about all those people who chose to make their hope active, to seize alternatives to the destructive practices of late modernity — people from all over the U.S., that great delegation from China, and others from far and wide, and they will say: "that was my turning point, our turning point, the reason why we persist in our hope that we can change the world."

ENDNOTES

1   Pieter Tans, http://grist.org/news/we-just-hit-400-ppm-co2-in-the-atmosphere-for-a-whole-month/?utm_source=newsletter &utm_medium=email&utm_term=EDIT%20Weekly&utm _campaign=weekly.

2   Grist, http://grist.org/climate-energy/were-about-to-push-the-earth-over-the-brink-new-study-finds/#.UA1m42dOqUw.email.

3   Elizabeth Kolbert, "Can Climate Change Cure Capitalism," in *The New York Review of Books* (December 4, 2014).

4   John Oliver, "Climate Change Debate: Last Week Tonight with John Oliver (HBO), published May 11, 20014 (https://www.youtube.com/watch?v=cjuGCJJUGsg).

5   http://www.alternet.org/environment/ethics-climate-hope-naomi-kleins-response-elizabeth-kolberts-review-changes-everything.

6   Derrick Jensen, "Beyond Hope," *Orion Magazine* (May/June 2006); https://orionmagazine.org/article/beyond-hope.

7   John B. Cobb, Jr., "Seizing an Alternative: Toward an Ecological Civilization" a Foundational Paper for the Seizing an Alternative Conference (July 2014. http://www.ctr4process.org/whitehead2015/about/background-material/).

8   In *Modes of Thought,* Whitehead writes, "The notion of potentiality . . . is fundamental for the understanding of existence, as soon as the notion of process is admitted," 99.

9   Alfred North Whitehead, *Adventures of Ideas,* 1933 (NY: Free Press, 1967), 19.

10   Ibid., quoting Plato, 120, 129.

11   Alfred North Whitehead, *Religion in the Making,* 1929 (NY: Fordham UP, 1996), 100.

12   Alfred North Whitehead, *Modes of Thought,* 1938 (NY: Free Press, 1968), 116.

13   Whitehead, *Adventures of Ideas,* 272.

14   Donella Meadows, "Envisioning a Sustainable World," written for the Third Biennial Meeting of the International Society for Ecological Economics, October 24–28, 1994, San Jose, Costa Rica; online at: http://donellameadows.org/archives/envisioning-a-sustainable-world/.

15   http://www.theguardian.com/commentisfree/2014/jun/16/saving-the-world-promise-not-fear-nature-environmentalism.

16   Whitehead, *Adventures of Ideas,* 272.

17   These are the terms favored by Nigerian-American journalist Dayo Olopade, see: http://www.npr.org/sections/goatsandsoda/2015/01/04/372684438/if-you-shouldnt-call-it-the-third-world-what-should-you-call-it.

18   Whitehead, *Adventures of Ideas,* 264.

19   Rebecca Solnit, "Hope in the Dark," first posted on Tom Dispatch.com, May 19, 2003; online at: http://www.tomdispatch.com/post/3273/the_best_of_tomdispatch_rebecca_solnit.

Participants in Section V, Ecological Civilization, included: Jeanne Nakamura, "The Psychology of Wellbeing and Its Ecological Implications"; Marilyn Hempel, "Population and Women"; Brianne Donaldson, "Seizing an Alternative: the Future of Meat without Animals"; Dean Freudenberger, "Agroecology as Foundational for Ecological Civilization"; Barbara Muraca and Fubin Yang, "Birth-pangs of Ecological Civilization"; China and Ecological Civilization (Xiaoting Liu and Tao Yang, chairs).

6

REIMAGINING AND REINVENTING THE
WISDOM TRADITIONS: WORLD LOYALTY

Mary Elizabeth Moore

EDITORS' INTRODUCTION: *Sections VI and VII of the conference were different from the others. In a conference on ecological civilization, what is often called "religion" (what we called the Wisdom Traditions) is an important topic. But it does not work to talk about it the way we talk about education or society. There are no major schools of education or sociology that have teachings that help or harm the prospects of ecological civilization. But there are complexly organized traditions with millions of followers that have been teaching about relevant matters for thousands of years. Some general theses can be formulated about all of them, but what is practically important is that each of them reconsiders its teachings in light of our global crisis. To some extent they have been doing so, especially since 1970. Some may have done rather little critical work until Mary Evelyn Tucker prodded them to do so in a remarkable series of conferences held at Harvard. Neither that series nor the "tracks" in this conference are comprehensive, but they go far to indicate the variety of movements involved in this re-thinking and that are hoping to play a positive role.*

The earlier plan was to represent these in just one section. But there were too many groups and too many approaches to contain in a single section. We divided the section into two, and that required two plenary addresses. Whitehead wrote a book entitled Religion in the Making, *and although his relevance to the topics of these sections is not limited to what he wrote here, we have focused on this book. Our term "Wisdom Traditions" points to what Karl Jaspers spoke of as the Axial traditions stemming in general from the middle of the first millennium BCE. Whitehead, writing earlier, referred to the same traditions as "rational religion," and this constituted his chief interest.*

Whitehead noted the distinction between theistic and nontheistic forms of rational religion. When we needed to make two sections out of the discussion of Wisdom Traditions, we followed this distinction. However, it should be clear that we included in the theistic side only the Abrahamic traditions: Judaism, Christianity, and Islam. There is much talk of "gods" in the Indian and Chinese traditions, and there is some talk also of a single God. Calling them all nontheistic is seriously misleading. Still, God does not play the central role in them that, until recently, God has played in the Abrahamic traditions. However, in fact, the two sections consisted of the Abrahamic tradition and "Others"—the latter not a satisfying title, so for the conference itself we settled upon Wisdom Traditions A and B.

Whitehead gave a variety of characterizations of rational religion. We selected two. The first is much more relevant to the Abrahamic traditions than to the others. That is World Loyalty. The Abrahamic traditions all call for personal and collective devotion to God and, of course, loyalty to God. In their mature form this is the one true God to whom is attributed the creation of all things. In all its forms, this family of traditions attributed to God a positive concern for the whole of creation. So devotion and loyalty to God should mean, and to some extent has meant, loyalty to humanity as a whole, but also to creation as a whole. That Whitehead featured this half a century before the ecological crisis was forcing the Wisdom traditions to re-think their relation to the natural world is remarkable and profoundly helpful. It assures us that what is most central to the Abrahamic traditions can play a crucial positive role if it is taken with deep seriousness. Allowing our belief in God to distract us from attention to the needs of the world has been a serious failure to understand the biblical message.

IN THIS FRAGILE MOMENT OF TIME, the world is torn with violence, and ethnocentrism has become a dominant pattern, whether in the political debates of the United States or in Syria's purging of citizens. The abuse of power is horrific globally, witnessed in city streets, prisons, small town movie theaters, and quiet villages. Efforts toward a just, peaceful, and ecologically sustainable universe are thwarted by those who accept the inevitability of injustice, who argue against any possibility of peace, and who deny climate change and all other threats to the planetary ecosystem. Adding to the trauma, religion is often used as an excuse to devastate the earth or ignore human responsibility, and to commit atrocities of injustice and violence. Religion often becomes the excuse to love one's own kind and denigrate or blame all others for the ills of the world. In such a world, can religion possibly be a source for a larger vision of the world and a deeper wellspring of hope?

Every religion of the world has within it a wisdom tradition, and these traditions characteristically point to a world that is larger than the adherents of that particular religion. Wisdom traditions (often plural within and across religious communities) have many and diverse meanings, and the very definition of wisdom tradition is multifarious. The heart of these traditions, and the meaning I intend in this chapter, is *a spiritual knowing that evokes insight, raises questions, and points beyond egocentrism, ethnocentrism, and anthropocentrism to a larger global and spiritual reality.* This definition undergirds the chapter, though it contrasts with definitions that equate wisdom traditions with universal or perennial truths. Wisdom traditions often do evoke insights that are shared across religions, but they also evoke questions, paradoxes, and wonderment. Jay McDaniel describes many of the particular wisdom traditions in his chapter, which follows. The present chapter focuses on the potential of religious wisdom traditions to expand human consciousness and human commitment to the universe. I will also attend to the dangers inherent in these same traditions.

Holding the tensions tenderly, we turn to the interplay of wisdom and world loyalty, exploring the potential of the human community to embody world loyalty and the role played by imagination and re-invention in evoking and sustaining such a loyalty to the wholeness of reality. In particular, the chapter explores the interplay of wisdom and world loyalty in a process-relational worldview; in the complicated movements of history; in embodied human narratives; and in practices that potentially foster world loyalty.

WISDOM AND WORLD LOYALTY: A PROCESS-RELATIONAL VISION

Wisdom traditions can potentially turn people toward a larger cosmos and to the richness of peoples and traditions in relation to one another, holding together the macro- and micro-realities that comprise human experience. Alfred North Whitehead's understanding of world loyalty is particularly helpful in naming the potential of human beings to see the connections of all aspects of the universe and to treasure the dignity of every being while seeking to value the whole. In his Lowell Lectures of 1926, he spun a vision of world-loyalty. He made a case that religion merges individual attention with attention to the universe, and he makes the bold claim that "religion *is* world-loyalty (emphasis mine)."[1] World loyalty thus emerges from religious experience, and it makes a claim on the lives of people.

The early Whiteheadian vision of world loyalty is resonant with his later reflections on creativity as the ultimate principle of reality, in which an emerging occasion embodies all of the universe that has gone before, and then contributes to those occasions that have yet to emerge.[2]

The very nature of the universe is to be interconnected, emergent, and co-constitutive. The relational process continues to weave an interconnected universe. This expansive vision suggests a great deal of positive potential built into the creative cosmic processes, and Whitehead did indeed see that potential. He also recognized the underside, both in the creative process and in moral advocacy. He recognized, for example, that intolerance can result from moral fervor,[3] even in positive human and religious advances, and neither religious nor ethical views of the universe will be free of dangers.

Others have built on Whitehead's vision of world order. Warren Copeland argues that to love God is to love the world — both human and nonhuman — and thus to be concerned for public life.[4] He describes world loyalty as "loyalty to the character of all relationships within the world and an intent to promote, insofar as it falls on us, relationships that enhance rather than destroy the creatures or individuals related."[5] Copeland does recognize the inevitable fragmentary nature of human actions, but he also recognizes the real possibility for individuals and communities to promote relationships that are mutually enriching, and to do so in ways that interweave the private and public dimensions of life.[6] Similarly, Jay McDaniel, in one of his early works, relates world loyalty with ecological spirituality. To cultivate the possibility of world loyalty, people need to develop the capacity to see the world from others' perspectives. McDaniel calls this practice "imaginative ego-transcendence," or the practice of transcending one's ego "to place oneself in the position of another subject, and to try to perceive the world from that being's point of view."[7]

The views of world loyalty described here offer a vision that is far from the reality that people experience every day. The world in which we live is fraught with destruction, fear, blame, and violence. René Girard has analyzed this phenomenon through literary and religious traditions and has described a persisting scapegoating phenomenon that spans centuries of human existence. Scapegoating is a process by which one group of people projects its anguish and fear upon another, blaming the denigrated other and inciting violence against them.[8] In a similar vein, Grace Jantzen argues that violence is rooted in a preoccupation with death, necrophilia, which can be traced throughout Western history in literature and religious sources. For Jantzen, the antidote to violence is to cultivate a new social imaginary that is centered on life or natality.[9] I would argue that the concept of world loyalty can contribute to such a social imaginary by spinning a vision for a world beyond scapegoating and beyond death-preoccupation. This is the vision that both Girard and Jantzen paint with different words; it is the vision of Copeland's loving God and loving the world and the vision of Jay McDaniel's imaginative ego-transcendence. That vision is far from daily reality, but oh so compelling!

WISDOM AND WORLD LOYALTY IN THE FLOW OF HISTORY

The unrealized vision calls for a detailed exploration of history, which extends beyond the present chapter. It also calls for engaged imagination in the very process of looking back and looking forward; thus, I ponder the complexities of history poetically rather than empirically. In this way, I seek to acknowledge the complexities without detailing them. I seek to ponder the phenomena of wisdom and world loyalty over time.

> In the beginning was wisdom and a world
> And wisdom permeated, even created, that world
> And the world was filled with wisdom,
> But wisdom was flighty and hard to find
> It shone in rituals and stories
> And every tribe had its own — oh so beautiful — ways
>   to sing and dance the wisdom of the ages!
> People *evoked* wisdom and they *invoked* the Holy
> But people loved their evocations and invocations more than
>   the Holy
> And each clan created and clung to its own.
>
> Today we inherit all of those rituals and stories,
>   And the clinging and creating.
> We have the potential to receive and hallow the rituals and
>   stories of our people

And the rituals and stories of others—
To hold these precious gifts of wisdom and to create anew
We have potential to embrace a larger world
To be global, even cosmic, citizens,
We have communication that connects us
Complex ideas that weave simplicities into
brilliant complexities
Trade that allows us to share and receive from one another
Public deliberations that allow us to draw ideas
from one another
And create something new.
But the new we have created is torn with violence
And with abundance held by a few while the many starve
And with desecration and desolation of the environment.
Global consciousness has become global*ism*
Conflicts between clans have become global wars
Culture-sharing has become colonialism
Resource sharing has become resource hording
Reason has become a sophisticated way to objectify and
dominate others
Critical thinking about culture creates justifications for one's
own people,
One's own values, one's own culture as superior to others.
In that milieu, is world loyalty possible?
Is it even a value to hold
when it is so easily distorted into dominance and destruction?
One is tempted to retreat to pre-modern worlds,
But even those were isolated and insulated from one another.
At least the dangers were more contained
And the simplicities were grounded in more embodied
existence—
Good efforts to hunt or grow food, to live in tune
with one's people and the land.

But peoples of long ago were perhaps not so isolated;
  Peoples crossed one another in ancient China
    In the lands of the Mediterranean
      In the lands of the Pacific
    In virtually every land.
And when they met, they sometimes warred
  They sometimes traded,
    They sometimes destroyed one another,
      They sometimes kept distance — as much as they
        were able
But they inevitably met, and when they did
  They reinvented themselves again and again.

World loyalty is about reimaging and reinvention — meeting a new moment and being thrown into terror, meeting a new moment and choosing hope. Reimagining is dreaming a new world. Mahatma Gandhi envisioned a world in which his people and *all* people were free. His Holiness the Dalai Lama envisions a world of peace. In the United States, the young Bill McKibben dreamed 350.org and it grew into a planet-wide organization with 20,000 rallies across the globe. Then he dreamed a movement of resistance to the Keystone Pipeline and a movement of demand for fossil fuel divestment. Every act began with a dream — a glimpse of what was possible. Dreams are the clay from which new shapes are molded. But the dreams are not themselves the full story. If the world is to be made new and if world loyalty is to become a reality, we need to draw upon ancient, modern, and postmodern wisdom to reinvent a world that does not yet exist.

World loyalty begins with a seed of hope and a commitment. It requires that we commit ourselves to the flourishing of the universe and not just to our own selves and our own people. But world loyalty *does* require that we commit ourselves to the flourishing of ourselves and our people and the natural world of our homelands because each part of this universe is crucial to the whole. The Tongva people of the Los Angeles Basin and the Chumash people of the Southern California coasts have nourished world loyalty by tending to their distinctive culture and religion, and to their long history of loving the earth. The choice between local and global is not a choice. The choice between indigenous traditions and grand civilizations is not a choice. The choice among pre-modern, modern, and post-modern is not a choice. The choice between one religious tradition and another is not a choice. We live in a universe of many textures, and that universe will suffer if the whole is not preserved with all of its fullness and manyness. However, we do not live in a universe that knows *how* to appreciate the cosmos and every part of it. That is our task—to reinvent a world, at least to reinvent our understanding of that world and our ways of living in it.

Arguments about an axial age identify a liminal period of global history during which civilization-shaping movements took place in religion, culture, and patterns of human thinking. Scholars locate the beginning of the axial age between 900 and 700 BCE and the ending between 300 and 100 BCE, with most of the major cultural shifts taking place between 600 and 300. What is most important in this analysis is that the world changed in dramatic ways during this period; dramatic changes took place in the ways people thought about and shaped their civilizations. The emergence led to greater awareness of worlds beyond one's own, increased critical analysis of cultures and religion, new understandings of the Holy as concerned with the whole earth and not just one's own people, and newly emerging ethical norms that responded to the whole known world and not just to one's own tribe. According to Karl Jaspers, and echoed by John Cobb in his writing on world loyalty, axial civilizations across the globe developed new capacities, grounded in reason.[10] These new capacities generated major cultural developments and inspired humanity in general toward a greater sense of the whole.[11] We need to recognize, however, that many of these civilizations also developed the capacity to overtake and dominate in empires of impressive grandeur and oppressive destruction.

One can see why some inheritors of axial civilization and religion suspect the inheritance and, instead, long for the pre-modern, simpler sensibilities. The pre-modern and postmodern almost touch as the pre-modern images and ideas are dimly discerned and brought into dialogue with postmodern questions. The question of world loyalty is a large and complex one, but its embodiment is urgent. Thus, I turn now to narratives of people who might be seen as embodying world loyalty. An analysis of those narratives will illumine the larger picture. I will come back then to propose human practices that can cultivate world loyalty in a world in which world loyalty can potentially lead to ecological care, justice, and peace, but can also be twisted into wanton destruction, rationalized injustice, and violation of others.

WORLD LOYALTY EMBODIED IN HUMAN LIVES

Human lives can reveal much about world loyalty in embodied form. Here we will explore the narratives of three people whose lives are beacons of world loyalty, albeit in very different forms. The three are Sojourner Truth, Abraham Joshua Heschel, and Vincent Machozi — people of radically different backgrounds and strikingly similar commitment to living in faith and making the world a better place.

Sojourner Truth

Sojourner Truth (c. 1797–1883) was born into slavery in New York with the name Isabelle Baumfree. At the age of 9, she was sold in auction, and she was to experience a harsh childhood with daily beatings. She was sold twice more, and then promised freedom by her owner, who was seemingly influenced by the movement to abolish slavery that was well underway in New York during that era (1799–1827). Isabelle's hope for freedom was short-lived, however, and her owner retracted his promise. She immediately began planning her escape, determined not to abandon hope. With her infant daughter, she did escape in 1826. Sometime later, she learned that her 5-year-old son Peter had been illegally sold to a slaveowner in Alabama. Isabelle Baumfree sued for his release, with the help of the Van Wagenen family for whom she worked at that time. She won the case (one of the first successful cases of an African American woman against a white man), and Peter was released.

Not long after this legal case was resolved, Isabella Baumfree had a Christian conversion experience. A few years later (1843), she had another life-changing religious experience, which inspired her to change her name to Sojourner Truth. At that time, she also dedicated herself to be a traveling preacher advocating for the abolition of slavery. Soon after, she became involved in women's rights, as well, and was invited to speak in the first National Women's Rights Convention in 1850. Shortly after, she moved to Ohio to continue her advocacy for women, slaves, and civil rights. There, in 1851, she delivered her famous "Ain't I a Woman" speech at the Women's Convention in Akron, Ohio.

Through the rest of her life, Sojourner Truth continued to advocate for the freeing of slaves and the vote for women. In the 1850s, she became a staunch advocate for desegregation — riding on streetcars that were labeled for whites. She also worked politically to obtain land grants for former slaves and she advocated for prison reform and abolition of the death penalty. She was a world changer who drew from the lessons of her own life to imagine a world that was better for everyone who had ever been oppressed by slavery, gender, poverty, or entanglement with the legal system.

Abraham Joshua Heschel

We turn now to a man who lived in another century, was from a different religious heritage and, in his early decades, lived on another continent. Abraham Joshua Heschel (1907–1972) was deeply grounded in his love of God and family. He was the youngest of six children, the offspring of Moshe Mordechai and Reizel Perlow, and the descendant of prominent European rabbis on both sides of the family. As a boy, Heschel had an excellent Yeshiva education and then studied for the Orthodox rabbinate. He completed a doctoral degree at the University of Berlin and also studied at *Hochschule fuer die Wissenschaft des Judentums,* where he later taught Torah and received a second ordination in the liberal tradition. Shortly thereafter, Joshua Heschel was arrested by the Gestapo and sent to Warsaw, where he taught for almost a year. With encouragement from others, he escaped Warsaw, but only six weeks before the Germans invaded Poland. As the Holocaust unfolded, Heschel lost many family members: his sister was killed in a German bombing, his mother was murdered by the Nazis, and his two sisters died in concentrations camps.

During these years, Heschel was emerging as a spiritual mensch in the United States. He became widely known as a public intellectual and teacher, first at Hebrew Union in Cincinnati, Ohio, and then at the Jewish Theological Seminary in New York City. He also wrote bountifully, focusing on the prophets and on the God-human relationship in particular. This is the period, for example, when he wrote *God in Search of Man,* and *Man is Not Alone.* During this period he also became absorbed by the Civil Rights Movement, marching with Martin Luther King, Jr.

As a teacher, social commentator, and spiritual mentor, Heschel worried that religion was becoming irrelevant and oppressive. His response was to ponder the depths of his own spiritual tradition and offer that wisdom to the larger human community. In so doing, he returned repeatedly to a few key themes: the social-religious significance of prophetic witness, the precious gift of wonder and awe, the grounding power of prayer as communion with God, and the gift of Sabbath practice to the community and the world. He also made strong connections between his life of prayer and religious observance and his life of public witness. After marching with King and a throng of others, he famously testified that "I felt my feet were praying."

Heschel was ardent in linking deep religion and deep concern for society. He wrote John F. Kennedy a telegram in 1963, saying "We forfeit the right to worship God as long as we continue to humiliate negroes. . . . The hour calls for moral grandeur and spiritual audacity."

This telegram later influenced the title of a collection of his essays, *Moral Grandeur and Spiritual Audacity* (1996). In one essay of that book, he explains his involvement in the peace movement:

> The more deeply immersed I became in the thinking of the prophets, the more powerfully it became clear to me what the lives of the prophets sought to convey: that morally speaking, there is no limit to the concern one must feel for the suffering of human beings, that indifference to evil is worse than evil itself, that in a free society, some are guilty, but all are responsible.[12]

The connections that Heschel made between his religious tradition and the issues of his time were nowhere more apparent than in his speech to the Conference on Religion and Race, 14 January 1963:

> (1) At the first conference on religion and race, the main participants were Pharaoh and Moses [audience laughter and clapping]. Moses' words were: 'Thus says the Lord, the God of Israel, let my people go that they may celebrate a feast to me.' While Pharaoh retorted: 'Who is the Lord, that I should heed this voice and let Israel go? I do not know the Lord, and moreover I will not let Israel go.'

> (2) The outcome of that summit meeting has not yet come to an end. Pharaoh is not ready to capitulate. The exodus began, but is far from having been completed. In fact, it was easier for the children of Israel to cross the Red Sea than for a Negro to cross certain university campuses.

> (3) Let us dodge no issues. Let us yield no inch to bigotry, let us make no compromise with callousness.

We see here a man for whom the connections between religion and global citizenship are obvious and deep.

Rabbi Heschel never ceased his efforts in race relations, and his world-changing efforts later extended to building interreligious relationships. Of particular note is the work he did on Roman

Catholic-Jewish relations with Cardinal Augustin Bea. Bea was a German scholar of the Hebrew Bible who had witnessed the effects of the Holocaust. He headed the Roman Catholic Church's efforts to reconcile with Jews in the Second Vatican Council. Rabbi Abraham Joshua Heschel was by his side in these efforts. Then, in 1972, Heschel was invited to participate in an interfaith conference that included Muslims. He was in frail health by this time, but he insisted on making a final trip to Rome. He left his witness to the value of interfaith relationships, as he had earlier and continually made his mark on race relations.

Vincent Machozi

The third story is of a man who has recently been martyred in the Democratic Republic of Congo (DRC). Near midnight on March 22, 2016, Father Vincent Machozi was in his home village. A military vehicle pulled up and 12 armed men, wearing military uniforms of the Congo army, went looking for him. Father Machozi was a recent graduate of the Boston University School of Theology. He had come to the school to study the church's role in human rights and peace-making. As a Roman Catholic priest in the order of the Augustinians of the Assumption, Father Machozi's intended to complete his ThD and return home as a pastor and professor. He described his vision in an interview before he returned home:

> I would like to continue teaching part time and work on social and economic issues affecting the grassroots trans-formation of society when I return to my country. I would also like to work in a village, training catechists and helping the poor to make a living. I want to bring the story of the Congo to the world through the continued development of the website.[13]

He further emphasized the need to focus on issues, especially poverty, and to place hope in young people.

After some time, Father Machozi felt a strong tug to return home with the doctoral degree unfinished, though he was later awarded the Master of Sacred Theology. Machozi could see that human rights abuses were growing by the day in his country, and he heard God calling him to step up and advocate for justice, human rights, and peace. Thus, Father Machozi returned to his homeland with a clear sense of mission: to tend his parish and seminary, and to document human rights violations in the eastern Congo so the people of the Congo and the world would be aware. He started a human rights website while a student at Boston University, and he continued to build it after his return home. His last posting on the internet was an online article denouncing the presidents of the Congo and Rwanda for their roles in the massacres of innocent civilians. Shortly after posting this article, the twelve soldiers found Father Machozi and killed him in a hail of bullets. His last words were, "Why are you killing?"

Father Machozi glimpsed a world in which dictators would cease their killing, and people of the Congo and around the world would stand against all acts of murder and violence. Father Machozi knew that his ministry was dangerous. He had experienced seven attempts on his life before he was assassinated. He knew the risks, but trusted God's future—a world in which everyone matters and differences are honored.

Notice in these three brief narratives that Sojourner Truth, Abraham Joshua Heschel, and Vincent Machozi endured enormous hardships, yet they found deep meaning and purpose in their respective faith traditions. One can see some parallels in their lives. All three reinvented themselves throughout their lives. They imagined that the world could be more just and compassionate, and they gave themselves fully to those visions, drawing from the wellsprings of their faith traditions and the wonder of the Holy. These themes are congruent with those in other narrative accounts of peacebuilders, such as Marc Gopin describes in his biographical studies.[14] Though each story is unique, the themes that emerge from them are strikingly similar in regard to world loyalty. They also suggest action—practices that have potential to cultivate world loyalty.

PRACTICES TOWARD WORLD LOYALTY

The pathways to world loyalty are visions, but they are also practices. Sojourner Truth, Abraham Joshua Heschel, and Vincent Machozi did not plan their lives in advance and take unwavering steps toward preconceived goals. Their lives were filled with experiencing, questioning, and wondering. All three were part of theistic religious traditions, so their wonder was grounded in awe of God and in the possibility of bettering the world. Their practices opened their consciousness to their own experience and to those of their people. Their practices also opened an ever-enlarging world to them. I will name some of those practices here, drawing from Truth, Heschel, and Machozi. The themes and practices have also been informed by a larger study of 55 oral histories with people known as world-changers in their local or global communities.[15]

Remembering the Traditions of One's People and the Traditions of Others

This entire chapter has considered the interplay between religious wisdom traditions and world loyalty. Strikingly, Truth, Heschel, and Machozi were all deeply affected by their religious traditions — both by the traditions they inherited and the mystical experiences of the Holy that were opened to them through those traditions. Their relations with God led them into an ever-expanding range of social consciousness and an ever-expanding range of action. For Sojourner Truth, the preaching of her faith and the advocacy for slaves and women were parts of one whole. As she became increasingly engaged in the ministry of proclamation and advocacy, her own sense of the issues expanded, and she found herself advocating also for civil rights, desegregation, land reform, and prison reform. Her religious fervor and her social passion were of one piece, and the power of the two together propelled her into radical action in the legal system, political debates, and public witness.

Similarly, Heschel was deeply grounded in his tradition, which was the orienting focus of his social passion. He cultivated a sense of wonder in God's presence, and that wonder fed his respect for the religious traditions of others; it also awakened him to the plight of others. This man, who had lost most of his own family in the Holocaust and who knew persecution and exile, allowed his own experience to awaken him to the hurt of others. He could not resist joining the civil rights march from Selma to Montgomery, and his own religious traditions gave him the insights to interpret that march and all it stood for. He also could not resist building relations with people in other faith traditions because his own wonder before the Holy awakened him to the wonder of others.

Likewise, Father Vincent Machozi discovered his calling to the priesthood early, and he drew deeply from the wells of his Roman Catholic faith, as well as the wells of Congolese peoples. His passion for the wisdom from both drove him home when he felt the urgency of his human rights work, and it kept him in the forefront of action even as he endured repeated attempts on his life, the last being successful.

Relating with Self, Earth, and Human Family

A second practice is relating with oneself, with the earth, and with the human family. Violent relationships led Sojourner Truth to walk out of slavery. More positive relationships with another white family helped her to sue for the freedom of her son Peter from slavery. Brief encounters with President Abraham Lincoln allowed her to advocate for abolition with the highest levels of government. She worked for land grants for freed slaves, recognizing that freed slaves needed to build new lives in relation to the land. Sojourner Truth's relationships with diverse peoples expanded her action to include women's suffrage and advocacy against the death penalty. Throughout her life, her practices led to new relationships, which led to new practices.

Similarly, Heschel moved toward ever-expanding relationships within the Jewish community of his childhood, the academic community of his training, the Jewish communities and friendships of his adulthood, the civil rights leadership, and the people of other faith traditions who came to be friends and mentors.

Machozi was also connected to everyone he met, including his people in the Congo and the people he came to know in multiple church and academic communities in Boston, Massachusetts. In the Congo, he helped establish the social center, "My Beautiful Village," where he was meeting with Nande tribal chiefs on the night he was gunned down; they were meeting to discuss their shared peace efforts. He was also deeply connected with those who were suffering and dying, as his website attests. In sum, Machozi was related to his village where he had established a social center; he was related to other leaders for peace; and he was related to the larger political structures in his country and around the world.

All three of these figures embodied a world loyalty that was nourished by relationships with those closest to them and with people they would never meet. They recognized the reality and importance of connections in a relational world.

Rethinking the Status Quo

A third critical practice is rethinking the status quo, which includes the status quo of ecological and social structures and dominant systems of thought. Sojourner Truth, Abraham Joshua Heschel, and Vincent Machozi were clearly rethinking the status quo at every turn. Truth refused to believe that slavery was a necessary or inevitable way of life; Heschel counteracted dominant assumptions about materialist worldviews and the alienation of peoples from one another. Machozi documented human rights violations to communicate atrocities to the world and enlist help in ending them. Note that every time these three people practiced one kind of rethinking, whether about slavery or about civil rights or peace-building, they opened themselves to rethinking all over again. And every act of rethinking expanded the range of their concerns, opening them to an ever-expanding perspective on world loyalty and to the reimagining and reinventing that go with it.

In his forthright address of ecological destruction, Pope Francis has made similar moves, drawing from his own Franciscan religious tradition, but also from more recent philosophical and social scientific ideas. Many of his statements and actions on ecology and economics echo the thinking of Karl Polanyi, who wrote *The Great Transformation*. In that book, Polanyi argues that economic systems originally emerged to serve human needs, but have become the dominant force to which humans have to adapt. He distinguishes between an economy that is "embedded in social relations" and one in which social relations are "embedded in the economic system." To raise such questions is to question the status quo, to rethink the world, and to imagine a new kind of future.

Repenting and Mourning the Destructions by One's People

In the three remaining practices I will be briefer because the seeds of these practices are already foreshadowed in the first three. Repenting and mourning are important elements in the practices of Truth, Heschel, and Machozi, and their mourning over abuse, injustice, and destructive social structures motivated all of their actions. Global citizenship not only breeds repentance and mourning, but also humility. We are small creatures in a world of huge need, and we ourselves participate in many of the most dangerous ecological and social problems, with and without our knowledge and with and without our consent. Repentance and mourning are ongoing.

Revisioning the Future in Light of the Best of the Past

What we see in Sojourner Truth, Abraham Joshua Heschel, and Vincent Machozi are continuing and ever-changing practices of engaging the world, seeing it through sober eyes, and discerning the ancient and modern wisdom that will guide the possibility of new visions for the future. For Sojourner Truth, this was expressed in her preaching and speaking, as in "Ain't I a Woman?" For Heschel, it was expressed in his voluminous writing as well, as in his teaching, speaking, public commentaries, and marching. For Machozi, it was expressed in his human rights website, together with his collaborations with peace leaders and his daily tending of human need.

Reconstructing the World

What we also see in Truth, Heschel, and Machozi is an *ongoing practice* of reconstructing the world wherever they found themselves. This practice was so important to Heschel that he traveled to an interfaith gathering at the very end of his life. It was so important to Machozi that he continued his work even after seven attempts on his life. These three people were exemplars of world loyalty, *engaged in practices of knowing and loving the world that only ended at their deaths*. As is evident in their stories, the process did not end there either. Their legacies have inspired and informed all of those who come after with the possibility of world loyalty. These three people not only imagined a better world, but they decided to hope in the midst of the overwhelming devastations of slavery (Truth), the Holocaust (Heschel), and genocide (Machozi). In so doing, they contributed to actual changes in their worlds. They also stir our collective imagination and challenge each of us to allow the wisdom traditions of our cultural and religious communions to shape our spiritual depths and turn us toward world loyalty.

ENDNOTES

1   Alfred North Whitehead, *Religion in the Making,* 1926 (New York: Fordham University Press, 2003, 1926), 60.

2   Alfred North Whitehead, *Process and Reality: An Essay in Cosmology,* 1929, Corrected Edition edited by David Ray Griffin and Donald W. Sherburne (New York: Free Press, 1978), 85, 211.

3   Whitehead, *Adventures of Ideas* (New York: Free Press, 1933), 50.

4   Warren R. Copeland, *Issues of Justice: Social Sources and Religious Meanings* (Atlanta: Mercer University Press, 2005), 84.

5   Ibid., 84–85.

6   Ibid., 85.

7   Jay B. McDaniel, *Earth, Sky, Gods and Mortals: Developing an Ecological Spirituality* (Eugene, OR: Wipf and Stock, 2009, 1990), 117.

8   René Girard, *Violence and the Sacred*, trans. Patrick Gregory (Baltimore: The Johns Hopkins University Press, 1977); Girard, *The Scapegoat,* trans. Yvonne Freccero (Baltimore: The Johns Hopkins University Press, 1986).

9   Grace M. Jantzen, *Foundations of Violence: Death and the Displacement of Beauty* (London: Routledge, 2004).

10   Karl Jaspers, *The Origin and Goal of History,* trans. Michael Bullock (New Haven: Yale University Press, 1968), 88–96.; John B. Cobb, Jr., "World Loyalty," paper presented as preview to Seizing an Alternative Conference, Claremont, CA, 4–7 June 2015; see: http://www.pandopopulus.com/world-loyalty/ (accessed 15 April 2016).

11   John B. Cobb, Jr., 2015; Kurt Salamun "Karl Jaspers' Conceptions of the Meaning of Life," *Existenz: An International Journal in Philosophy, Religion, Politics and the Arts,* 1:1-2 (2006), 1–8; see: http://www.bu.edu/paideia/existenz/volumes/Vol.1Salamun.pdf (accessed 12 September 2015).

12   Abraham Joshua Heschel, *Moral Grandeur and Spiritual Audacity* (New York: Farrar, Straus and Giroux, 1996), 224; originally published in 1973.

13   See interview with Father Vincent Machozi at: http://www.assumption.us/about-us/portraits/224-fr-vincent-f-machozi-aa-1965-2016 (accessed 16 April 2016). The website to which Father Vincent refers is: www.benilubero.com.

14   Marc Gopin, *Bridges across an Impossible Divide: The Inner Lives of Arab and Jewish Peacemakers* (New York: Oxford University Press, 2012).

15   Mary Elizabeth Moore, Oral History Project, conducted at Emory University, 2003–2008, and Boston University, 2009–present. Interviews collected at Emory are deposited in the Pitts Theology Library; interviews conducted at Boston are being prepared for deposit.

7

THE WORLD'S RELIGIONS AND

ECOLOGICAL CIVILIZATION

Jay McDaniel

EDITORS' INTRODUCTION: *Speaking in broad generalities, the Wisdom Traditions of India and China focused on the cultivation of the inner life of individuals more than on issues of to whom we owe devotion or loyalty. Although all had communal ceremonies, what the Abrahamic traditions understood as worship was not common. Whitehead gave much of his attention to religion as "the art and theory of the interior life." Whitehead was not saying that the Abrahamic traditions failed in this respect, and neither are we, but it is in this regard that today so many heirs of the Abrahamic traditions are finding help in Indian and Chinese traditions. It should also be emphasized that all the rational religions think in universal terms and tend to work against limited loyalties.*

One of the important contributions of Karl Jaspers was to enable us to see the philosophical development in Greece as a partner of what had been called the religious traditions. It expressed itself in communities of followers for a while, but these largely disappeared. Still the influence of the axial thinkers of Greece remains of great importance. They initiated the idea that individuals could think through fundamental questions of the meaning of life for themselves rather than identifying with traditional communities. In this respect the Greek philosophical tradition has never been more influential. This is where Whitehead himself is to be located. This tradition could be discussed equally well in either section.

Finally, we are outgrowing both Jaspers and Whitehead. Neither of them recognized the importance of pre-axial forms of wisdom for us today. More than any of the rational or axial traditions, the most ancient traditions, those of hunting and gathering societies, focused on the intimate inclusion of the human within the natural. This is an understanding that many of us would like to recover in a new form. In any survey of the contributions, potential and actual, that traditional wisdom can offer us today, this must be given a prominent place.

CAN THE WORLD'S RELIGIONS help contribute to ecological civilizations? The answer is fairly straightforward. They can do so if they remind us that we live together in a larger community of life on Earth — the Earth community — which is our common home. They can do so if they inspire us to live with respect and care for the community of life, humans much included. And they can do so if they inspire us to help build local communities that are creative, compassionate, participatory, ecologically wise, and spiritually satisfying with no one left behind. And they can do so if they inspire leaders to develop public policies conducive to these end. I am saying nothing that is not already said, quite beautifully and accurately, in Pope Francis' *Laudato Si*.

In order to do this, the religions must do something a bit more philosophical, also implied by *Laudato Si*. They must help us challenge certain assumptions of contemporary life that prevent us from appreciating our common home, living with respect, and building these communities. They must help us move (1) from a shallow empiricism that focuses only on sense experience to a deep empiricism, that we may appreciate the wide range of experiences that yield wisdom concerning the natural world; (2) from an overemphasis on individualism to a recognition that we are persons-in-community, whose well-being depends on the well-being of greater wholes; (3) from an anthropocentrism that focuses primarily on the value of human life to a recognition of the value and indeed a love of all life, or biophilia; (4) from exclusivist loyalties to our nations or ethnic groups toward world loyalty; and (5) from selective compassion to inclusive compassion. The world's religions can contribute to ecological civilizations if they help us make these shifts. At least this is how things look to those of us influenced by the philosophy of Whitehead. My aim in this essay is to elaborate on some of these ideas, introducing readers to aspects of Whitehead's thinking along the way.

WHITEHEAD ON RELIGION

Whitehead is important for the ideas he had about religion and for the ideas his philosophy inspires. In *Process and Reality* he proposes that religion deals with the subjective side of life: that is, with the formation of attitudes toward life and emotional responses to life. But his most systematic treatment of religion is in his book *Religion in the Making*. In that book he talks about "rational religion," which corresponds roughly with the wisdom traditions arising in the axial period. He discusses theistic and nontheistic forms of religion, which generally correspond with the Abrahamic and the other axial religions. He gives many different definitions of rational religion, the best known of which is "what the individual does with his solitariness."[1] The latter phrase suggests that rational religion arises out of intentional choice rather than cultural conformity. He offers two additional definitions which apply roughly to the Abrahamic and other axial religions. One of them is "religion as world loyalty." This idea fits well with the Abrahamic traditions, with their emphasis on a divine reality whose care and concerns includes the whole of creation. Another definition focuses on the disciplined structuring of the inner life, which fits especially well with some of the South Asian traditions that emphasize personal liberation of the self from the rounds of samsara. There is a hint throughout the work of an appreciative pluralism which recognizes that the aims and emphases of particular religious traditions can be different but complementary, each adding a certain sort of wisdom and beauty to the human experience. This appreciative pluralism is one of the many aspects of Whitehead's thought upon which Whiteheadians have built. I turn, then, to what it can mean to think about religion in a Whiteheadian way.

RELIGIONS AS WAYS OF LIVING

Readers unfamiliar with the wide range of the world's religions might naturally ask: How many are there and what are they? The matter is complicated by the fact that, in most settings, it is impossible to distinguish religion from culture and that new religions are frequently emerging, such that scholars of religion now speak of New Religious Movements as a category of its own. Indeed, some scholars — the late Wilfred Cantrell Smith, for example — argue that there are as many religions as there are people, because each human being has a unique journey through life shaped by what he or she considers most important.

There is wisdom in Smith's approach. As noted above, Whitehead himself says: "Religion is what an individual does with his own solitariness."[2] Nevertheless, Whitehead also emphasizes that no individual is an island and that solitariness itself, as lived from the inside, is a social reality. The physical and cultural worlds outside our bodies are inside our experience and our experience is inside these worlds. We are persons-in-community, not individuals in isolation; and we are inevitably shaped, positively and negatively, by cultural and religious traditions that surround us and dwell within us.

Moreover, many people throughout the world *claim affiliation* with one or another of these traditions in various degrees and ways, which intensifies the role that religions play in human life. Accordingly, if we are interested in religion and ecological civilization, it is not enough to focus on individual choices; we need to keep in mind the various religious traditions and how they influence people.

The traditions are both actual and imagined. They exist in actual fact in concrete history and as ideas or what Whitehead calls "lures for feeling" in people's minds. To say that people imagine their religions is not to say that their religions are false. It is to say that they are experienced as ideals or goals by which people feel called forward in life. Religions are not only historical facts; they are callings, influencing people's subjective aims.

What, then, are the various religious groupings? Here it helps to turn to a typical survey of the world's religions. Consider *World Religions Today* published by Oxford University Press.[3] Its chapters are:

Indigenous Religions

The Many Stories of Judaism: Sacred and Secular

Christian Diversity and the Road to Modernity

Islam: The Many Faces of the Muslim Experience

Hinduism, Jainism, and Sikhism: South Asian Religions

Buddhism: Paths Toward Nirvana

East Asian Religions: Confucianism, Daoism, Shinto, Buddhism

Globalization: From New to New Age Religions

As we peruse these chapters, we quickly realize that none of these religions are about belief alone. The building blocks of any and every religion include core experiences, shared rituals, myths and stories, a sense of community, ethical guidelines, material realities (icons, music), and beliefs. In many of these religions the shared rituals and sense of community are more important than shared beliefs. This is to be expected for those of us influenced by Whitehead's way of thinking. Influenced by his account of experience in *Process and Reality* we come to think of a religion not so much as a belief system, but rather as a *way of living* involving all of the elements of experience or (to use Whitehead's word) concrescence. From a Whiteheadian perspective a way of living includes physical feelings, intellectual feelings, emotions, attitudes, bodily practices, social relations, subjective aims, remembered pasts, and hopes for the future. Religion is an experiential process. It is an activity of identity-formation, community involvement, worldview development, imaginative exploration, and ritualized practice—rather than as a settled and static fact.

Moreover, as scholars of religion increasingly recognize, the very word "religion" can be problematic if it suggests a special compartment of life distinguishable from the culture, or a way of living focused on a single divine reality, or obedience to guidelines from a written text, or even a sense of the sacred. Many of the religions treated in *World Religions Today* are not like this at all. Some of them—prophetic Judaism, for example—are more interested in ethics than in a sense of the sacred. Others—Zen Buddhism, for example—explicitly eschew a dichotomy between the sacred and the profane. Some—Theravada Buddhism, for example—are explicitly interested in demythologization. Some—the Indigenous traditions, for example—are oral rather than textual. Given some of its connotations, the very word "religion" can keep us from understanding religion. This is one reason it can be more helpful simply to speak of these religions as Ways of Living or as Wisdom Traditions.

Even phrases such as Ways of Living and Wisdom Traditions can be problematic if they suggest homogeneity, stasis, or independence. If we study the world's religions with Whiteheadian eyes, three points are especially noticeable. First, each of these traditions is internally diverse, such that those who feel allegiance to them may practice the religion in different ways. Second, each is evolving through time, such that none are fully defined by their pasts. Third, all the traditions are historically situated, such that what they mean for their adherents, and how they are practiced, will be profoundly influenced by contexts. In our time there is one context that all the religions face, regardless of their local situations. It is the potential calamities that the whole world faces today if we do not seize an alternative: political disintegration, economic breakdown, war and the threat of nuclear war, and environmental collapse, including global climate change. A central question is: Can they offer wisdom that helps us respond constructively to this context?

COMPLEMENTARY PLURALISM

The wisdom needed in our time must be embodied wisdom: that is, a *felt sense of the world* that is ritualized and translatable into practical action. As noted above, this wisdom needs to include a sense that we belong to a dynamic and complex Earth community, filled with many forms of life, each of which has some kind of intrinsic value, and all of which add beauty to the whole. And it needs to encourage us to build communities that are creative, compassionate, participatory, ecologically wise, and spiritually satisfying, with no one left behind. Can the wisdom traditions contribute to this kind of wisdom?

It is important to recognize at the outset that these traditions are already "wise" about different but complementary matters. At least this is what those of us influenced by Whitehead propose. Consider the taglines for the chapters in *World Religions Today*: Hinduism and other South Asian traditions can be wise about *many paths to liberation*; Buddhism can be wise about the *paths to nirvana*; Confucianism can be wise about *powers of human cultivation* of virtues required for civic society; and Daoism can be wise about *capacities for natural harmony*. There is no need to assume that these different forms of wisdom are identical, nor is there need to think that they are contradictory. At least this is how those of us influenced by the philosophy of Whitehead approach matters. If, as Whitehead suggests, the universe is a creative advance into novelty, then we would expect that myriad cultures and peoples on our planet would have novel aims, all of which make the whole of human life richer. In Whitehead as in so many forms of Hinduism, multiplicity is not to be feared, it is to be welcomed.

Indeed, Whitehead's philosophy goes even further, presenting a plurality of realities that are "ultimate" or "irreducible" in their own ways: God, Creativity, the Cosmos, the Present Moment. Thus we are encouraged to consider the possibility that, in the course of human history, different communities in different circumstances have been attuned to different kinds of ultimate realities, each of which leads to distinctive forms of human well-being that are valuable in their own ways. To put the matter boldly, there may be multiple ultimate realities and multiple forms of salvation or meaning-making that may well be complementary not contradictory. Awakening to Nirvana as final peace may bring a certain kind of satisfaction to human desire, and faithfulness to the God of social justice may likewise bring satisfaction. For one religion to be "right" about something, the others do not have to be "wrong." They can be "right" about different things.

WISDOM FOR ECOLOGICAL CIVILIZATION

Still, especially in our time, it is important to recognize that the Earth is our common home and we must learn to live together for the sake of the well-being of people, animals, and the Earth. Thus, amid the diverse forms of wisdom offered by the religions, we rightly ask: Is there a particular form of embodied wisdom that is especially needed today, if we are to seize an alternative for the common good? I will call it *wisdom for ecological civilization*. This kind of wisdom is trans-modern in that it critiques and moves beyond certain habits of thought that characterized ways of thinking that were considered "modern" in Western Europe and the United States for three centuries, and that have been exported throughout the world. Modern ways of thinking emphasized the primacy of individual autonomy over relational selfhood; the primacy of scientific ways of knowing over traditional, spiritual, and artistic ways of knowing; and the primacy of human life over other animals and the larger web of life. These modern ways further assumed that, deep down, the universe as a whole and the earth in particular are best understood on the analogy of a machine with replaceable parts, rather than a living organism with a creativity of its own. Ultimately, so it seemed, the whole universe could be reduced to nugget-like atoms that were devoid of creativity and whose sole mode of interaction was collision.

One value of Whitehead's philosophy is that it offers a trans-modern way of thinking that builds upon the better sides of modernity but moves beyond the worst. It knows that there are predictable and machine-like dimensions of the world; it knows that collisions are real; it knows that human beings have intrinsic value deserving care; it knows that science yields knowledge important to us all. Still, it is one sided and needs to be expanded. John Cobb suggests that there are five attitudes toward life needed today that move beyond modern thinking, guiding us toward a more just and sustainable world.

Deep Empiricism. Our need is for a shift from sense-based empiricism (focused on conscious sense-perception alone) to *deep empiricism*, in which the cognitive disclosures of memory and anticipation, emotion and feeling, conscious and unconscious experience, bodily experience and cerebral experience, are appreciated. This can be complemented by an appreciation of multiple forms of intelligence: verbal-linguistic, logical-mathematical, visual-spatial, rhythmic-musical, kinesthetic, and emotional.

Persons-in-Community. Our need is for a shift from Western-based individualism to a more *community-based way of living*, in which we understand ourselves as persons-in-community, not individuals in isolation. This can be enriched by recognizing that community itself includes the more than human world: hills, rivers, other animals, trees, stars.

Biophilia. Our need is for a shift from anthropocentrism to *biophilia*, amid which we recognize that all forms of life, not human life alone, are worthy of respect and care. This is rightly enhanced by a recognition that there is something like subjectivity or aliveness in all things, all the down into the depths of matter.

World Loyalty. Our need is for a shift from we/they thinking to *world loyalty*, amid which the health and well-being of all human beings (and other living beings as well) matters as much, if not more, than local allegiances to village, city, town, and nation. This can be facilitated by a recognition that there is a horizon or consciousness that includes or embraces the whole of things with, in Whitehead's words, "tender care."

Inclusive Compassion: Our need is for a shift from conventional morality to *inclusive compassion*, amid which capacities for empathy are expanded to include justice for all, with special focus on the vulnerable and other animals. This includes social justice.

If Cobb is right, then we can ask: How might the various wisdom traditions help guide us into these alternative forms of embodied wisdom?

We best recognize at the outset that particular traditions may be helpful in one or some areas, but not in others. Consider Judaism, Christianity, and Islam. With their faith in a transcendent God whose horizons of concern include the whole world, the prophetic traditions of Judaism, Christianity, and Islam may be especially helpful in promoting world loyalty but not as helpful in encouraging the quietness of mind necessary to sense the aliveness of all things or in fostering a sense of respect for animal life. In the latter regard Buddhist meditative practices may be more helpful. When it comes to the five foundations, different traditions may have different gifts and, for that matter, different liabilities. Truth be told, we need all the traditions, perhaps especially the oldest: the Indigenous Traditions.

WISDOM FROM INDIGENOUS TRADITIONS: RELATIONAL KNOWING

Indeed the Indigenous Traditions of the world may be most important since so many of them highlight a sense of aliveness throughout the whole of the world, recognize multiple forms of knowing, emphasize persons-in-community, and recognize eco-community as part of what "community" means. But equally important, they invite us to recognize that wisdom itself is not simply "about" one subject or another, but a way of living in its own right, fully relational. More often than not indigenous peoples think of knowing itself, not as a mode of objectifying apprehension focused on data received from the senses in a neutral way, but rather as a way of living in the world that draws deeply from emotion and intuition, in relation to people, animals, the earth, and spirits. This is close to Daoism in some ways, but the Indigenous traditions offer it more concretely in local, communal settings, thus linking community life and spirituality in ways not characteristic of the more eremitic Daoist sensibility. Understood in Indigenous ways, wisdom is not so much about externalized knowledge as it is how a people live in the world:

> Perhaps the closest one can get to describing unity in Indigenous knowledge is that knowledge is the expression of the vibrant relationships between people, the ecosystems, and other living beings and spirits that share their lands. . . . All aspects of knowledge are interrelated and cannot be separated from the traditional territories of the people concerned. . . . To the indigenous ways of knowing, the self exists within a world that is subject to flux. The purpose of these ways of knowing is to reunify the world or at least to reconcile the world to itself. Indigenous knowledge is *the way of living* within contexts of flux, paradox, and tension, respecting the pull of dualism and reconciling opposing forces. . . . Developing these ways of knowing leads to freedom of consciousness and to solidarity with the natural world.[4]

If there is to be a shift in consciousness from sense-bound epistemology to deep empiricism, then Indigenous peoples add a dimension to deep empiricism that might otherwise be absent. Deep empiricism is more than recognizing multiple forms of knowing (aesthetic, artistic, intuitive); it is a form of knowing that emerges through lived relationships with the world and that is always ongoing. Indigenous peoples teach the whole world about this form of knowing; the need on the part of the world is to honor, protect, and defend their rights to become more fully themselves, on their own terms and for their own sakes. At least this is what those of us in the Whiteheadian tradition propose. Diversity makes the whole richer; and some forms of diversity are essential to the very future of the whole.

SOUTH AND EAST ASIAN TRADITIONS

This does not mean that other traditional ways—say those of East Asia and South Asia—are unimportant. To be sure, all of the world's religions encourage and offer practices concerning the cultivation of character and the inner life. But the traditions of East and South

Asia can play a special role. Hinduism invites us to embrace plurality itself, recognizing what Diana Eck calls the manyness of God: that is, the multiple faces and names by which the divine reality, understood in personal or transpersonal terms, can be known and felt. Insofar as an ecological civilization includes a healthy respect for diversity, Hinduism offers its special voice. Buddhism invites us to recognize that, when push comes to shove, it is not the amount of material goods we possess that gives us our freedom, but rather the twin virtues of wisdom and compassion that make us whole. Insofar as an ecological civilization is built upon a wise recognition of the interconnectedness of all things, and a compassionate response to all living beings, Buddhism offers its special voice. Jainism encourages us to live with deep ahimsa, with radical nonviolence, thereby widening our sense of who deserves our compassion. Insofar as an ecological civilization requires inclusive compassion, Jainism offers its special voice. Daoism encourages us to sense a qi-like energy throughout the whole of the universe, incarnate among other places in our own bodies, to which we can awaken and live healthy lives. Insofar as an ecological civilization requires sensitivity to the energetic dynamics of life and sensitivity to the inner lure toward holistic health, Daoism offers its distinctive voice. Confucianism invites us to see human beings within a larger cosmic context—a trinity of heaven, earth, and humanity—and then to live within our own context in humane, reciprocal ways, informed by a sense of li or appropriateness. Insofar as an ecological civilization entails this kind of relational living, this sense of being a person-in-community, Confucianism offers its unique voice. These are but some of the South and East Asian traditions and these gifts are but a few they offer to the better hope of the world. Their contributions are complementary to, not contradictory of, the gifts also offered by the Abrahamic traditions. We need them all.

In an age of cultural globalization, it is important to avoid cultural exploitation, to avoid cultural strip-mining. As the lessons learned from these and other traditions are acquired, we need to be attentive to the context in which their gifts emerge. Still, at this stage in history, with an increased awareness of the earth as our common home, we cannot but be grateful for the ways in which these "ways of living" might enrich the wider world and help us avoid the catastrophes—or at least build new communities after the disasters. The world's religions are cultural treasures but also, in their ways, oceans of possibility. It is just these possibilities that we need today.

ENDNOTES

1   Alfred North Whitehead, *Religion in the Making,* 1926 (NY: Fordham University Press, 1996), 47.

2   Ibid.

3   John L. Esposito, Darrell J. Fasching, and Todd T. Lewis, *World Religions Today,* 5th Edition (NY: Oxford University Press, 2014).

4   Quoted by Battiste and Henderson, 390. *Protecting Indigenous Knowledge and Heritage: A Global Challenge,* Purich's Aboriginal Issues Series (Saskatoon: Purich Publishing, 2000), 42.

8

ARE WE REALLY RELATED?

The Impact of Whitehead's Organismic
Philosophy on Our View of Education

Franz Riffert

EDITORS' INTRODUCTION: *The previous chapter considered aspects of shaping the interior life as the province of what we often call religion. Today, however, personal formation is often thought of not as spiritual, but as the task of secular education. For Whiteheadians, any attempt to isolate the spiritual from other aspects of formation is a doomed proposition, for the whole process of human development is a unity. Nevertheless, within that unity it is possible to highlight different aspects. Accordingly, this chapter continues the focus on formation, but from the perspective of schooling. Chapter 9 will deal with the process holistically, bringing the physical dimension to the fore.*

Throughout the discussion, we have emphasized relatedness. We have complained that the modern world has exaggerated the separateness of individuals and sought to revise our thinking so as to take account of our interconnectedness. But we have not dealt with the profound philosophical problem that ~~has~~ underlies and intensifies the individualistic tendencies of modernity. Modern philosophy has not been able to explain how we are genuinely related to anything.

Although our common sense notions have kept us assuming that we are related, the lack of theoretical justification still affects both theory and practice. This chapter will explain how this has worked in education. Whitehead's greatest philosophical achievement may have been to give an explanation of causality and relationship that justifies common sense and common practice and explains both normal and unusual experiences. The remainder of these chapters will progressively develop his contribution.

Foundational to this is what Whitehead calls causal feelings or pure physical prehensions. The latter term is a technical one. Since this is an aspect of reality not noticed by previous philosophers, he needed a new term. But since a new term carries no connotations at all, he indicated that the term "feeling" can also be used. A causal feeling is a feeling of being caused in some respects.

Whitehead's intention is to talk about an aspect of ordinary experience. Since we all have, or are collections of, ordinary experiences, it should not be so difficult to grasp his meaning. Once one does so, one can begin to understand Whitehead's overall philosophy—and even wonder why it has taken so long to name and describe this feature of experience.

The problem, we think, has been that Western philosophy has privileged vision as the basis of knowledge of the external world. As Hume indisputably demonstrated, the world as given us in vision offers no hint of causality. Some patterns repeat themselves, so we can expect some to be followed by others. Hume said we could call that cause and effect. But of course there are regular successions that we do not think of as causal. Day always follows night, and night, day, but we do not think they cause one another. Clearly, the common sense of causality does not derive from the succession of visual patterns.

Let's consider other aspects of our experience. A thought experiment may help. Try to imagine that your experience starts in the present, that no past experiences preceded it. We expect you will say that you cannot do so. That the present arises out of a past is indubitable. Why? Perhaps it is because much of the content of the present is experienced as given, not simply generated in the moment. Suppose in the present moment you are hearing the end of a musical phrase. You hear it as the end of the phrase, not as an isolated sound. The previous chords are still present in the new experience supplemented by an additional one.

This is where Whitehead suggests we look for causality. What we hear in one moment has an effect on successor moments. It has this effect by continuing to resonate in the successor moment. The analysis of the second moment of experience discloses the causal presence of the past. We cannot think about a moment that is not past, because so much of the experience in the moment is the causal presence of the past.

This causal presence is what Whitehead calls a pure physical prehension. The present moment of experience is, actually, causally related to one's personal past. But not only to that. If you try to imagine your experience as disembodied, you will have similar problems. If you have a toothache, you will definitely experience yourself as in pain because of events in your tooth. Once we understand that the past of our personal experience and of our bodies *informs what we are, we can discern less immediate and intense causal presences.*

In subsequent chapters we will see that our relation to the world is not limited to pure physical prehensions. If it were, then the Cartesian deterministic view of the world would be correct. But before we undertake to correct Descartes and the science that is so extensively formulated in Cartesian terms, we need to see the large extent to which it is validated. The causes science seeks are real and play an overwhelming role, especially, but not only, in the inanimate world. That causality is physically and psychologically—and even spiritually—effective is immensely important. It binds us to one another and to the whole world. Yes, we are really related, and Whitehead enables us to understand how.

Riffert's paper locates this rather simple philosophical idea as a crucial breakthrough in the history of thought. That is surely important, and we hope readers will take the time to do the extra work involved here in studying the philosophy. But in this book we are focusing on how Whitehead's philosophical ideas contribute to the changes needed in the way society functions. Riffert has devoted years to implementing Whitehead's ideas in education. Accordingly, in this chapter the reader is treated not only to a summary of Whitehead's contribution to educational theory but also to an account of how Riffert has implemented the implications of Whitehead's theory in the field of educational testing. No other chapter in this book goes so far in demonstrating the changes that specifically result in practical affairs when Whitehead's thought is taken seriously.

IN THIS ESSAY, I will deal with one of Whitehead's most creative and groundbreaking contributions to philosophy, his concept of prehension—in particular, physical prehension. This concept of prehension allows us intimately to relate human beings to their surrounding—to integrate them fully and truly into nature. But before going into further detail, we should remember what Whitehead once said about new ideas and their reception: "If you have had your attention directed to the novelties in thought in your own lifetime, you will have observed that *almost all really new ideas have a certain aspect of foolishness* when they are first produced" (1967c, 47). And since Whitehead's concept of prehension is "one of the supreme intellectual discoveries," (Hartshorne 1972, 127) this warning has to be taken seriously, when presenting it. Therefore, it seems to be appropriate to start this discussion by dealing with the better known ideas of three (still) influential traditional approaches: rationalism, (sense) empiricism, and Kantian transcendentalism. I will focus first on René Descartes—the French master of rationalism at the turn of the sixteenth to the seventeenth century, then on David Hume—one of the three great English-speaking empirical philosophers of the eighteenth century, and finally with Immanuel Kant—the Prussian philosopher of the Enlightenment of the eighteenth century.

Since Whitehead was convinced that the just-mentioned philosophic traditions were not only deficient, but downright harmful, he developed a radically different alternative—his "philosophy of organism." This is based on his concept of physical prehension, which, his followers believe, offers a much better worldview. The still dominant modern philosophies leave us with a world of individuals with no real relations to one another or the natural world. They encourage the extreme individualism that has done so much damage. Understanding this problem and its seriousness may motivate one to do the unaccustomed thinking required by Whitehead's radically new, 'foolish'-looking, ideas.

René Descartes, by selecting doubt as the methodological guide in his rigorous search for truth, tried to lay the foundations for a system of thought which should enable human beings to attain knowledge beyond any doubt—reliable and secure. Sense perceptions, which obviously produce deceptions and illusions, were no candidates for satisfying this criterion of truth; so they could not function as evident axiomatic cornerstones for a system of thought from which by use of logical proof further true statements could be deduced. Only specific *judgments* met this criterion of certainty—the most well-known one: "*Je pense, donc je suis*" [I think, therefore I am]. From such ideas, which qualified as "*clare et distincte*" [clear and distinct], i.e., as self-evident, Descartes built a radically dualist philosophic system, containing material stuff and mental substances. (Actually, Descartes affirmed God as a third type of substance, the only real *causa sui*.) Among the created beings, only humans have a mind which accompanies their bodies; all other creatures are simply bodies and therefore insentient machines or automata. All these creatures "eat without pleasure, *cry without pain*, grow without knowing it; they desire nothing, *fear nothing*, know nothing" (Malebranche 1689/1841, 394). This quotation is from one of Descartes' followers, Nicolas Malebranche. That it correctly expresses the implications of Descartes' thought is supported by the following quote from Descartes himself.

> I desire, I say, that you should consider that these functions in the machine [i.e. the animal body] naturally proceed from the mere arrangement of its organs, neither more nor less than do the movements of a clock, or other automaton, from that of its weights and its wheels; so that, so far as these are concerned, it is not necessary to conceive any other vegetative or sensitive soul, nor any other principle of motion or of life, than the blood and the spirits agitated by the fire which burns continually in the heart, and which is no

wise essentially different from all the fires which exist in inanimate bodies. (Descartes 1662, 427)

It is not surprising that many philosophers accused Descartes of holding a position which is a "monstrous thesis" (Kemp Smith 1963, 135f) or—not much more friendly—an "irredeemably fatuous belief" (Clark 1977, 37; for a different view see: Cottingham 1978). Nevertheless, the strong influence of Descartes' concept of animals as insentient automata on modern Western societies can be illustrated by Western laws. Here I turn to Austrian law, the one I know best. In Austria animals were dealt with in the domain of so-called "Sachenrecht [i.e., property law]"; that is, "the law of things," if translated literally. So animals legally were treated as insentient things. This was not changed in Austria until 1990. But even since then, animals are still widely treated as insentient matter.

Whitehead was convinced that Descartes bifurcated nature, i.e., separating it into one part, in which mental operations and values play a crucial role, and another part that is devoid of any feelings and values, and in which all action is by blind mechanical forces. Whitehead believed that this bifurcation of nature has disastrous consequences, of which the automaton theory of animals is but one. To avoid these consequences, Whitehead created an alternative metaphysics. At its basis he introduced the concept of physical prehensions. Physical prehensions grasp their environment and thereby interconnect everything that exists—human beings and all other nature.

David Hume, on the other hand, claimed—in strict opposition to Descartes—that everything that is in our mind must before have been in our senses. Indeed, he taught that for anything to exist, it must be perceptible with our senses: *esse est percipi (aut percipere)* [to be is to be perceived (or to perceive)]—as George Berkeley (1710/2003) put it. When Hume undertook an analysis of everyday human perception, he came up with a result that had far-reaching implications. When ordinary people (non-philosophers) perceive the world around them, they get the impression that they live in a reality of permanently existing "stable" objects (such as stones, houses, trees, tables). These stable, enduring objects seem to carry features that may change (more or less quickly). But, when analyzing our everyday mode of perception and its contents, Hume could not find any hint of a stable substrate (or substance) underlying these changing features (qualities). And since, according to his sense-empiricism, only what is perceivable exists, underlying stable substrates do not exist. All that did exist for Hume was a stream of sense impressions (qualities). Further, these sense impressions are connected only externally by their relations in time and space. For instance, an analysis of two billiard balls,[1] shows that a round black form approaches an unmoved circular red form; when their shapes come so close that they may seem to make contact, the red round shape may start moving while the black round shape may stop. Nothing in the whole situation gives us the right, Hume thought, to postulate any causation between the two shapes. So, according to Hume, there is no reason to postulate any causal forces or pushes as they are presupposed in Newton's physics. Another inconvenient consequence following from Hume's radical sense-empiricism is that there is no indication of any memory and therefore—as a devastating result—no diachronic identity in the human person.

Despite these strange consequences, Hume's ideas found their way into psychology, informing associationism and behaviorism. Here again, unfortunate effects unfolded, as in associationist and behaviorist learning theories. Ivan Pavlov, for instance, introduced the so-called "equipotentiality principle" (Pavlov 1927, lecture 2). This principle claims that any arbitrary, so-called neutral, stimulus can equally well be associated with any unconditioned stimulus at any point in time, issuing in a conditioning process, i.e., in transforming the neutral stimulus into a conditioned stimulus. This implies that learning processes are arbitrary: any random combination of any stimuli can be learned at any time by anyone with the same result.[2]

Whitehead rejected Hume's radical sense empiricism for several reasons. Most important, in our context, he rejected the behaviorist and associationist learning approaches: "The pupil's progress is often conceived as a uniform steady advance undifferentiated by change of type or alteration in pace . . . I hold that this conception of education is based upon a false psychology of the process of mental development which has gravely hindered the effectiveness of our methods" (Whitehead 1967a, 17). Instead, learning "is a process completely of its own peculiar genus. Its nearest analogue is the *assimilation of food by a living organism*" (33).[3] Whitehead's view of learning is not that of a uniform steady progress but that of a cyclic rhythm of assimilation. At the level of metaphysics, the educational concept of "assimilation" is explained by Whitehead's new concept of physical prehensions.

Let us turn now to the third thought tradition: transcendentalism. Immanuel Kant said that Hume woke him from his "dogmatic slumber"(Kant 1783/2004, 4, 260, 10). But if Hume was right and there was nothing in the mind that had not before been in one's senses, how then was it possible that Newton could predict future events (make so-called synthetic *a priori* statements) as, for instance, solar eclipses? Kant's solution was to split nature into the *noumena*—things as they are in themselves (the so-called "*Ding an sich*")—and the *phenomena*—the world for the perceiver. Kant taught that the phenomenal word is actively constructed by the subject (the perceiver) in that she/he imposes the two intuitions [*Anschauungsformen*]—space and time—and a selection of the twelve categories upon the noumenal world. And that is why we are able to predict these features: because they are already in the perceiver—prior to any concrete perceptive act. But the price that had to be paid for this solution was high: There is an insurmountable gap between the world as known by us and the world in itself (which is not detectable by any means)—human beings are caught solipsistically in their constructions of the phenomenal world without any possibility of reaching the world beyond these constructions.

In addition to this unacceptable consequence, Kant's position suffers a severe inconsistency: (Vaihinger 1892). In order to perceive something, the perceiver has to apply a selection of the twelve categories of perception along with the two "*Anschauungsformen*" [two pure forms of intuition] of space and time to the scene (Kant 1781/1929,

A253). But, how does the perceiver (consciously or unconsciously) know which of the twelve categories are the correct ones to be selected if this act of perception is the only connection to the so far unknown scene? This problem seems to be entirely insoluble if we do not postulate a more fundamental (non-categorical/non-conceptual and therefore direct or immediate) type of perception. Without that we end up with a radical constructivist position.

This fundamental problem is present in modern cognitive science, which is strongly influenced by Kantian ideas. Noë and O'Regan, for instance, describe the problem as follows:

> [T]o see detail in the environment, you must direct your attention to it. But how can you direct your attention to an unperceived feature of the scene? Surely in order to direct your attention, you must already perceive that to which you direct your attention. This Paradox would seem to threaten the very possibility of perceptual awareness. (Noë & O'Regan 2000)

In order to cope with this fundamental problem the authors find themselves forced to postulate a primitive form of perception which they call "perceptual sensitivity"; this primitive mode of perception has to be distinguished from our everyday "visual perception." While the latter is well known to us from our conscious everyday encounter with the world, the earlier one is a more primitive pre-attentive and sub-conscious type of perception. The authors describe it as a "perceptual *coupling* of animal and environment that consists in the animal's access to environmental detail thanks to its mastery of the sensori-motor contingencies that govern the way it explores the environment."[4]

This concept of "perceptual coupling of animal and environ-ment"—as we shall see—comes astonishingly close to Whitehead's theory of perception. Whitehead developed a bold new theory of per-ception. He developed it in a philosophical rather than a psychological manner, but since he was convinced that philosophy has to deal with the world in which we find ourselves living, a theory of perception had also to be—at least in consequence—a psychological theory.

Whitehead's philo-psycho-logical theory of perception is bold in postulating a primitive mode of perception — unconscious, emotion-laden and pre-attentive — that before him was only rarely grasped and nowhere (to my knowledge) systematically explored and related to the higher modes of perception: he calls this perception in the mode of *causal efficacy*. This primitive perceptive mode of causal efficacy can also be called a pure physical prehension.

Whitehead was well aware that such a bold position was in need of empirical confirmation: "This wider definition of perception [which includes causal efficacy] can be of no importance *unless we can detect occasions of experience exhibiting modes of functioning which fall within its wider scope*" (Whitehead 1967b, 180).

Ending this short discussion of rationalism, empiricism, and transcendentalism, I will outline Whitehead's process philosophy, summarize his theory of perception, and sketch its implications for education (learning and teaching) as well as standardized testing.

SOME BASIC FEATURES OF WHITEHEAD'S PROCESS METAPHYSICS

Let me start with a short introduction to Whitehead's basic philosophic outlook. For Whitehead, the world is constituted by a multiplicity of micro-processes, which he called actual entities. An actual entity is in essence the process of growing together of all the actual entities which constitute its immediate past environment. So, since actual entities are intimately connected to each other, the world is a pulsating, *vibrant web of processes*. By grasping this immediately past environment, every actual entity constitutes itself according to a self-set aim (Whitehead calls this the "subjective aim"). Whitehead's technical term for this "grasping" is "prehension," and Whitehead claims that one can arrive at his concept of prehension either from physics or from psychology (Whitehead, 1967c, 152). Therefore, taking the psychological path, he also terms prehensions "feelings."[5] There are different types of prehensions: the two most basic ones being physical prehensions and conceptual prehensions. Each process of growing together — Whitehead here introduces the technical term "concrescence"—of an actual entity starts with physical prehensions. These prehensions passively receive the pressures of the immediately past world, which largely shape the developing actual entity. However, the reception is selective based on the actual entity's own unique aim. These passive physical prehensions are present at the very start of *every* growing together of any actual entity. They constitute the physical pole of each actual entity, which Whitehead also calls the conformal phase because it reenacts what is given by the past.

So prehensions can be defined as "Concrete Facts of Relatedness"; (Whitehead 1978, 32) by being prehended, an actual entity that has just reached its full realization becomes an ingredient in a just-developing, new actual entity. Therefore, prehensions can be conceived as "vectors," Whitehead writes, "for they feel what is there and transform it into what is here."[6] This characterization comes close to Whitehead's metaphor of an act of assimilation: by incorporating (in the literal sense of the word) external elements, an organism constitutes itself.[7]

WHITEHEAD'S TRI-MODAL THEORY OF PERCEPTION

Whitehead turned our attention to the fact that we are in need of empirically confirming phenomena for this very primitive mode of perception (causal efficacy). Since it is a very primitive mode, the following domains should be good candidates: early phases in the development of life (the phylogenetic dimension); early developmental phases in humans (ontogenetic dimension); and any state that shows a kind of regression into more primitive phases of development in individuals. It is also possible to produce deficient forms of perception artificially. For instance, a very quick and short stimulus presentation via tachistoscopes can be rendered subconscious by forward and/or backward masking. Empirical research along these lines has increased during the last 30 years.[8]

There are also other hints available in favor of causal efficacy from the domain of everyday perception. Whitehead, for instance, points to the following commonly known phenomenon: if we are in the dark and a strong flash is surprisingly triggered, our eyes will blink, and, Whitehead continues, "The man will explain his experience by saying 'The flash *made me* blink; and if his statement be doubted, he will reply 'I know it, because I felt it'" (Whitehead 1978, 175).

We noted that Kant's perceptive approach ran into severe difficulties not being able to explain how a perceiver knows which selection of the twelve categories should be applied in a specific act of perception. Whitehead, by introducing the perceptive mode of causal efficacy, has solved this problem.

Descartes as a methodological principle only accepted something as a certain truth which could be grasped clearly and distinctly. If Whitehead is right, this methodological rule by definition will lead us into error, since the basic facts are at the subconscious level and therefore will never be grasped *"clare et distincte."* Here, the abyss between Whitehead and Descartes becomes fully visible—and this difference has tremendous practical consequences, particularly for education!

We have seen that Whitehead's theory of perception also departs from Hume's theory of perception, which is based on pure sense perception understood by Whitehead as presentational immediacy. Whitehead agrees that, since there is no causal relation possible between the contents of sense impressions, they are related only by random spatio-temporal associations. By introducing the perceptive mode of causal efficacy Whitehead is able to save causation and, along with it memory, and the possibility to explain the diachronic identity of human beings.

WHITEHEAD'S CONCEPT OF THREE-PHASED LEARNING CYCLES

As already noted, according to Whitehead, learning is not an arbitrary summation of random items but, as Piaget too later insisted (1937), an act of assimilation. Assimilation is incompatible with any arbitrary incorporation of food: if we eat the wrong food at the wrong time we won't keep it for long; it may make us ill or even kill us.

> It must never be forgotten that education is not a process of packing articles in a trunk. . . . Its nearest analogue is the assimilation of food by a living organism: and we all know how necessary to health is palatable food under suitable conditions. When you have your boots in the trunk, they will stay there till you take them out again; but this is not at all the case if you feed a child with the wrong food. (Whitehead 1967a, 33)

Based on this metaphor of assimilation Whitehead sketched a descriptive theory of learning and a prescriptive theory of instruction in clear opposition to traditional associationist and behaviorist learning theories. Whitehead claimed that learning is essentially a rhythmic and phased process by which true assimilation takes place.

The idea of rhythm is fundamental for Whitehead's thinking. Cyclic or periodic rhythms pervade not only learning but all human life and even all other domains of reality. Even in his early mathematical work, *An Introduction to Mathematics*, he remarked:

> The whole of Nature is dominated by the existence of periodic events, that is, by the existence of successive events so analogous to each other that, without any straining of language, they may be termed recurrences of the same event. The rotation of the earth produces the successive days. . . . Again the path of the earth around the sun leads to the yearly recurrence of the seasons. . . . Another less fundamental periodicity is provided by the phases of the moon. . . . Our bodily life is essentially periodic. (Whitehead 1911, 134f)

Indeed, actual entities, the basic elements of reality, are pulsations, growing out of preceding actual entities and, when they reach their culmination, becoming a member of the preceding actual entities for new actual entities. This rhythm underlies all of reality, at all its different levels, and makes it a pulsating web.

PHASED LEARNING PROCESSES

Given this understanding of reality, it is by no surprise that learning is also rhythmic. A complete cycle of learning comprises three phases, which Whitehead termed (1) romance, (2) precision and (3) generalization.[9]

In the *stage of romance* the student for the first time is confronted with new stimuli, a new problem. This stage is one of discovery: "The stage of romance is the stage of first apprehension" (Whitehead 1967a, 17). Such apprehension does not take place in *vacuo;* the student brings to it all previously acquired knowledge and uses it in this process. "It is a process of discovery, a process of becoming used to curious thoughts, of shaping questions, of seeking for answers, of devising new experiences, of noticing what happens as the result of new ventures. This general process is both natural and of absorbing interest" (32). If students feel the new stimuli to be relevant they will be interested. "Education must essentially be a setting in order of a ferment already stirring in the mind: you cannot educate mind in *vacuo*" (18). However, at this stage the relations and connections of the new stimuli among themselves and to the student still remain vague and fleeting intuitions, at the verge of consciousness. Such an intuition "holds within itself unexplored connexions with possibilities half-disclosed by glimpses and half concealed by the wealth of material" (17). These half-disclosed relevant connections of novel situations are emotion laden. "Romantic emotion is essentially the excitement consequent on the transition from bare facts to the first realization of the import of their unexplored relationships" (18).

This first phase of a learning process can hardly be overestimated. It ignites in the learner excitement and emotional arousal towards new possibilities that flash up in the learner: curiosity is triggered in the student. Without this intrinsic arousal one cannot expect the student to show further interest in exploring the new situation.

This *descriptive* aspect of *learning* has to be taken into account when developing a *prescriptive* theory of *teaching*: if teachers do not allow enough room and time for the stage of romance, their students will lack intrinsic motivation. Traditional education has violated this central postulate of Whitehead's process theory of teaching because of its linear piecemeal account of learning.

The *second stage* of a full learning cycle is termed *precision*. At this stage, students investigate and elaborate the relationships of the new stimuli among themselves; in relation to other, already well known stimuli; and to their already available knowledge base. "In this stage, width of relationship is subordinated to exactness of formulation. It is the stage of grammar, the grammar of language and the grammar of science" (Whitehead 1967a, 18). This stage requires discipline; in its ideal form such discipline is *self*-discipline motivated by the lures introduced by the stage of romance.

It is of decisive importance that the phase of precision always *follows* and never precedes the phase of free-floating romance. If this central rule is violated—as, in fact, it is in traditional linear piecemeal education—the result is inert knowledge. (Whitehead 1967a, 1). "Without the adventure of romance, at the best you get inert knowledge without initiative, and at worst you get contempt of ideas—without knowledge" (33).

But, of course, there is also the opposite danger: over-emphasizing the stage of romance. Whitehead repeatedly stresses the fact that romance has to be complemented by the stage of "precision,'" or "discipline." And in doing this he draws our attention to the fact that there "are right ways and wrong ways, and definite truths to be known."[10] So the stage of disciplined precision is important too. According to Whitehead, it is beyond question that "a certain pointing out of important facts, and of simplifying ideas, and of usual names really strengthens the natural impetus of the pupil" (Whitehead 1967a, 33).

The *third and final stage* of each learning cycle is termed *generalization*. It marks at the same time the culmination of the learning cycle in question and the start of a new cycle; it is the "return to romanticism" (Whitehead 1967a, 19). Now, the detailed and interrelated knowledge calls for application to new, more complex situations. And again new exciting perspectives and fascinating half-disclosed insights are flashing up: a new cycle of learning is starting.

Whitehead sums up the general character of a full learning cycle in the following words: "There is the general apprehension of some topic in its vague possibilities, the mastery of the relevant details, and finally the putting of the whole subject together in the light of the relevant knowledge" (Whitehead 1967a, 48).

In Western education, the first and third phases of learning are missing. Despite empirical data in favor of this cyclic learning approach, only precision is emphasized.[11,12] Things have not improved in recent decades; on the contrary: due to the trend towards standardized testing, they are getting even worse.

WHITEHEAD ON STANDARDIZED TESTING
AND ITS IMPACT ON LEARNING

Whitehead also dealt with the phenomenon behind standardized testing although the terms "standards" and "standardized testing" were unknown in his days. In England, education had been in the hands of the Church until the mid-19th century, when the state started to expand its role. It undertook to break the monopoly of the Church "through the introduction of grants for the erection of new buildings, for the training of teachers, and for the encouragement of attendance, first in rural schools, and then in all schools" (Wiliam 2010, 6). In return for its engagement, the state introduced the so-called "payment by results":

> The Commission's report, published in 1861, recommended, among other things, that the amount of public money paid to each elementary school should depend on three factors: the condition of the school buildings, student attendance, and the performance of the students attending the school in an oral examination, undertaken by one of the national school inspectors of every child in every school to which grants were to be paid. (Wiliam 2010, 6)

At the upper secondary level such examinations were arranged around a so-called "syllabus" which consisted of "a list of all things that can be tested in the examination (Wiliam 2010, 9). These examinations were based on carefully prescribed syllabi. Accordingly, Whitehead was responding to a situation quite similar to our modern standardized testing.

When Whitehead talks about this testing, he uses the words "external testing" or "uniform testing," often combined as "uniform external testing." I will now turn to his position on standardized testing and its impact on the learning processes in school.

ON THE CONNECTION BETWEEN LEARNING AND TESTING

Teaching, according to Whitehead, is a complex undertaking. "The best procedure [of teaching] will depend on several factors, none of which can be neglected, namely, the genius of the teacher, the intellectual type of the pupils, their prospects in life, the opportunities offered by the immediate surroundings of the school, and allied factors of this sort" (Whitehead 1967a, 5). External standardized testing cannot do justice to these situation specific factors and their unique local combinations. "With this educational ideal nothing can be worse than the aimless accretion of theorems in our text books, which acquire their position merely because the children can be made to learn them and examiners can set neat questions on them" (80).

Standardized testing can have further unfortunate consequences: If the test is important, i.e., if high-stake decisions are based on its results, then of course there is a strong urge towards teaching, even cramming, to the test. Such *teaching to the test* has but one aim: passing the (entrance) examination. It is not aimed at clarifying general concepts and creatively applying them on new problems. It also does not stimulate the spirit of adventurous research. Instead, it carries within itself the danger of stressing simple pattern recognition. Do enough test-specific problems so that when you see a problem in the exam, you can recall the specific trick, the special integrating factor, the substitution, or whatever else may be required, to obtain the correct answer.

Further, this specialized training usually is done at the expense of teaching and learning other content: If you need much of the available time for cramming test-relevant contents, there is no time to inspire curiosity and encourage adventurous exploration.

Such one-dimensional learning to the test further tends to create unfortunate attitudes as well: The practice of drilling affects the students' general attitudes towards the education process. Such attitudes are reflected in their performance, in the narrowness of vision, in passivity, and finally in boredom. Gone is the love for creative learning and spontaneous curiosity. The students wait in the lectures for the bottom line, the formulae they can learn by heart or the recipe they can follow blindly for solving the examination problem. As Whitehead has put it: "The evocation of curiosity, of judgement, of the power of mastering a complicated tangle of circumstances, the use of theory giving foresight in special cases — all these powers are not to be imparted by a set rule embodied in one schedule of examination" (Whitehead 1967a, 5).

So Whitehead's criticism of external standardized testing concerns the unfortunate effects such testing has on the learning process and on the attitudes of the students towards creative learning. Whitehead is not alone in this criticism of standardized testing; in the 1970s, Jerome Bruner made the same point:

A method of instruction should have the objective of leading the child to *discover for himself*. Telling children and *then testing them on what they have been told* inevitably has the effect of producing *bench-bound learners* whose motivation for learning is likely to be extrinsic to the task — pleasing the teacher, getting into the College, artificially maintaining self-esteem. The virtues of *encouraging discovery* are of two kinds. In the first place, the child will make what [s/]he learns his [her] own, will fit his [her] discovery into the interior world of cultures that [s/]he creates for [her]himself. Equally important, discovery and the sense of confidence it provides is the proper reward for learning. (Bruner 1971, 123f)

Nevertheless, Whitehead recognized that testing and evaluation are needed. The issue is who should test and for what. Whitehead defined the *individual school* as the *essential educational unit*: "When I say that the school is the educational unit, I mean exactly what I say, no larger unit, no smaller unit" (Whitehead 1967a, 14). Whitehead opts for a great liberty for schools to develop according to their specific circumstances and possibilities. He complains about the fact that "[n] o headmaster has a free hand to develop his general education or his specialist studies in accordance with the opportunities of his school, which are created by its staff, its environment, its class of boys [pupils], and its endowments" (13).

Whitehead held that this liberty is essential to secure an optimal situational frame for creative learning processes. So the most important step in educational reform, according to Whitehead, is to grant liberty to individual schools: "[T]he first requisite for educational reform is the school as a unit, with its approved curriculum based on its own needs, and evolved by its own staff. If we fail to secure that, we simply fall from one formalism into another, from one dung-hill of inert ideas into another" (Whitehead 1967a, 13). Only the liberty to adjust the curriculum to the needs of a particular school with its specific constellation of teachers and the unique potentials of its students and equipment can provide the basis for a flexible creative learning process. So he argues that "[e]ach school should grant its own leaving certificates, based on its own curriculum" (13).

Whitehead is well aware that such liberty has to be counter-balanced by evaluation:

The standards of these schools should be sampled and corrected. . . . Each school must have the claim to be considered in relation to its special circumstances. The classifying of schools for some purpose is necessary. But no absolutely rigid curriculum, not modified by its own staff, should be permissible. Exactly the same principles apply, with proper modifications, to universities and to technical colleges. (Whitehead 1967a, 13–14)

If external tests are conducted for some purpose—and Whitehead explicitly accepted the need for external tests—they have to be adjusted to the situation specific conditions of the school in question: "The external assessor may report on the curriculum or on the performance of the pupils, but never should be allowed to ask the pupil a question which has not been strictly supervised by the actual teacher, or at least inspired by a long conference with him" (Whitehead 1967a, 5).

But is this possible? How can tests on the one hand meet scientific test standards such as objectivity, validity, and reliability, and on the other hand do justice to the unique situation of the particular school? This question is addressed in the next section.

EVALUATION IN A WHITEHEADIAN SPIRIT: THE "MODULE APPROACH TO SELF-EVALUATION OF SCHOOL-DEVELOPMENT PROCESSES" (MSS)

In what follows I will present a very brief outline of a more than ten-year research project I have undertaken together with my colleague Andreas Paschon at Salzburg University and in collaboration with fourteen schools (Riffert & Paschon 2005). Around 2000 in Austria, individual schools were granted autonomy to develop their own profile according to their needs and wishes. In order to be able to do so the Austrian *Ministry of Education and Cultural Affairs* granted to each school the freedom to change one-third of the curriculum; the other two-thirds were still prescribed by the Ministry to secure a basic standard in all schools and to secure that students could change schools without major problems. So schools—i.e., the so-called school-partners: teachers, parents, and students—could modify the curricula of subjects, develop and implement new subjects, and even create unique school branches (for instance with a focus on languages, arts, or science). This liberty, however, had to be counter-balanced by obligatory self-evaluation of these newly introduced changes in order to detect unforeseen negative side effects and to make visible to what extent the school approached its own self-set goals. The Module Approach for Self-Evaluation of School Development Projects (MSS) was developed to meet this challenge.

First, the MSS takes seriously Whitehead's point that the school is the essential educational unit! And so it is designed to be flexible enough to do justice to the different developments possible in school programs. It is based on an intimate cooperation between the school-based experts (the teachers, parents and students) and the scientists. According to Whitehead, no standardized testing of students should take place without being "either framed or modified by the actual teacher" (Whitehead 1967a, 5). So far the MSS has been conducted in fourteen Austrian schools, and its concept has been permanently optimized on the basis of feedback from the expert-practitioners of the involved schools.

The core idea of the MSS-approach is its *module conception*. A single module covers one specific school-relevant domain. A module-pool consists of several single modules ranging from single statements up to elaborate inventories and validated, reliable scales as, for instance, on test anxiety, self-efficacy convictions, social and moral competences, tasks of international achievement studies such as TIMSS and PISA, leadership practice inventory, and teacher-parent interaction. modules. At the moment, the MSS consists of more than 150 modules which in turn consist of many more sub-modules.

The MSS is an instrument for *self- or internal evaluation* and not for external evaluation (i.e., initiated and conducted from outside the school). This means: (1) the initiative for an evaluation must come from the individual school. (2) The expert knowledge of the school-partners (teachers, parents, students) is highly valued and given primary importance. The school partners (teachers [T], parents [P], students [S]) are the experts concerning their own school and their knowledge has to be taken seriously. And since the schools are defined as the three groups of school partners it is obligatory for the MSS team that all three groups (T, S, P) must freely accept a MSS study and sign a contract. All three groups also must come to a freely reached conclusion concerning the modules that they select for their unique evaluation.

Some examples may help illustrate this point.

1. The school partners want to examine the field of educational aims. They in particular want to know how all three school partner groups experience the aims which are in fact realized in their school and want to compare them with the ideal, i.e., with those educational aims which should be aimed at. That is they want to undertake an 'Is-Ought'-comparison on the specific aims of education of their school.

2. Further, some parents and the school psychologist report that there has been an accumulation of test anxiety during the last school year, while other parents and some teachers cannot confirm this impression. So the school partners discuss if they should not select a scale, for instance the AFS (Anxiety Questionnaire for Students), for examining this issue of test-anxiety (Wieczerkowski et al. 1980).

3. The math teachers have implemented a new method for teaching mathematics (for instance: Freudenthal's method of "realistic mathematics") (Freudenthal 1977, 1983) and they now would like to know how their students are doing on PISA-tasks (which are operationalizations of Freudenthals theoretical concept).

4. Since it is known that self-efficacy convictions are of major importance for achievement in the future for physical, psychical, and social health, etc. (Bandura 1994), the school partners want to know how well developed these convictions are in their students and if there is any need to set forward steps in order to improve them.

5. Social competencies acquire more and more importance in business and at university. The school partners decide

to evaluate one aspect which is especially stressed in their school's mission statement, namely teamwork.

6. The parents want to know how teachers and students evaluate their involvement in school activities.

7. The headmaster wants to improve his competencies in leadership, and because he sees himself as a moderator between the three groups, he wants a diagnosis from all three groups: colleagues, parents, and students.

8. Since literacy belongs to the key competencies in life and the school has a high percentage of non-native speakers, the schools partners discuss the possibility of diagnosing the situation in their school in order to be able to draw more reliable conclusions for future changes in this field.

9. The language teachers want to get individual feedback from their students on their teaching and on their project "Learning Abroad." They insist that the results be reported only to the individual teachers, but that they get the average percentage on each statement for comparison with their colleagues.

It is important at this point to note that although standardized testing of student achievement is possible within the MSS, it is *only one* aspect of the wide range of possibilities of the MSS. The scope of the MSS is much broader. In principle, all activities relevant to a school's development, in its full complexity, can be the subject of an MSS study. In principle, any of the over 150 modules can be chosen and combined to form a school-specific measurement tool. Usually the process of choosing the topics is already a very important activity in the development of the school. At the beginning of this selection process, the school partners often want to choose many topics, and it is one major task of the MSS team to warn them to focus on those modules most relevant for their school at this time.

School-specificity: School partners normally are not able to conduct standardized testing according to scientific and technological standards, so the MSS team offers help. (1) It provides a great number of different modules on topics that *might* be of interest for a specific school. The school partners, on the basis of their expert knowledge of their own school, can select whatever module is relevant for their purposes. In some instances, the team even creates new modules to meet the felt needs of a particular school. (2) The MSS team provides help in selecting the modules from a methodological (technological) and theoretical (scientific) point of view: What does a certain scale measure? What are its limits? What further independent variables might be of interest? The different perspectives of teachers, parents, and students are taken equally into account.

Anonymity is granted to each person taking part in the evaluation and to the school as a unit. This secures that everybody (especially students, but also parents and teachers) can answer without any fear of meeting negative sanctions (for instance, students from teachers or teachers from colleagues).

Comprehensive data collection. In order to give each person the chance to contribute his/her opinion to the school development process, the collection/measurement is not based on a sample; this also offers a possibility to analyse the selected data down to single classes! The detection of, for instance, sources of violence is possible, and preventive initiatives can be placed with great accuracy.

Further, the MSS allows for *analysis of so-called discrepancies*: (1) discrepancies between "Is" and "Ought" (existing fact and aimed-at ideal) can be calculated; e.g., concerning the educational aims of a school; or (2) discrepancies between strengths and weaknesses of the school as viewed from each perspective of the school partners can become the subject of the measurement.

Thereby the MSS makes the formulation of aims of the school development process easier: all three *perspectives* of the person groups are available in "Is-Ought dimensions; no more guessing is necessary as to what others *might* want or how they *could* see the situation; so many possible sources of frustration can be avoided. Further, the analysis of discrepancies shows on what topic there is high agreement between the three groups, which therefore lends itself easily to change processes. It also shows on what topics the partners disagree. More discussions are necessary before any steps towards changes in these fields are meaningful.

The MSS collects *quantitative* as well as *qualitative data*. In the context of the MSS, "quantitative" means: answers to closed (i.e., pre-formulated) questions. "Qualitative," on the other hand, means: answers to open questions, which allow a free response. Both types of data are presented to the school.

Cross section analysis: By any single measurement—and the MSS here is no exception—one can only obtain a kind of "snapshot" of the "measured" situation at a certain point in time. This certainly is a disadvantage. The distortion to which such cross-sectional snapshot data collections may give rise, however, can and must, in fact, be counter-balanced by the experts of the school partners. To give but one illustrating example: a good and competent teacher has been given a "difficult" class a few weeks before the MSS measurement takes place and now gets "bad" feedback from his "difficult" class. The specific situation of this teacher is well known to his colleagues, to the headmaster, and to the parents, and this knowledge must counter-balance the results obtained by a single measurement at a certain point in time.

A *longitudinal analysis* is possible with MSS; the MSS questionnaire only has to be conducted repeatedly to gather data along different points in time. Such repeated measurements also contribute to correction of the possible distortions of a single measurement (snapshots).

FINAL REMARK

Whitehead was a very exceptional thinker; he came up with creative ideas in so many different domains of research—from logic and mathematics to physics, from philosophy to education. At the core, as Charles Hartshorne indicated, we find his concept of prehension. This radically new concept opens the perspective for creative thoughts in different domains. In this chapter I could only deal with a few of them in the domains of education and perception. Every time I read Whitehead, I am amazed by the freshness of these new ideas and their complex interrelations, which form an alternative to the still reigning paradigms.

ENDNOTES

1   Hume's choice of billiard balls for a discussion of causation must be seen in the intellectual context of his day: Sir Isaac Newton had introduced a billiard ball concept of the final constituents of the world: "God in the Beginning form'd Matter in solid, massy, hard, impenetrable, moveable Particles" (Newton 1704, Query 31); therefore a discussion of billiard balls and their interaction could easily be generalized to causal relations in general and therefore was of great importance; see also: Temple 1984.

2   M. Seligman (1971) challenged the equipotentiality assumption of radical behaviorism by pointing toward the empirically established fact that there are certain types of stimuli (as for instance snakes, spiders, . . .) which can more easily be transformed by the conditioning process into fear-triggering stimuli than others (as for instance telephone receivers or pencils). In order to explain this difference, he had introduced the concept of preparedness, which in turn is linked to the evolution process.

3   It is interesting to note that Jean Piaget developed a groundbreaking new psychological approach which centers on the concept of assimilation. For details concerning the surprising parallels between Piaget's genetic constructivism and Whitehead's process philosophy see: Riffert, *Whitehead und Piaget*, 1992.

4   Noë & J. K. O'Regan, "On the Brain-Basis of Consciousness: A Sensorimotor Account," 569; see also: E. Myin & J. K. O'Regan, "Situated Perception and Sensation in Vision and Other Modalities: From an Active to a Sensorimotor Account," 185–200; J. K. O'Regan, "The 'Feel' of Seeing: An Interview with J. Kevin O'Regan," *Trends in Cognitive Sciences*, 278–79.

5   But here some caution is appropriate: Whitehead warns that he stretched the meaning of this word 'feeling' to its utmost limit when using it in the metaphysical domain. See Whitehead, *The Function of Reason*, 79–90.

6   Whitehead, *Process and Reality*, 133; for a detailed discussion of Whitehead's concept of prehension also see: J. Cobb, "Prehension," paper presented at the philosophy department of the University of Budapest, March 7, 2002; available at http://www.anthonyflood.com/cobbprehension.htm.

7   Whitehead also draws attention to the fact that a concrescing actual entity does not only positively integrate the previous world (actual entities), but also negatively prehends (i.e., excludes) some of the available actual entities. This also is true for any process of assimilation as conceptualized by Piaget (see Jean Piaget, "Piaget's Theory," in *Carmichael's Manual of Child Psychology*, 707.

8   For a discussion of examples see: F. Riffert, "Whitehead's Theory of Perception and the Concept of Microgenesis," 2004; and Riffert, "Whitehead's Wahrnehmungstheorie im Lichte Empirischer Befunde der Mikrogenese und Perzeptgenese-Forschung" [Whitehead's Theory of Perception in the Light of Empirical Results from Microgenetic and Perceptgenetic Research], 2007.

9   He also referred to them as the phases of freedom (romance and generalization) and (self-)discipline (precision); see *Aims of Education,* 30.

10 Ibid., 34. This quote makes obvious that Whitehead did not hold a radical constructivist learning theory. (see Riffert, "Process Philosophy and Constructivist Education—Some Basic Similarities," 1999.)

11 F. Riffert, J. Kriegseisen, T. Hascher, & G. Hagenauer, "Testing Whitehead's Theory of Learning Empirically: A Report from a Pilot Study," *Tattva—The Journal of Philosophy* 1 (2009); T. Hascher, G. Hagenauer, F. Riffert, & J. Kriegseisen, "Lernzirkel im Physik und Chemieunterricht in der Sekundarstufe 1" [Learning Cycles in Physics and Chemistry Teaching at Secondary 1 Level], *Erziehung und Unterricht* (2009); and G. Hagenauer, A. Strahl, J. Kriegseisen, & F. Riffert, "Emotionen von Schülern und Schülerinnen im Physikunterricht auf Basis des Lernzyklenunterricht—Befunde einer zweijährigen Interventionsstudie" [Emotions of Students in Physics Classes on the Basis of Learning Cycle Instruction —Results of a Two-Year Intervention Study] (2018).

12 The learning cycle approach holds another advantage: it models the research process in the sciences and so very naturally offers

the students opportunities to become familiar with the nature and procedure of scientific research. (see Riffert, "Whitehead on Cycles of Learning and Cycles of Research," 2014.)

BIBLIOGRAPHY

Bandura, A. (1994). *Self-Efficacy: The Exercise of Control*. New York: Freeman.

Berkeley, G. (1710/2003). *A Treatise Concerning the Principles of Human Knowledge*. Dover Publications. Online: http://www.gutenberg.org/files/4723/4723-h/4723-h.htm (access: 06/22/2015).

Clark, S. R. L. (1977). *The Moral Status of Animals*. Oxford: Clarendon.

Bruner, J. (1971). *The Relevance of Education*. New York: Norton.

Clark, L. R. (1977). *The Moral Status of Animals*. New York: Oxford University Press.

Cobb, J. (2002). Prehension. Paper presented at the philosophy department of the University of Budapest, March 7, 2002. Online: http://anthonlyflood.com/cobbprehension.htm.

Cottingham, J. (1978). 'A Brute to the Brutes?': Descartes Treatment of Animals. *Philosophy* 53, 551–59.

Davies , G. & Ostrom, E. (1991). A Public Economy Approach to Education: Choice and Co-Production. *International Political Science Review* 12(4), 313–35.

Descartes, R. (1662). *Traite de l'homme. [Treatise on Man]* Leiden: FlorentSchuyl. Online: http://www.biusante.parisdescartes.fr/sfhm/hsm/HSMx1987x021x004/ HSMx1987x021x004x0381.pdf (access: 06/22/2015).

Freudenthal, H. (1977). *Mathematik als pädagogische Aufgabe [Mathematicsas an Educational Task]*. (Vol. 1 & 2) Stuttgart: Ernst Klett.

Freudenthal, H. (1983). *Didactical Phenomenology of Mathematical Structures*. Dortrecht: Reidel.

Hagenauer, G., Strahl, A., Kriegseisen, J. & Riffert, F. (2018). Emotionen von Schülern und Schülerinnen im Physikunterricht auf Basis des Lernzyklenunterricht—Befunde einer zweijährigen Interventionsstudie [Emotions of Students in Physics Classes on the Basis of Learning Cycle Instruction—Results of a Two-Year Intervention Study]. In. G. Hagenauer & T. Hascher (Eds.). *Emotions and Emotion Regulation in School and at University.* Münster: Waxmann (forthcoming).

Hartshorne, C. (1972). *Whitehead's Philosophy: Selected Essays, 1935–1970.* Lincoln: University of Nebraska Press.

Hascher, T., Hagenauer, G., Riffert, F. &Kriegseisen, J. (2009). Lernzirkel im Physik- und Chemieunterricht in der Sekundarstufe 1 [Learning Cylces in Physics and Chemistry Teaching at Secondary Level 1]. *Erziehung und Unterricht* 9–10, 2021–27.

Hume, D (1738). *Treatise on Human Nature.* London: Longmans, Green & Co. Online: https://archive.org/details/atreatiseonhum-a01grosgoog (access: 06/22/2015).

Kant, I. (1781/1929). *Critique of Pure Reason.* London: Macmillan.

Kant, I. (1783/2004). *Prolegomena to Any Future Metaphysics.* G. Hatfield, revised ed. Cambridge: Cambridge University Press.

Kemp Smith, N. (1963). *New Studies in the Philosophy of Descartes.* New York: Russell & Russell.

Malebranche, N, (1689/1841). *Oevres completes.* [Complete Works] Vol. II: *Feuillet de Conches. Méditations Métaphysiques et Correspondance de N. Malebranche. Neuvième Méditation.* 1689/1841, Paris: J. Vrin.

Myin, E., & O'Regan, J. K. (2008). Situated perception and sensation in vision and other modalities: form an active to a sensorimotor account. In. P. Robbins & A. Aydede (Eds.): *Cambridge Handbook of Situated Cognition.* Cambridge: Cambridge University Press, 185–200.

Newton, I. (1704/1995). *Opticks.* Reprinted in: I. B. Cohen & R. S. Westfall (Eds.): *Newton: Texts, Backgrounds, Commentaries. Critical Edition.* New York: Norton.

Noë, A. & J. K. O'Regan (2000). On the brain-basis of conscious-ness: A sensorimotor account. In A. Noe & E. Thompson (Eds.): *Vision and Mind. Selected Readings in the Philosophy of Perception.* Cambridge, MA: MIT Press, 567–98. Online: http://faculty.virginia.edu/perlab/misc/ReadingMeeting/Noe.ORegan.pdf (access: 06/22/ 2015).

Noë, A. & O'Regan, J. K. (2000). Perception, Attention and the Grand Illusion. *Psyche* 6.15, no pagination specified; online: http:// journalpsyche.org/files/oxaa87.pdf [access: February 20, 2018]

O'Regan, J. K. (2001). The 'feel' of seeing: an interview with J. Kevin O'Regan. *Trends in Cognitive Sciences*, 5(6), 278–79.

Ostrom, E. (1990). *Governing the Commons: The Evolution of Institutions for Collective Actions*. Cambridge: Cambridge University Press.

Pavlov, I. P. (1927). *Conditioned Reflexes. An Investigation of the Physiological Activity of the Cerebral Cortex*. London: Oxford University Press.

Piaget, J. (1937). *La construction du réel chez l'enfant*. [*The Construction of Reality in the Child*] Neuschâtel: Delachaux et Niestle.

Piaget, J. (1970). "Piaget's Theory." In *Carmichael's Manual of Child Psychology*, 3rd Ed., Vol. 1. P.H. Mussen, ed. 703–32, New York: Wiley.

Riffert, F. (1992). *Whitehead und Piaget: Zur interdisziplinären Relevanz der Prozessphilosophie*. [*Whitehead and Piaget: On the Inter-disciplinary Relevance of Process Philosophy*] Vienna: Lang.

Riffert, F. (1999). Process Philosophy and Constructivist Education—Some Basic Similarities. *SalzburgerBeiträge zur Erziehungswissenschaft* 3(2), 68–77.

Riffert, F. (2004). Whitehead's Theory of Perception and the Concept of Microgenesis. *Concrescence. Australasian Journal of Process Thought* 5. Online journal: http://www.concrescence.org/index.php/concrescence/article/view/63/44 (access: 06/22/ 2015).

Riffert, F. (2007). Whiteheads Wahrnehmungstheorie im Lichte empirischer Befunde der Mirkrogenese- und Perzeptgenese-Forschung [Whitehead's Theory of Perception in the Light of Empirical Results from Microgenetic and Perceptgenetic Research. In. S. Koutroufinis (Hrsg.): *Prozesse des Lebendigen. Zur Aktualität der Naturphilosophie A. N. Whiteheads*. [*Processes of the Living. On the Actuality of A. N. Whitehead's Philosophy of Nature*] Freiburg: Alber, 183–216.

Riffert, F. (2014). Whitehead on Cycles of Learning and Cycles of Research. In. D. Sölch (Hrsg.): *Erziehung, Politik und Religion.*

Beiträge zu A. N. Whiteheads Kulturphilosophie [*Education, Politics and Religion. Contributions to A. N. Whitehead's Philosophy of Culture*]. Freiburg: Alber, 73–100.

Riffert, F. & Paschon, A. (2001). Zur Kooperation zwei errivalisierender Paradigmata—Der Modulansatzzur Selbstevaluation von Schulent-wicklungsprojekten (MSS) [On the Cooperation between Two Rivaling Paradigms—The Module Approach to Self-Evaluation in School Development Projects]. *PädagogischeRundschau* 55(3), 335–56.

Riffert, F. & Paschon, A. (2005). *Der Modulansatz zur Selbstevaluation von Schulentwicklungsprojekten* (MSS): Ein Praxisbuch für Schulpartner [The Module Approach to Self-Evaluation of School Development Projects: A Manual for School Partners)]. Münster: Lit.

Riffert, F., Kriegseisen, J., Hascher, T. & Hagenauer, G. (2009). Testing Whitehead's Theory of Learning Empirically: A Report from a Pilot Study. *Tattva—The Journal of Philosophy* 1, 45–56.

Riffert, F., Hagenauer, G., Kriegseisen, J. & Strahl, A. (2018). Testing the Efficiency of the Learning Cycles Instruction in Science Classes (Physics and Chemistry). In preparation.

Seligman, M. E. P. (1971). Phobias and Preparedness. *Behavior Therapy* 2, 307–21.

Temple, D. (1984). Modal Reasoning in Hume's Billard Ball Argument. *History of Philosophy Quarterly* 1 (2), 203–11. Online: http://www.jstor.org/discover/ 10.2307/27743679?sid=21106006087083&uid=4 &uid=2&uid=3737528&uid=2129&uid=70 (acess: 06/22/2015).

Vaihinger, H. (1892). *Commentar zu Kants Kritik der reinenVernunft*. Vol. 2, Stuttgart: Union deutsche Verlagsgesellschaft.

Whitehead, A. N. (1911). *An Introduction to Mathematics*. London: Williams & Norgate. Online: https://www.gutenberg.org/files/ 41568/41568-pdf.pdf (access: 06/22/2015).

Whitehead, A. N. (1929/1958) *The Function of Reason*, Boston: Beacon Press, (1929).

Whitehead, A. N. (1967a). *The Aims of Education and Other Essays*. New York: Free Press (1929).

Whitehead, A. N. (1967b). *Adventures of Ideas*. New York: Macmillan (1933).

Whitehead, A. N. (1967c). *Science and the Modern World*. New York: Free Press (1925).

Whitehead, A. N. (1978). *Process and Reality*. Corrected Edition. D. R. Griffin and D. W. Sherburne, eds. New York: The Free Press (1929).

Whitehead, A. N. (1985). *Symbolism. Its Meaning and Effect*. New York: Fordham University Press (1927).

Wieczerkowski, W., Nickel, H., Jankowski, A., Fittkau, B. & Rauer, W. (1980). *Angstfragebogen für Schüler* [Anxiety Questionnaire for Students]. Braunschweig: Westermann.

Wiliam, D. (2010). Standardized Testing and School Accountability. *Educational Psychologist* 45(2), 107–22. Online: http://eprints.ioe.ac.uk/5845/1/Wiliam2010Standardized107.pdf (access: 06/22/2015).

ぐ 9 ぐ

DO IDEAS MATTER?

John Sweeney

EDITORS' INTRODUCTION: *Chapter 8 introduced technical philosophy
into this book. It focused on one concept original to Whitehead—the
feeling of causal relations, technically named "pure physical prehensions."
The chapter showed how this concept solves problems that characterize
the dominant philosophies of the modern world, including educational
philosophy. Pure physical feelings, or prehensions, create binding connections through time and explain that we are all products of the world. No
actual thing exists in isolation.*

*Prehension, however, is not limited to pure physical or causal feelings.
For example, while we cannot understand learning apart from causal
prehensions, we cannot reduce learning to these causal feelings, either.
In this chapter, and the two that follow, we will explain some of these
other prehensions. This chapter focuses on two: hybrid physical feelings
and conceptual feelings.*

*Most philosophers have noted that there is a difference between a
stone and a thought. Of course, there is a difference also between a stone
and a star or a chair, but we can think of all of these as physical things,
whereas a thought is different in kind. This more radical distinction
is that traditionally made between "objects" and "ideas," or between
"matter" and "mind," or between the "physical" and the "mental."*

165

Whitehead favors this last, adjectival distinction. He focuses on experienced relations, that is, "prehensions." In the preceding chapter, we introduced physical prehensions. In this chapter, we introduce the mental aspect of experience, beginning with what Whitehead called "conceptual prehensions." Physical prehensions are feelings of what is actual. Conceptual prehensions are feelings of what is potential. Pure mental prehensions are feelings of concepts, or pure potentials in abstraction from the role they play in the world. That is, we think of what may or may not be present now simply in terms of the fact that it could characterize something at some time. Whitehead was a mathematician, and mathematics is a good example of dealing with ideas of this kind.

In introducing Whitehead's philosophy, it seems to work best to identify first the purely physical aspect of experience and then the purely mental one. Of course, concretely, in our experiences, these are usually mixed in a variety of ways, and subsequent chapters will describe some of these so as to explain our ordinary experience. In this chapter, we introduce prehensions in just one of these mixed modes. Whitehead calls these "hybrid." Because their data are actual entities, they are "physical feelings," but because their data include the conceptual feelings of these prehended actual entities, these hybrid physical prehensions are distinguished from the "pure physical prehensions" dealt with in the preceding chapter.

Pure physical feelings are prehensions of earlier events that appropriated their *physical feelings from previous events. The world studied by physics is constituted primarily by the physical feelings of physical feelings of physical feelings, ad infinitum. These are an extremely important part of the world, overwhelmingly important for the understanding of the inanimate world, but important for understanding human experience as well. Nevertheless, this purely physical world is not, as so many scientists seem to suppose, all that we feel.*

A good, if difficult, exercise is to examine your own experience in a moment. Most of it is the reenactment of past experiences, especially, immediately past ones. If I was worried in the previous moment, that worry is very likely to persist into the present. However, the past experiences we appropriated included not only physical feelings but also conceptual feelings. That worry had conceptual content. Perhaps I had noted that someone I was expecting was late, and I knew that he was not a good driver. I also knew the roads were slippery from the recent rain. I imagined a possible accident. My reenactment of the past worry usually includes the reenactment of knowledge and imagination that accompanied it. These hybrid physical feelings, that is, the continuations into the present of the mental aspect of the past experience, play a large role in most human experiences. Indeed, they play the dominant role in conscious memory. The purely physical aspect of the feeling remains vague and difficult to identify. Accordingly, most philosophers have given some attention to the mental content of memory, while they have missed the causal feelings apart from which memory cannot be understood.

One important philosophical question is "action at a distance." Most scientists reject that. They are comfortable with the idea that for one event to affect another it must be adjacent. On the other hand, when I recall a conversation that I had yesterday, it does not seem that I am limited to what was contained in all the intermediate moments of experience. I seem to remember the past experience directly.

Whitehead suggests that both I, in my sense of direct derivation from yesterday's experience, and the scientists opposition to the idea of action at a distance, have a point. He proposes that pure physical feelings may well be limited to contiguous events. Hybrid physical feelings, on the other hand, do not depend on contiguity. This means that energy is transmitted only by immediately proximate events, but my recall of the conceptual content of yesterday's conversation may still be quite direct. It is our judgment that when scientists are open to considering hybrid feelings of noncontiguous occasions as playing a role in the world, there can be significant advances in explaining the evidence they now exclude. Rupert Sheldrake, thus far unsuccessfully, appeals for this expansion of science.

IN THE CONTEXT OF A LENGTHY DISCUSSION of the anticipated conference John Cobb wrote as follows:

The Section Plenary will deal with "conceptual" and "hybrid feelings." The main reason that the kind of thinking to which this section is devoted is largely excluded from the university is that it assumes that ideas have consequences, that subjective experience has effects in the objective world. The central dogma of the dominant Cartesian science is that the objective world is a closed system. The standard model has no way of conceptualizing the causal efficacy of subjective experience such as thought on what is understood as "nature."

Whereas physical feelings are feelings of the feelings of others, conceptual feelings are feelings of forms or potentialities. Hybrid feelings are feelings of the conceptual feelings of others. It is by means of this analysis of various types of feelings that Whitehead works out the mutual relations of what Cartesians think of as "mind" and "matter." A special contribution of Whitehead is that by his discussion of hybrid feelings he shows that continuity is not necessary for influence. Telepathy and other phenomena considered "anomalous" by those shaped by the dominant metaphysics are fully intelligible.[1]

So, do ideas matter? Of course, or at least most of those who attended the conference thought so. Otherwise, I suspect that few people would have come. In one of his later books, *Adventures of Ideas*, Whitehead made clear that he believed that ideas matter, and that ideas have made a significant difference in history. For example, Whitehead demonstrates that the growth of "the humanitarian ideal,"—that is, the idea that humans have souls—contributed to the rise of the abolition movement and the battles against slavery. As the continued existence of slavery shows, the effect of new ideas is rarely total. Also, Whitehead notes that any dramatic change, such as the effort to value all human beings and to eliminate slavery, rarely occurs without trauma; the Civil War in the U.S.A. being but one example.

Another example of the ongoing influence of an idea comes from the Constitution Center in Philadelphia, Pennsylvania. Within the Constitution Center, one of the themes noted in a number of displays is how the phrase "all men are created equal" is constantly being interpreted and reinterpreted—perhaps another sign that "the humanitarian ideal" is still at work, and how difficult that work can be.[2]

In exploring ideas and how they matter, the remainder of this chapter is organized as follows: (1) why Whitehead did not treat ideas as fundamental to his philosophy; (2) Cartesian dualism and its role in the development of modern paradigms, illustrated by its impact on topics discussed in this section of the conference; (3) a presentation of some aspects of Whitehead's philosophy of organism, including the notions of hybrid physical feelings and conceptual feelings, and how they contribute of the discussion of the same topics, and (4) concluding remarks.

REGARDING "IDEAS"

In *Process and Reality*, when Whitehead introduced the mental aspect of reality, he avoided the term "idea." It had too many uses in the tradition. Whitehead specifically points out that Locke uses the word in at least two ways—one way referring to traditional universals or abstractions and the other way referring to particular objects in consciousness.[3] Whitehead also notes that "the term 'idea' has a subjective suggestion in modern philosophy, which is very misleading for my purposes; and in any case it has been used in many senses and has become ambiguous."[4]

Accordingly, Whitehead notes that instead of using the term "idea" he is using a variety of other terms and phrases, such as "eternal objects," "pure potentials," and "forms of definiteness." To replace Locke's "ideas" he uses "objectification of eternal objects" and "ingression of eternal objects into actual entities."[5] For Whitehead, pure potentials (or eternal objects) occur throughout this world. Further, since most of what happens in this world occurs nonconsciously, most of the ingression of these eternal objects into actual entities does not involve consciousness. When he uses the term "ideas" in *Adventures of Ideas*, Whitehead is speaking in ordinary language about what we call conscious human ideas. These are a special feature of the high-grade mentality that depends on the conceptual feelings we are now considering. Without the novelty introduced by conceptual feelings, there could be no discussion or influence of the human ideas and ideals he discusses in this book. Here he talks about the role they play in human history. This is a question of critical importance as we hope to shift the direction taken by humanity in a sustainable direction.

So, "Do Ideas Matter?" Whitehead certainly thought so and developed his metaphysics to support and ground that conviction. He concluded: "For the vitality of thought is in adventure. *Ideas won't keep.* Something must be done about them. When the idea is new, its custodians have fervor, live for it, and, if need be, die for it."[6]

REGARDING CARTESIAN DUALISM

Cartesian dualism is a complex idea that has had a profound effect on the development of modern worldviews. The idea of Cartesian dualism, aided and abetted by other ideas — Newtonian physics, Kantian metaphysics, misinterpretations of Adam Smith's economic/ethical theories, and other assorted co-conspirators — is a prime factor in the issues addressed by the conference for which this essay was written. Cartesian dualism, along with all its "accessories after the fact," also reveals itself as a key factor in a variety of bifurcations: male-female, machine-organism, simplicity-complexity, straight-queer, external relations-internal relations, mental health-physical health, and so on. In the realm of Cartesian dualism, there are no continuums; there are only either-or-but-not-both options.

Cartesian dualism divides the world, metaphysically, into two kinds of stuff, two substances. A substance is, by definition, "that which needs nothing but itself to exist." The two substances are (1) a physical/material/extensional substance and (2) a mental/spiritual/psychic substance. Hence, there is a mental substance that needs nothing but itself to exist, and there is a physical substance that needs nothing but itself to exist.

A dualistic tendency has been around for a long time, perhaps from the establishment of civilization — cf. Zoroaster, Plato, Gnostics,

Buddhists,[7] the Bible, Confucius, and many others. But people tended also to see multiple levels in the world, rather than just two. In the Middle Ages, the "great chain of being," with its many levels, was more typical than a strict dualism. Often the division between the animate and the inanimate, or the sentient and the insentient, or plants, insects, and animals was considered as basic as the division between mind and matter. Descartes did not introduce dualistic thinking, but mind/matter dualism in its fully developed form as a major belief system was new. Cartesian dualism "stuck" and was reinforced by Kantian philosophy, now in epistemological terms.

Descartes described the body as a machine, and a machine cannot feel. On the other hand, the spiritual/mental substance is the home of emotions, thought, imagination, feeling, and the like, and a soul is composed of this spiritual substance. Descartes provided reasons for his contentions that human beings had souls and that animals did not have souls. These reasons included the human abilities to use language in non-imitative ways and to solve complex problems. Animals, according to Descartes, can neither use language appropriately nor solve complex problems. Also, please note that without a soul, animals cannot feel pain or anything else. When an animal appears to be feeling, that appearance is merely the "gears in the machine" doing what they do. Hence, Cartesian Dualism provides support for the practice of vivisection.

A puzzle that arises immediately from this dualism is how the human soul interacts with the material body. To define body and soul as completely independent from each other makes this an acute puzzle. Descartes was aware of the problem and suggested the pineal gland as the location of, and mechanism for, all the interaction that occurs. This suggestion failed to convince many people. In Western thought a variety of ideas have been suggested to deal with the problem of interaction between two completely independent substances. The proposed solutions include double-aspect theory, parallelism, dualistic interactionism, and epiphenomenalism. The two simplest solutions are idealism and materialism. Both "idealism" and "materialism" are responses that give up the notion of real interaction. There are only ideas or there is only matter; any appearance of interaction between them is just that, appearance.

"Materialism" is the most important solution because it became, and remains, the core of the modern scientific paradigm. Materialism, along with the body-as-machine metaphor, has become the most influential ripple from Cartesian dualism. The scientific enterprise is based upon materialism; so if anything cannot be explained according to current materialistic, reductionistic, scientific criteria, then "it" does not exist, whatever "it" may be. For example, parapsychological phenomena are ruled out *a priori* as is the placebo effect. Despite the evidence for both, neither can be explained in modern, scientific ways.

Yet, the scientific enterprise is not completely dominant. Many folks are wary of science, or at least of some aspects of science. In *Bad Faith*, Paul Offit discusses how this wariness of science shows itself in medical circles, for example, in the persistent belief that vaccines contribute to autism. Joel Achenbach notes a variety of issues in which the results of scientific investigation are doubted. For example, a majority of Americans still do not accept "that human activity is the dominant cause of global warming."[8] Process thought is critical of some scientific theories, but the process critique is that science is not empirical enough, ignoring evidence that does not fit the modern, materialistic paradigm.

The most fundamental debate today is about paradigms. That is, given the success in many areas of the modern, materialistic, scientific, body-as-machine paradigm, it is today widely accepted. But process thinkers believe it is now leading human beings in self-destructive ways; therefore, they propose a different paradigm. As Kuhn has demonstrated, paradigm change can be quite difficult.

For each of the track topics in this section, I will note an effect or two of Cartesian dualism, with an emphasis on materialism, which is its most important legacy. After further consideration of Whitehead's alternative paradigm, I note ways in which the discussion can benefit.

Bodies Count: Embodiment and the Effects of Bodily Activity

From a materialist perspective bodies, and only bodies, count. The reason is that is all there is—bodies are composed of matter, more specifically matter in motion following universal, natural laws. The Cartesian view that the body is a machine has had, and continues to have, great influence on Western culture. A machine cannot think, feel, emote, imagine, dream, etc. For consistent materialists, there is matter, in the form of material particles, in motion, and that is all. Hence, there is no human agency.

Much of academia reflects a bit of schizophrenia in that both idealism, which values the mind, and materialism, which does not value the mind, are valued. So, both the mind and the body are important, yet in different, sometimes contradictory, ways.

A further complication occurs for materialists in that while their claim is that only matter, following natural laws, exists, they act as if what they choose to do makes a difference. They choose to publish books, debate with others, and generally act in ways that seem at odds with their body-as-machine paradigm. Their theory, of course, is that all those activities are the results of matter in motion following universal laws, but it is not clear that they really believe that.

Another ripple, in response to the materialism associated with the rise of science, gives rise to some forms of idealism, those worldviews in which the mind/soul/spirit is all that exists. This implies that the condition of the body, or even its sheer existence, is grounded in its being thought or imagined. Examples of modern idealism include Christian Science, Science of Mind, and some forms of New Thought.

Rethinking "Sexuality"

Cartesian dualism and its effects give substantial support to the idea that there are only two sexes—male and female, as well as only two sexual orientations—queer and straight. Any other physical manifestations of sexuality are anomalies, aberrations to be ignored, or perhaps even ruled out *a priori*; they cannot count, even should their anomalous existence be acknowledged.

Further complicating this discussion is a patriarchal paradigm: (1) mind/soul is better than body (for dualists); (2) male is closely associated with the mind/soul; (3) female is even more closely associated with the body; (4) the mind/soul involves degrees of freedom; (5) the body is causally determined. Accordingly, within this patriarchal paradigm, males are better and freer than females. Please note that this paradigm places mind/soul "above" body, which would seem to conflict with the materialism of science, but no one said we humans are, or need to be, fully consistent.

The Quest for Wholeness: East and West

The dominance of the body-as-machine idea in the West, especially in the medical field, is obvious. This is true of psychiatry as well, leading to a preference for chemicals rather than talking in psychotherapy. The body-as-machine idea continues to dominate. Perhaps this is to be expected, given the success of this idea in dealing with diseases, broken bones, and the like.

However, there is increasing interest in a broader approach to bodily and mental wellbeing. The recognition that other cultures have effective ways of treating health problems has, for example, heightened interest in holistic approaches. These are demonstrably helpful in aiding recovery, alleviating pain, and the like. Westerners have also developed some surprisingly successful methods. Norman Cousins laughed his way to health after doctors diagnosed him with *ankylosing spondylitis,* or reactive arthritis, in 1964, and gave him only a short time to live. It is increasingly difficult to ignore the role of emotions, beliefs, and other apparently not material factors.

EXTRAORDINARY CHALLENGES TO THE MODERN PARADIGM

The modern materialist paradigm rules out parapsychological phenomena, *a priori*; the body-as-machine worldview rules out all parapsychological phenomena. Regardless of evidence, "action at a distance" does not occur, because it is not possible within the modern scientific paradigm.

Some supernaturalists accept this impossibility so far as nature is concerned, but argue that God, as the creator of nature and the imposer of natural law, can violate it. On the theistic, dualistic side, some parapsychological phenomena are possible, but only as directly caused by the supernatural.

Mystical Disciplines, Ritual, and Worship

The materialism rippling out of Cartesian dualism shows itself in at least two ways. (1) Religious experiences of ecstasy, of the Divine, of enlightenment, etc. are explained away as merely chemical reactions in the body-machine. They are often understood to be chemical reactions to music, to chanting, to whatever is happening in both the body and the larger environment. (2) Whatever happens in mystical disciplines, ritual, and worship is merely the result of molecules in motion following universal laws; matter just does what it does. Neither divine nor human agency is involved.

Eco-Feminism

The eco-feminist movement has led society in rejecting Cartesian dualism. This is partly because eco-feminism takes actual experience, especially the experience of women, seriously. This experience is of the rich and complex interaction of mental and physical elements in experience and in the world. Underlying the polemic against Cartesian dualism is the recognition that it undergirds the ruthless exploitation of nature. Since women are thought to be closer to nature, Cartesian dualism also undergirds their subordination to supposedly rational men. Eco-feminists have yet to break the hold of materialism on the natural sciences, but elsewhere they have made major changes in society.

REGARDING PROCESS THOUGHT, CONCEPTUAL FEELINGS, AND HYBRID PHYSICAL FEELINGS

In response to Cartesian dualism and the various ideas that ripple therefrom—body-as-machine, materialism, idealism, and assorted dualisms—Whitehead suggests a complex of ideas, frequently known as process thought or process philosophy, among which are "ideas" concerning metaphysics, the power of the past, novelty, conceptual feelings, and hybrid physical feelings. As opposed to the distinct substances proposed by Cartesian dualism, process thought suggests an event-based metaphysics within which both the mental and the physical are found integrated into each and every event, as these events occur and as they influence future events.

The ideas mentioned above are discussed in the following paragraphs, in the order listed: metaphysics; the power of the past; novelty; conceptual feelings; and hybrid physical feelings. Of course, there are interrelationships among these ideas, but the focus in each section is on one idea. The final slice of this portion of the paper indicates a few of the ways in which adopting a Whiteheadian metaphysics may readjust the discussion on the topics discussed in this section.

Metaphysics

As mentioned above, a process metaphysics is an event-based metaphysics. The basic events are called "actual entities" or "actual occasions" or "occasions of experience." These basic events combine in various ways, resulting in all that exists—quarks, redwoods, dirt, chairs, humans, etc.

These occasions of experience are composed of an integrated complex of feelings—both physical feelings and mental feelings. Physical feelings are influences from the past, pushing for their repetition, wanting to happen again. Mental feelings, of which there are varieties, are the sources of such novelty as may occur—from minimal novelty to much novelty. All occasions of experience, no matter how simple or how complex, are composed of an integration of physical and mental feelings. There always is an element of repetition from the immediate past, and there is always some element of novelty.

Physical feelings are feelings by a current actual occasion of past actual occasions. Conceptual feelings are feelings by a current actual occasion of eternal object(s) or forms. Hybrid physical feelings are feelings by a current actual occasion of a novelty (form, potentiality, eternal object, idea) that is found in a past actual occasion that need not be either contiguous or immediately continuous with the current occasion. "The universe, thus disclosed, is through and through inter-dependent. The body pollutes the mind, the mind pollutes the body."[9]

The Power of the Past

In process philosophy, the past exercises a powerful influence on the present. The past insists on having itself repeated in the present, and into the future. The past occasions demand to be physically felt by the present ones.

One of the sources of this power of the past is in the sameness that occurs between previous events and subsequent events; sameness increases influence. The "power of the past" is especially evident in repetition. Repetition involves patterns of thought and patterns of behavior—including linguistic behavior—being repeated and repeated. Repetition involves individuals incorporating only minimal change into themselves. With ongoing repetition, the power and influence of the pattern being repeated builds. With sufficient repetition, the pattern becomes a habit and correspondingly more difficult to alter; the more intense the repetition, the more difficult it becomes to alter that habit.

One more facet of the power of the past, implicit in the discussion above and important for the discussion below, is that each experience that occurs then becomes part of the past that, in turn, influences the present, and whose influence carries into the future: "the many become one, and are increased by one."[10] All that an individual does, thinks, feels, says becomes part of the past and of potential use for that individual and for others in their future development.

The power of the past is neither completely deterministic nor completely detrimental. The power of the past is responsible for the stability of the world in which we live. For example, the chairs and tables that we are using today and the building in which we are meeting maintain their stability due to the power of the past, due to the events that compose these tables, chairs, and this building repeating themselves with little novelty. Individuals with less freedom, or less awareness of freedom, are more likely to repeat the patterns of the past. However, eventually, in time, the chairs, the tables, and the building will deteriorate and collapse, unless there are novel interventions to keep the chairs, the tables and the building stable.

Consider the various habits that we human beings develop. There are habits that we would like to change, for example, those that harm one's health, such as overeating. There are habits of which we humans tend to be unaware, such as breathing or the use of language. We rarely become conscious of these habits unless they are interrupted in some way. The ongoing repetition of previous patterns can be, and often is, such that changing those patterns in any significant way is very difficult.

Novelty

Alongside the power of the past, process philosophy affirms the possibility of "novelty." One of the primary ways by which novelty occurs involves the role of individual freedom. Some philosophies, such as scientific materialism, hold that the power of the past, as found in efficient causality, automatically results in a complete determinism. In contrast, process philosophy integrates the self-creative role of the individual within the network of connections that constitute reality. As part of the description of "freedom," Whitehead suggests that each actual occasion has the ability to contribute something, however minimal, to its own creation as well as to the future creation and self-creation of other individuals. The feelings and relationships are integrated in various ways with varying degrees of complexity. Despite the power of the past, individuals have the ability to affect themselves and future individuals. Freedom also involves the individual's being able to select from among the various repetitive and novel experiences that are flowing into the developing individual. Complex individuals, such as human beings and orangutans, have more potential freedom than do less complex individuals, such as sea slugs and subatomic particles, in choosing from the available options.

One of the benefits of a process view of novelty and freedom is that it allows that human beings are, in varying degrees, morally responsible beings. A complication of the process view of novelty and freedom is that moral responsibility, in varying degrees, also occurs in some nonhuman creatures. In a completely deterministic system, no matter the source of the determinism, there can be no moral responsibility, since there is no real self-determination.

Process philosophy balances the power of the past, which is the basis of order and permanence, with novelty, as it occurs through an individual's choosing from among the possibilities presented in their experience. While the past provides an inhibiting context, the individual's own inherent freedom provides for opportunities for change. These opportunities come from two basic sources, each of which is discussed below: (1) conceptual feelings of forms and (2) hybrid physical feelings of the previous occasions of experience.

Conceptual Feelings

Whereas physical feelings are feelings of the feelings of other past events, conceptual feelings are feelings of forms or potentialities. Whitehead suggests that physical feelings refer to the influence of past events on the current occasion of experience, and that influence is most direct from the immediately preceding occasion(s) of experience. However, physical feelings from a more distant past also can exert influence through the continuous transmission of influence, of energy from past occasions, through intervening occasions, and into the current occasion of experience.

For each occasion of experience, in addition to the physical feelings from the past, there is a conceptual or mental aspect. This mental aspect involves the current occasion's own self-determination involving its opportunities for novelty. The sources for novelty include a realm of forms or possibilities from which the developing occasion can select some new way of actually modifying the past influences with which the occasion began.

For theists, including Whitehead himself, the source of novelty involves the primordial nature of the Divine and the ideals presented in each occasion of experience by God. In feeling the Divine feeling of an ideal, a creature feels it, at least initially, with a desire to realize that suggestion in this world. However, the finite subject, as constituted by its feelings of the Divine and of the past world, then decides, mostly unconsciously, how to form its own becoming, deciding what to make of its endowments. "It is our freedom to depart from the divine ideal (as well as past finite causation) that explains why we have the experience not only of 'ideals aimed at' and 'ideals achieved,' as Whitehead put it, but also of 'ideals defaced.'"[11]

HYBRID PHYSICAL FEELINGS

Whitehead affirms that, in addition to pure physical feelings and conceptual feelings, there also are hybrid physical feelings. A pure physical feeling feels the physical feelings of antecedent occasions of experience. This is the vector transmission of energy for repetition. Hybrid physical feelings feel the mental pole, or the conceptual feelings, of a previous occasion of experience. Whitehead further suggested that this feeling can occur contiguously or at a distance.[12] That is, it is possible for hybrid feelings to feel the conceptual feelings of noncontiguous events directly, without transmission through intervening events.

Sometimes this "noncontiguous feeling" has been called "action at a distance" and has been ruled out, *a priori*, by the Cartesian metaphysics that supports modern science. However, some quantum phenomena, such as quantum entanglement, seem to call for modifying the modern paradigm. Whitehead's suggestion of hybrid physical feelings can explain quantum phenomena quite well, and also provide a way of understanding such psychic phenomena as mental telepathy. For example, feeling the death of a loved one without conscious awareness of the death, and from a distance, becomes possible. In the modern paradigms, such experiences are not possible.

CONCEPTUAL FEELINGS AND HYBRID
PHYSICAL FEELINGS—A SUMMARY:

Within individuals, and the occasions of experience of which individuals are composed, (1) physical feelings are the influence from the past that push for repetition; (2) conceptual feelings are feelings of forms or potentials, a source of ideas and of novelty for that individual; (3) hybrid physical feelings are feelings that come from conceptual feelings of past occasions, both the immediate past and the more distant past. Hybrid physical feelings are then another source of ideas. Since the data of hybrid feelings need not be spatiotemporally contiguous, they can explain many extraordinary events that the modern paradigm declares impossible.

Adjusting the Track Topics

Whitehead's clarification of conceptual feelings or prehensions and how past feelings of this sort can be the objects of hybrid physical feelings opens the way to a richer discussion of the topics treated in this section. I will identify some of the new possibilities.

1) Bodies Count: Embodiment and the Effects of Bodily Activity: A process paradigm allows for a more holistic view of the body. The "racialized, speciesed, gendered, abled, and sexually-oriented bodies" that have been emphasized in the modern paradigms (dualistic or materialistic or idealistic) can be re-conceptualized. The influence of Cartesian dualism, bifurcating the world as it does into white and black, humans and animals, male and female, abled and disabled, straight and gay, and so on, is changed by process thought into continuums with many so-called "races," with gradations of genetic overlap among all animals, and so on.

Process thought provides an alternative to the deterministic aspect of modern materialism. If offers explanations for elements of experience that are incompatible with materialism. Such elements include creaturely freedom, consciousness, the power of belief, as found for example in bio-feedback, and emotional displays by both human and nonhuman animals.

2) Rethinking "Sexuality": Rather than dividing humans into only two sexes (male-female) and only two sexual orientations (queer-straight), process thought promotes openness to the evidence indicating that there are more than two sexes. (I have heard of the possibility of dozens of biological sexes based upon how the XY(Y) chromosomes really intermingle with each other.) Further, the variety in sexual orientations is becoming more and more evident.

3) The Quest for Wholeness: East and West: The body-as-machine image has dominated Western medicine, including psychiatry, and is a prime example of the materialistic modern paradigm. While the success of body-as-machine model is unquestioned, there have been areas in which it has blocked progress. It cannot explain the placebo effect, or Norman Cousins' cure by laughter, or the success of acupuncture, to name a few such areas. The slowly increasing role of holistic, a.k.a. complementary, medicine indicates that the body-as-machine paradigm is limited. The process paradigm is inclusive enough to allow for explaining far more of the phenomena.

4) Extraordinary Challenges to the Modern Paradigm: As noted above, in the modern paradigms the phenomena explored in transpersonal psychology and parapsychology cannot be explained. Within a process paradigm, transpersonal and parapsychological phenomena are not ruled out *a priori*. These extraordinary phenomena are possible because the incorporation of past conceptual feelings is not solely dependent upon the directly contiguous and continuous incorporation of feelings from the immediately preceding occasions of experience. Hybrid physical feelings can feel events that are neither contiguous nor continuous. That means that praying for someone in another part of the city may have an effect. There can be "action at a distance," extrasensory perception, shamanic healing, and so on.

5) Mystical Disciplines, Ritual, and Worship: In a process paradigm, the contact with the Divine reported throughout the types of religious experience is explainable. This contact can occur via either conceptual feelings (sometimes referred to as Divine lures) or hybrid physical feelings (Divine lures, once removed). Developing spiritual disciplines, including rituals and worship, can help one feel the Divine lures, as well as improve our response to them. Spiritual disciplines can also open us to creative contributions from the wider past.

6) Eco-Feminism: Perhaps the most encompassing, most inclusive, critique of the modern paradigms has been eco-feminism. It responds directly to materialism, dualism, and patriarchy. It notes that there is much more to life than merely matter in motion; emotions and spirit are ever-present throughout all of nature. Eco-feminism challenges the strict divisions of male-female, queer-straight, human-natural, etc. and proposes an intimate interrelatedness among all that exists. Eco-feminism also counters, in a variety of ways, the patriarchal paradigm that continues to dominate the world by challenging the assumptions and the myths that support patriarchy, myths such as that men are identified with mind, women with body, and so on. All of these challenges are supported by process thought, which also provides philosophical explanations for much that eco-feminism finds experientially.

CONCLUDING REMARKS

So, "Do Ideas Matter?" Given all the information above, yes. Within a process metaphysics, ideas can spur action, both immediately and over historical periods. Also, as a part of a past that is ever-present and ever-expanding, ideas are always available as an influence in a wide variety of experiences.

Even in paradigms that devalue the notion that ideas matter, ideas matter. The ideas of which modern scientific materialism is composed emerged out of the ideas proposed by Descartes, Newton, Kant, et al. They are incorporated into Cartesian dualism, whose extensive negative consequences we have been discussing.

Whether it be the idea of a billiard ball universe within a space-time container, or the idea of a deity-controlled cosmos, or the body-as-machine idea, ideas have been and continue to be powerful ways to influence behavior. Further, many people influenced by these ideas are not conscious of them. Still the ideas that have dominated can be altered, though to what degree and how quickly is hard to know. Given the power of the past, changeability would seem more difficult the longer the ideas — and the paradigm of which the ideas are a part — have been in place.

We wonder whether the ideas generated and discussed in our conference can have enough influence soon enough to delay, prevent, ameliorate the oncoming environmental disasters. Clearly, most of us hope that these ideas and their ripples will become as influential as Cartesian dualism and its ripples have been — the sooner the better.

ENDNOTES

1   John B. Cobb, Jr., "Seizing an Alternative: Toward an Ecological Civilization" a Foundational Paper for the *Seizing an Alternative* Conference (July 2014; http://www.ctr4process.org/whitehead2015/about/background-material/), 39–40.

2   See Kuhn, *Structures*, 1970, regarding the difficulties in changing paradigms.

3   Whitehead, *Process and Reality: An Essay in Cosmology*, 52, 149.

4   Ibid., 44.

5   Ibid., 149.

6   Price, *Dialogues*, 100.

7   Loy, "Awakening."

8   Achenbach, "Why Do Many," 2015.

9   Whitehead, *Religion*, 85.

10   Whitehead, *Process and Reality*, 21.

11   Griffin, *Panentheism*, 23–33. "But this doctrine of necessary confor-mation applies only to the first phase of an occasion of experience, which is its *physical* pole. Each occasion's physical pole is followed by a *mental* pole, which involves self-determination. In this pole, the subjective forms of the inherited feelings can be modified. . . . Rather

than total conformation, there is only "initial confirmation."

. . . Following this initial conformation, the occasion, in its mental or conceptual pole, determines the final subjective forms of its various feelings in the process of determining its overall aim, called the "subjective aim." This subjective aim may diverge drastically from the ideal presented to it by God, which Whitehead calls the "initial subjective aim," or simply the "initial aim."

In feeling the divine feeling of an ideal, a creature feels it, at least initially, with a conformal subjective form — that is, with appetition to realize it. This divinely derived feeling is only the *initial* subjective aim, rather than the subjective aim as such, because the causality from God, like the causality from other actual entities, is not all-determining. The finite subject, once constituted by its prehension of God and the past world, is then "autonomous master" of its own becoming, deciding precisely what to make of its endowments. The subject, therefore, "is conditioned, though not determined, by [the] initial subjective aim." It is our freedom to depart from the divine ideal (as well as past finite causation) that explains why we have the experience not only of "ideals aimed at" and "ideals achieved," as Whitehead put it, but also of "ideals defaced."

12   Whitehead, *Process and Reality*, 308

BIBLIOGRAPHY

Achenbach, Joel. "Why Do Many Reasonable People Doubt Science?" *National Geographic*, March 2015.

Buchanan, John H. "Mystical Experiences in a Whiteheadian Universe." A Paper for the Silver Anniversary International Whitehead Conference. Claremont, CA, August 1998.

Cobb, John B., Jr. *A Christian Natural Theology: Based on the Thought of Alfred North Whitehead*. Second Edition. Louisville, KY: Westminster John Knox Press, 2007.

Cobb, John B., Jr. "The Practical Need For Metaphysics." Paper available from the Center for Process Studies, Claremont, CA.

Cobb, John B. Jr. "Process Theology & Buddhism." *Ask Dr. Cobb.* February 2011. http://processandfaith.org.

Cobb, John B., Jr. *Whitehead Word Book: A Glossary with Alphabetical*

Index to Technical Terms in Process and Reality. Claremont, CA: P&F Press, 2008.

Cobb, John B., Jr. "Seizing an Alternative: Toward an Ecological Civilization." Foundational Document for Conference (2015). Claremont, CA.

Eisenstein, Charles. "Climate Change: The Bigger Picture." *UTNE Reader* (Winter 2014, No. 185), 68–72. Reprinted from http://www. resurgence.org/magazine/article4147.

Griffin, David Ray. *Panentheism and Scientific Naturalism: Rethinking Evil, Morality, Religious Experience, Religious Pluralism, and the Academic Study of Religion.* Claremont, CA: Process Century Press, 2014.

Griffin, David Ray. *Parapsychology, Philosophy, and Spirituality: A Postmodern Exploration.* Albany, NY: SUNY Press, 1997.

Griffin, David Ray. *Reenchantment without Supernaturalism: A Process Philosophy of Religion.* Ithaca, NY: Cornell University Press, 2001.

Griffin, David Ray. *Unsnarling the World-Knot: Consciousness, Freedom, and the Mind-Body Problem.* Berkeley, CA: University of California Press, 1998.

Hasenkamp, Wendy. "Brain Karma: Is Delusion Hardwired?" *Tricycle: The Buddhist Review* (Vol. XXIV, No. 1, Fall 2014), 65–67; 106–07.

Iyer, Pico. *The Open Road: The Global Journey of the Fourteenth Dalai Lama.* New York, NY: Alfred A. Knopf, 2008.

Kraus, Elizabeth M. *The Metaphysics of Experience: A Companion to Whitehead's Process and Reality.* New York, NY: Fordham University Press, 1998.

Kripal, Jeffrey J. "Visions of the Impossible: How 'Fantastic' Stories Unlock the Nature of Consciousness." *UTNE Reader* (Fall 2014, No. 184), 60, 61, 63, 64, & 66–69. Reprinted from *The Chronicle Review* (April 4, 2014).

Kuhn, Thomas S. *The Structure of Scientific Revolutions.* Second Edition, Enlarged. Chicago: University of Chicago Press, 1970.

Levy, Lawrence. "Let's Dance: Transforming Our Lives Through Meditation." *Tricycle: The Buddhist Review* (Volume XXIII, No. 4, Summer 2014), 30–31.

Loy, David. "Awakening in the Age of Climate Change." *Tricycle: The Buddhist Review* (Volume XXIV, No. 3, Spring 2015), 73-75 & 111–112.

Mesle, C. Robert. *Process-Relational Philosophy: An Introduction to Alfred North Whitehead.* West Conshohocken, PA: Templeton Foundation Press, 2008.

Offit, Paul A. *Bad Faith: When Religious Belief Undermines Modern Medicine.* Philadelphia, PA: Basic Books, 2015.

Price, Lucien. *Dialogues of Alfred North Whitehead.* Boston, MA: Little, Brown and Co., 1954

Suchocki, Marjorie Hewitt. *What Is Process Theology: A Conversation with Marjorie.* Claremont, CA: Process & Faith, 2003.

Sweeney, John M. *I'd Rather Be Dead Than Be A Girl: Implications of Whitehead, Whorf, and Piaget for Inclusive Language in Religious Education.* Lanham, MD: University Press of America, 2009.

Whitehead, Alfred North. *Adventures of Ideas.* 1933. New York, NY: The Free Press, 1967.

Whitehead, Alfred North. *The Aims of Education and Other Essays.* 1929. New York, NY: The Free Press, 1967.

Whitehead, Alfred North. *The Function of Reason.* 1933. Boston, MA: Beacon Press, 1958.

Whitehead, Alfred North. *Modes of Thought.* 1938. New York, NY: The Free Press, 1968.

Whitehead, Alfred North. *Process and Reality: An Essay in Cosmology.* Corrected Edition. David Ray Griffin and Donald W. Sherburne, Eds. New York, NY: The Free Press, 1978.

Whitehead, Alfred North. *Religion in the Making.* 1926. New York, NY: New American Library, 1974.

Whitehead, Alfred North. *Science and the Modern World.* 1925. New York, NY: The Free Press, 1967.

Whitehead, Alfred North. *Symbolism: Its Meaning and Effect.* 1927. New York: G. P. Putnam's Sons, 1959.

10

OVERCOMING THE IMPASSE IN
POLITICAL AND SOCIAL THEORY

Cliff Cobb

EDITORS' INTRODUCTION: *We have repeatedly emphasized the centrality of relations in Whitehead's thought and how that helps to overcome the individualism that is a problem both in physics and in human societies. For Whitehead, to be is to become a creative synthesis of prehensions of others. No actual entity could be independent of other actual entities. This point has been strongly reinforced by the emphasis on physical feelings in the two previous chapters.*

Nevertheless, Whitehead declares himself to be an "atomist." To be actual is to be an individual actual entity. We ourselves, and the things we normally think about, are not individual actual entities. We are societies of actual entities. Some societies, such as your experience in the course of a minute, consist in a temporal series of momentary experiences, each of which is a single actual entity. Other societies, such as a stone, can be analyzed into the subatomic actual entities of which it is composed, which are connected both spatially and temporally. This talk can lead the followers of Whitehead to join other "atomists" in considering this kind of analysis to be the proper role of scientific study, although Whiteheadians would always insist that the individuals into which the society is organized are highly social beings.

Whitehead's definition of "causal" intensifies the "atomism." One great contribution he has made to modern philosophy is clarifying the reality and actual experience of causality by pointing out that causality is felt. Causal feelings are feelings of the feelings of predecessor actual entities affecting our experience. Whitehead says they are physical feelings or prehensions. He further limits the definition of "causal." Some physical feelings feel the conceptual feelings of preceding occasions. These are not causal feelings. Causal feelings are pure physical feelings. Further, a causal feeling is always the feeling of a single actual occasion. He identifies this as a "simple" physical prehension," and this alone is designated as "causal."

Whitehead is, of course, free to define his terms. In this case, we think he is guided by his work in physics. The causes he is thinking of are the ones physicists seek, primarily the transmission of mass or energy. In physics there are laws of the conservation of mass and energy. If in addition to the energy in atoms there were additional energy in the molecules into which they are often organized, this law would not work. We take it that the energy of the molecule is the energy of the atoms that make it up. At least we judge that Whitehead thought so.

There is a problem. In ordinary language, when something makes a difference, we think of whatever caused that difference as an effect. It is obvious that the organization of the atoms into a molecule makes a difference. The molecule as molecule has a different effect on its environment from the effect the atoms would have if not making up a molecule. This is common sense, and we are confident that Whitehead would not disagree. However, in all his complex cosmology he has not provided the language for talking about it.

He does talk about how the causal efficacy of all the entities in our physical world give rise to our experience of the world as made up of entities that are in fact societies rather than individual actual entities. Our conscious experience is very rarely of the individuals that physics considers fundamental. The "individuals" of ordinary experience are complex societies of the individual actual entities. It is important to understand why we experience the society of molecules that make up a stone as one stone. Whitehead describes the way in our experience that

we objectify the stone as a unity. He calls this process "transmutation."
The data of conscious experience have almost all been transmuted in this
way, for Whitehead considers a transmuted prehension to be a physical
feeling, but it is not a "causal" feeling. Nevertheless, if dropped on a piece
of glass, the stone will have effects that the separate molecules would not.
Also, the visual experience of the stone may evoke human actions that
would not be evoked by a pile of molecules.

For the abstractions of physics, all this common sense may be irrelevant.
But these days there is much talk in the wider scientific community of
"emergent" properties, and these play an explanatory role in the sciences.
One may choose not to call this explanation "causal," but at some point,
we believe, the term is needed for any feature of reality that makes a
difference in what happens. Clearly, for Whitehead, the conceptual and
hybrid feelings introduced in the previous chapter make a difference.
The transmutation of many simple feelings into feelings of societies also
makes a difference. The various types of social order make a difference.
One Whiteheadian writer, Joseph Bracken, is particularly concerned to
do justice to the importance of institutions and social organization; he
has called his position neo-Whiteheadian because of Whitehead's failure
to make the social implications of his cosmology clear.

Whitehead's emphasis on how each individual is constituted by its
relations to other individuals already points insistently to the importance
of human and other societies. Whiteheadians want to support efforts to
help individual members of societies by improving the society as a whole,
as well as by helping individuals directly. Whiteheadian thought, once it
overcomes the confusion engendered by Whitehead's technical limitation
of the term "causal," can contribute significantly to clarification of why
and how directly affecting a society is important.

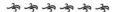

POLITICAL THEORY HAS REACHED AN IMPASSE. Although
progressives, libertarians, and conservatives might disagree on
moral questions and on the appropriate size and power of government,

they all agree on a set of unspoken and unexamined premises about the relationship of individuals to society. All of them are methodological and ontological individualists or reductionists. All of them assume that social explanation requires only knowledge of individual behavior and that "society" is merely an aggregation of individuals. "Society" is considered an abstraction that has no agency. Only individuals are agents who feel, think, plan, and act. Along with that premise is an accompanying belief that causality can only take one form: direct action.

In addition to providing direct services to individuals, governments can only decide what will be taxed, where the revenues will go, what to prohibit, and what to encourage. The market fundamentalists oppose taxation, redistribution, and government services; progressives, social democrats, and liberals favor high taxes on the rich, more redistribution, and more active government. Conservatives favor more punishment of criminals; progressives prefer less punishment and more rehabilitation. Essentially, politics boils down to a conflict between "tough love"—the rewards and punishments of an impersonal system—and "compassion"—policies that take some of the rough edges off that system.

Given their shared assumptions, almost all politically active citizens lie along a spectrum that embraces the basic tenets of 17th century classical liberalism. Most of those who are not on this spectrum are fascists who oppose liberal individualism in principle. But since fascists still define themselves in relation to liberalism, they are on the same plane as this spectrum. Even "climate deniers" base their stance less on skepticism about science than on market fundamentalism. They see the climate debate as just one more instance of phony compassion versus tough-minded economics.

The contest between compassion and toughness has been going on for approximately two centuries, with government policies varying along the spectrum according to popular moods. I call this an "impasse" because it means that no real change is possible. One can move to a different point along the line, but no one is even contemplating points that lie off the line or off the plane on which the line is found. Margaret Thatcher was more correct than she knew when she enunciated the view that "there is no alternative." As long as the basic premise of political thought is ontological individualism, as long as "society" is conceived as nothing more than an aggregate of individuals, it truly does seem that no real alternative is possible.

In the 1950s, economics subsumed classical republicanism within an individualist framework by constructing the concept of "public goods," showing that the aggregate value of certain goods (defense, highways, parks) with spillover benefits exceeds the amount individuals will pay for them in private markets. Even this very limited defense of government was contested by the market fundamentalists (Coase (1960) who contend that beneficiaries of public goods should negotiate in appropriate markets to determine the price they are willing to bribe polluters and other destroyers of public goods to leave them intact.[1]

In this way, several generations of economists, lawyers, and government officials have come to believe that public goods can also be treated as private goods in most cases. Consequently, today, even when one speaks of "the common good" (the stock phrase of classical republicanism, dating back to Aristotle and Machiavelli), it no longer has any philosophical meaning. It is just another means of appealing for more compassion by supporting government programs with broad benefits.

Since compassion runs counter to the logic of individual responsibility, each year, the net closes a little tighter, leaving a bit less intellectual room for defense of the compassionate view.

The most serious erosion of the compassionate alternative takes place in administrative and legal cases. In a legal or administrative context, there is no room for appeals to compassion or the common good. The limiting factors in most cases are decisions about what constitutes scientifically admissible evidence and procedures based on reductionist premises about causality. When philosophical premises that lie several layers beneath the surface become the fulcrum of decisions, the superficiality of political debate becomes apparent. Year after year, the rules of evidence and administrative procedures slowly shift away from social ideals and in the direction of purely individual benefits. Those who are caught up in the system can do nothing to change the direction of the drift, although some may fight a rearguard action to slow it down. In the Unites States, even the Supreme Court probably lacks the power to stem the tide of decision-making that is tied to ever more stringently defined individualism.

The public sees only a tiny fraction of what is going on and locates the issue in partisan politics. In the short run, politics can alter the course of this process, but over the course of a generation or two, the politics of ideas, fought in university departments and in academic journals, is decisive. The legislative and executive branches of government are limited in their scope by the judicial branch, and the judiciary is ultimately limited by the weight of scientific opinion.

In the 19th century, the conflict of methods (*Methodenstreit*) pitted methodological holists against individualists. Sociology began as a source of ideas about holism or emergence, and 19th century thought was full of holistic models, but 20th century social scientists completely eschewed such ideas. One might say there is another such struggle going on in academia, but it is entirely one-sided. A handful of scholars are investigating systems thought, which seems to offer space for some for social-structural explanations in opposition to the ideology of reductionism. When we include these, we can say that sociology is not completely dominated by individualist models. But the openness is limited. Even some of the systems thinkers embrace reductionism.

The victory of philosophical individualism or reductionism may, like climate change, be irreversible. The current worldview produces and affirms fragmentation of knowledge. It prevents effective responses to the raft of disasters now facing civilization. But the failure of a worldview does not cause it to change. Only a new worldview or paradigm can achieve that; and the current worldview discourages any effort to move in that direction. It is difficult to imagine what sort of intellectual breakthrough might alter the direction of thought in the natural and social sciences.

The most promising movement on the horizon is the growing interest in the concept of "emergence" of new properties of a system which are not derived from its components.[2] Accepting this idea does not require the complete abandonment of individualism. Rather, it calls for the embrace of reductionism *and* emergence on a case-by-case basis. Accordingly, this revolution in philosophy would be less dramatic than was the displacement of holism by individualism. If the shift occurs, it will likely take a century or more to be complete.

THE FAILURE OF CURRENT POLITICAL THEORY

After decades of growth of neoliberal ideology in the public realm and reductionist thought in academia, one might imagine that forces of opposition would have emerged to rebut the claims of those who have been whittling away at the principles supporting classical republicanism and concerns about culture and society. Although there have been numerous books, articles, and conferences decrying the external manifestations of the change, there is no sign of resistance at the level of underlying premises. Communitarians have tried to revive some of the principles of classical republicanism (duties along with rights, virtue education, and allegiance to the common good), but no one has effectively challenged the ontological premises of classical liberalism. As long as one accepts the individualistic premises of liberal thought and fails to provide an ontological basis for either social agency or social well-being, the drift toward individualist policies and institutions will continue.

Continental philosophy might seem at first to provide a source of resistance to the spread of liberal ideologies. The residues of Hegelian and Marxist thought in European social thought still offer some basis for thinking about society as a whole. But Hegelian thought is teleological in a deterministic sense and has lost ground. Marxism as a coherent system of thought is also in retreat. Postmodernism is strong in intellectual circles in Europe, but it rejects all forms of systemic thought, based largely upon its rejection of the "totalizing" character of philosophy for Hegel and Marx. This guarantees the inability of postmodern thinkers to offer any resistance to the fragmentation of thought that classical liberalism has already achieved. Indeed, some critics have called postmodern thought "hypermodern" because it accelerates the tendency toward fragmentation.

Anglo-American political theory is no better. John Rawls has set the agenda for the past four decades for normative discussions about law and politics. His influence continues to pervade the field. Yet, his methodology is based on nothing more than common sense reasoning, which means it can never deeply question classical liberal premises. Indeed, that was never Rawls's intent. Rawls's (1971) model of justice is fashioned closely on the principles of the welfare state that existed in the United State when he wrote. His purpose is not to design a just and equitable system but to devise a method of rationalizing the existing social and economic inequality by compensating those denied access to the benefits of the economic system. None of this should come as a surprise. The conservatism of his approach is built into a deductive methodology that necessarily draws upon culture-specific ideas.[3]

What is missing in Rawls is any sense of how humans relate to the world through history, culture, and other sources of identity. For Rawls, there is only pure reason. Although philosophers are loathe to accept any form of metaphysics at present, they are quite willing to follow a philosopher who constructs a world in the same manner as conventional metaphysics — out of a set of propositions deemed rational. What Rawls is aiming at, in other words, is a closed, timeless, universal system of justice based on eternal truths. Why this philosophy, with all of the old methods of constructing metaphysical systems, should be accepted by skeptical philosophers remains a puzzle. Perhaps the answer lies in the fact that Rawls said nothing new.

THE NEED FOR AN IDEA OF THE WHOLE

All of the problems associated with the thin account of justice provided by Rawls point to the need for a more encompassing vision.[4] It would be highly desirable to develop a political and social theory that will inform us about the kinds of institutions needed to create a sustainable society, including institutions that make use of emergent properties of societies. To do so, human action must be viewed in a natural and historical matrix, not just from the perspective of common sense derived from daily experience. In short, what is needed is a grand narrative, which is precisely what French postmodern thought has eschewed. To avoid the problem with past grand narratives, however, new ones should be open-ended and contingent, not closed systems seeking to represent eternal truths.

What is particularly needed is a philosophy that can explain a logical basis for Aristotle's intuition that the polis is an organic whole in which "the whole is greater than sum of its parts." Despite the tenacity of that intuition, its historic association with vitalism and collectivism has undermined its credibility. Recent work in systems theory and the concept of emergence are beginning to create the conditions under which it might regain intellectual standing, but applications of those ideas to human societies has only begun in the last ten or fifteen years.

The process philosophy of Alfred North Whitehead offers the best starting point available for the creation of a general theory from which political ideas might be derived. What is most significant in that regard is that Whitehead sought to construct a set of general principles that apply to all aspects of reality, not simply to human experience. Whitehead's "philosophy of organism" thus represents the potential basis for what Rawls referred to as a "larger theory," one that deals with questions about the ways humans are part of nature and not merely questions about the relationship of individuals to each other.[5] Indeed, since Whitehead introduced the term society in a way that is encompassing of all natural relations, any social or political theory derived from Whitehead will cover a wider range of phenomena than past theories have done.

Thus far, however, process thought has generally been used to justify pre-determined political and economic ideas, like eisegesis in biblical studies (rather than exegesis) or like historicism in historical studies. Hoffert (1975: 175–76) has discussed the limitations of treating process thought as nothing more than a tool of legitimating existing political philosophies:

> Tracing out the political content of an organic metaphysical posture should not begin by placing an *imprimatur* upon the available historical option which most nearly or most easily "fits" the pattern. Rather, it would seem to be more appropriate to construct a novel political vision reflective of organic philosophy's own paradigm. What would politics look like from within the organic model? Not, how would organic politics look like the liberal model? What would be the distinctly "political" content of life from an organic view? Not, what would be the distinctly "liberal" content of life from an organic view? The foundational task, it would seem, is not to search for the least troublesome available political category, but to construct a unique political response coherent with the metaphysical structure. The appropriateness of Whitehead's philosophy for politics is tested by its ability to articulate a coherent and persuasive political vision and not by its adaptability to pre-cast political horizons.

What Hoffert is proposing is that we start with Whitehead's philosophy of organism and see where it leads us. That is precisely what I am proposing as well.

A BASIS FOR POLITICAL THEORY IN PROCESS THOUGHT

Because we are accustomed to thinking in terms of distinct disciplines, we must first observe that Whitehead's method transcends disciplines and offers a basis for all of them. More specifically, Whitehead's thought provides the intellectual prerequisites for *any* sort of constructive political theory.[6] In the absence of Whitehead's philosophical realism and neo-naturalism, we are left with idealism (the "social construction of reality," which eventually devolves into solipsism), empiricism (which even Hume recognized as inherently incoherent), Aristotelian thought (which denies all modern science), or naïve realism (which is a confusing blend of dualism, materialism, and idealism). As in the case of Plato, Aristotle, Augustine, Hobbes, Locke, and others, political philosophy should conform to a broad philosophical framework. Viewed in that way, Whitehead wrote extensively on political theory. He questioned the dominant materialist philosophy of science and created a new understanding of nature. Every reading of nature is ultimately political because it is contested by others.[7] How we collectively interpret nature has enormous consequences for how society is organized. But the current intellectual monopoly obscures the political character of all human thought.

Many of the greatest scientists of the past century and a half have taken great pride in ridding intellectual discussion not only of religious belief, but of any hint that purposes enter into the outcome of events, even human action. In this way, modern science has instilled nihilism as central to contemporary thought. The cosmology of Stephen Hawking and the evolutionary biology of Richard Dawkins, for example, are major factors in modern political psychology. Most scientists agree is that the universe is a vast, aimless mechanism, governed by impersonal laws. Any belief that human purposes derive from or correspond with purposes outside of human consciousness is a product of wishful thinking. In fact, human purposes are nothing more than chemically induced drives, even if we imagine that we make our own choices.[8]

Countering those trends in 20th century philosophy, Whitehead addressed two belief systems that came to dominate thought among intellectuals and the general public: 1) Cartesian dualism, which separated humans from nature, and 2) Darwinian naturalism, which decisively restored humans within the natural order, but simply as an object of empirical analysis, without any distinctive mental or spiritual qualities. For Descartes, nature was comprised of inert substances, and real things are material objects that are observable or measurable by scientists, but he exempted the human soul from nature.

The Darwinian insistence that humans are fully natural overcame the problems of dualism by insisting that materialist categories should be applied with equal force to human life. Accordingly, humans are understood as purely material and devoid of feeling and experience. If engines and dogs are merely complex machines, acting purely on the basis of antecedent causes studied by physics and chemistry, then so are humans. The appropriate psychological or sociological study of humans is thus entirely in terms of either biochemistry or observed behavior. What poets call love or courage can be explained entirely in terms of physical causes. Diseases, both somatic and mental, are simply manifestations of physical abnormalities, to be corrected entirely with chemicals or radiation or surgery, not by forms of therapy that marshal the strength of the mind and of the immune system with nutrition, exercise, positive emotions, new surroundings, or balancing of energies. In this worldview, the idea that humans act on the basis of meaning and purpose is illusory, since brain chemistry is the sole explanation of behavior.

Although many scientists resist extreme reductionism (because no one actually lives entirely according to these nihilistic precepts), and some cling at least implicitly to Cartesian dualism, the reigning philosophy of science opposes them. Those who take materialism seriously regard humans as nothing more than decaying bodies that incorporate antiquated, chemically-based computers that are deficient in computational capacity.[9] The only value appreciated (although never recognized as a value) is pure logic. According to that standard, machines are superior to humans, who are weighed down by emotions and superstitions.

Whitehead's critique of scientific materialism and its associated worldview is political in the sense that it provides the grounds for believing that values exist as objectively as physical processes and that caring about the world is philosophically defensible. Process thought thus challenges nihilism, the deepest possible threat to social order.[10] To accomplish this, Whitehead transcends many common-sense notions of materialism. Specifically, process thought posits that everything has subjective experience and that what appears to be passive or inert is actively constituting itself from its surroundings. There is some small element of freedom, purpose, and subjectivity in every event, even in the highly repetitive experience of subatomic particles. The indeterminacy of quantum theory is not merely an epistemological gap, but rather a product of ontological freedom, however, minimal it might be.

For Whitehead, the human experience of freedom and purpose emerges out of natural processes and is not an illusion. Today, this is a revolutionary position. Whereas the position of most scientists implies that preferences for democracy, anarchism, or fascism are arbitrary, Whitehead asserts that our judgments matter. Whitehead's philosophy does not necessarily indicate which system of governance is preferable (as that would depend on the context), but given a context, one or another is really better. For him the way life is organized is never a matter of indifference.

Thus, relational philosophy provides political theory with a new lease on life. Since both scientists and the public routinely conflate science and 17th-century philosophy, we might say that process thought presents us with a "new science," which offers an intellectually defensible reason to care what happens in the world and to take seriously history and society. Process thought challenges the fragmentation of knowledge into meaningless facts. It argues that the connections that endow events with meaning are not simply "social constructs." If reality is viewed as being comprised of relational events that are both subject and object, political thought will not become drawn toward the fatalism instilled by positivism. Making that possible is already a huge contribution to political thought.

PROCESS THOUGHT AND TRADITIONAL QUESTIONS OF POLITICAL THEORY

Process thought does more than restore the intellectual legitimacy of believing that meanings and purposes exist throughout nature, not merely as human projections onto nature. It also helps answer some of the traditional questions of political theory. But process thought comes to the aid of political theory in a roundabout way, by provoking new questions and ways of thinking that would never be imagined if we merely continued drawing upon political ideas of the 17th century. There are numerous problems in our time that remain intractable given the present assumptions.

For example, economic theory has been attacked by dozens of authors for positing an agent with purely self-interested aims, *homo economicus*. Since the self is constituted socially for Whitehead, there can be no meaning to the concept of pure self-interest. But, the critique of *homo economicus* does not get us very far in rethinking economics. The only alternative framework that has received widespread attention assumes the exact opposite: Lenin's "new socialist man" was supposed to do everything for the good of others.

Whitehead's analysis of experience is more closely aligned with *homo economicus* than with Leninism: whereas most human behavior is guided by narrow self-interest, broader social conceptions of the good can be attained, but only with great difficulty. In any case, the unrealistic assumptions involved in the characterization of *homo economicus* are already widely discussed and debated *inside* the economics profession. The idea that values are social and not purely individual is not novel. What is lacking is a new general theoretical framework in which the implications of a social self are thoroughly worked out.[11]

The existing theoretical framework, which undergirds *all* modern political theories, even fascism, is classical liberalism. No philosophy since the 17th century has been able fully to transcend that framework.[12] For example, a fundamental feature of liberalism and anti-liberalism (fascism) is the dualism of public and private spheres. (Liberalism builds a gender hierarchy upon the dualism, and fascism seeks to abolish the private sphere. Both recognize the dualism ontologically as the starting point of analysis.) By contrast, Whitehead's ontology redefines the public-private relationship as a polarity (like the Chinese concept of yin-yang or mutual containment) that exists in every experience, not as a dualism to be reified in laws and practices.

If we dissect the liberal notion of the private and public realms, we observe that religion, purity, femininity, family, nature, conscience, emotion, and exclusive property rights are tied to the private, non-social domain, whereas culture, reason, power, justice, business, politics, war, and corruption are in the public domain. The distinction between purity and pollution explains how liberalism deals with questions of race and sexuality. These are classified as private matters. Treating them as appropriate topics for public discussion is a violation of liberal norms. Any serious transgression of the public-private boundary is a taboo.

Accordingly, liberalism is not merely a theory of how to conduct politics or economic relations. It orients every aspect of life toward ideals that are defined by implicit ontological commitments. As a way of life, it is protected by the unwillingness or inability of philosophers to question its ontological presuppositions. Because social scientists have so little curiosity about the premises that lie behind liberal thought, their work is largely afflicted with narrow research questions and precise, but unimaginative, methodologies that yield trivial results. Significant progress in social understanding awaits new frameworks.

Whitehead has generally been seen as a liberal individualist. The possibility that a truly social ontology might be derived from Whitehead has been simply inconceivable. For example, Rice (1989: 88) emphasizes Whitehead's thesis that all experience and valuation is embodied in individuals, thereby denying the possibility of social experience:

> While a society might in some *metaphorical sense* be said to enjoy value and embody aims and purposes, *a society is not a true actual occasion or center of experience.* The aims and purposes of a society are always aims originated, realized, and sustained only in the concrete occasions of individual members of that society. Thus, the value of any social and political order must be judged according to its provision for the realization of aims entertained by its individual members. (emphasis added)

But Rice does not stop with a simple reaffirmation of individualism. Instead, he points to a paradox at the heart of the problem of understanding human existence: a social dimension that cannot be reduced to individual experience:

> While all the life of a human society is in the life of its individual members, when we use the term "society" we clearly mean more than just the life of this or that member, and even something other than the sum of the lives of all the members of society. We have in mind a kind of entity which is not itself a subjective center of experience, but which nevertheless lies beyond any particular center of experience. Society has a kind of being of its own and yet that being is originated and sustained only by the being of its individual members.

But finally, for Rice (and many other commentators on a process political theory), the dialectic collapses back into a liberal model of society being created out of individual actions. Rice (1989: 89) claims that Whitehead

> warns in no uncertain terms against committing "the fallacy of misplaced concreteness" in social theory — against reifying the notion of society, forgetting that particular individual actualities are the sole authentic reality.

Rice further claims that Sturm's (1979: 400–01) communitarian reading of Whitehead contradicts Whitehead's explicit emphasis on the individuality of experience. Thus, Rice, like most Whiteheadians, is ultimately satisfied with liberal individualism, with a few minor reforms.

Whether Sturm (1979) is actually a communitarian is hard to discern because Sturm never defines it. The point at which Sturm (1979: 401) discusses the common good, he does so not in terms of the social character of the individual, but in terms of Whitehead's concept of Peace, a dynamic religious and political ideal that involves the continuing dialectic of harmony and discord, unity and diversity, contentment and risk. The one point at which Sturm explicitly addresses the ontological relationship of individuals and society, he does not show any particular support by Whitehead for a communitarian philosophy. Instead, Sturm merely shows that Whitehead ([1933] 1967: 63) opposed all previous forms of political philosophy:

> The whole concept of absolute individuals with absolute rights, and with a contractual power of forming fully defined external relations, has broken down. The human being is inseparable from its environment in each occasion of its existence. The environment which the occasion inherits is immanent in it, and conversely it is immanent in the environment which it helps to transmit. The favorite doctrine of the shift from a customary basis for society to a contractual basis is founded on shallow sociology. There is no escape from customary status. This status is merely another name for the inheritance immanent in each occasion. Inevitably customary status is there, an inescapable condition. On the other hand, the inherited status is never a full determination. There is always freedom for the determination of individual emphasis.

This passage makes clear that Whitehead is not a liberal individualist. He denies both the "absolute individual" and "absolute rights." Yet, even as he portrays individuals as primarily products of custom, he distinguishes his view from any form of conservatism that is slavishly devoted to custom or convention. It is clear from the final sentence that Whitehead also disavowed any support for collectivism that would deny human freedom. To determine if there is a communitarian thread running through Whitehead, we now turn to the question of how Whitehead conceived of human societies.

THE MEANING OF "SOCIETY" IN WHITEHEAD

We can start by observing the fact that Whitehead used the term "society" to refer to order at the most fundamental ontological level. A society is any group of actual entities with a common characteristic derived by each from others in the group. Societies may be organized in various ways. If the group is linear, with only one member at a time, then Whitehead calls it an enduring object. A photon is a series of occasions of this sort. Most of the objects of ordinary human experience are composed of many enduring objects. They are called corpuscular societies. Stones and pieces of wood are corpuscular societies. Many societies have much more complex order. What we call "empty space" is empty of societies, but it is still full of actual entities. Like societies, they constitute a nexus, but this kind of nexus is called "non-social."

Actual entities may introduce some characteristic that is not derived from their past. Those that do are called "living." Societies in which living occasions play an important role are called living societies. Enduring objects consisting of living occasions, where novelty is inherited alongside of repetition, are called "living persons." Part of the experience of living persons may be conscious. We typically identify ourselves with such living persons, made possible by the enormous complexity of human brains. Whitehead seems to suppose that the emergence of conscious experience requires such brains, but this is an empirical question.

Although societies are very important in his thought, and every actual entity is largely a product of the societies of which they are members, Whitehead locates causal efficacy in the individual entities. Societies do not have causal efficacy other than that of their members. Some societies, such as brains, produce actual entities whose causal efficacy is in some sense that of the society in its unity. This is our human experience. But most societies, even plants, lack members of this kind.

Perhaps the most interesting element in Whitehead's account of biological organisms is that "life" (the capacity for novelty of experience in an organism) is not found in the DNA of a cell or its other organelles, but in the "empty space." Since the societies within a cell are characterized by orderly repetition—without which they cannot endure over time—the novelty of new combinations cannot come from them. This implies that life is always an internal balance of chaos and order, not the homeostatic equilibrium that was once conceived as the primary quality of life. The observation that novelty arises from "empty space" (evanescent events) may be a clue to what happens in human societies.

Whitehead said little about these. It is quite easy to imagine, as Whiteheadian liberals have done, that human societies should primarily be understood as aggregations that have no subjectivity or agency in themselves. Whereas individual humans are living persons, there is no similar unity in a group of humans. Bees, ants, termites, and other social insects may have a unity of feeling, perhaps like the cells in a body, but all animals with nervous systems seem to be too fully distinguished from each other to have that level of fellow-feeling.

DO HUMAN SOCIETIES EXIST?

For almost two centuries, the ontological status of human societies has troubled sociologists and raised doubts about the validity of their findings. When England's Prime Minister Margaret Thatcher (1987) announced that "there is no such thing as society," she articulated a view that was widely held by libertarians and conservatives. In a note later appended to the interview, Thatcher (1987) added: "Society as such does not exist except as a concept. Society is made up of people. It is people who have duties and beliefs and resolve." If Whitehead echoed Thatcher's views and affixed them with an ontological finality, then process thought would be in danger of entering current political debates on the side of neoliberalism and market fundamentalism. At a minimum, process thought would contribute nothing to efforts to formulate alternatives to individualist ideologies. In short, the stakes here are very high.

No one would seriously contend that Whitehead's cosmology supports an extreme form of ontological individualism. The doctrine of internal relations obviates that possibility. Each event is largely constituted by relevant past events. Some aspects of the past are rejected and others accentuated, and finally each event includes a decision about just how it constitutes itself from that material. Thus, each person is largely a product of social conditioning.

Even though the concept of internal relations is one of the distinctive features of process thought, clearly differentiating it from the purely external relations of scientific materialism, most accounts of Whitehead's thought fail to explore its full ramifications, retaining the emphasis on voluntarism. But as Whitehead said, social custom ("inherited status" or "customary status") largely determines behavior. Personal freedom arises only at the margins, mostly when conditions permit it.

The question, as currently posed, is whether process thought can overcome what Halewood (2011: 49) calls the "difficulty caused by the ontological status of structure and agency and their causal correlation." He refers to the ongoing debate in sociology over whether social structures or individuals (agents) have primacy in influencing outcomes. Halewood may be correct in indicating that different theorists lean in different directions on this question, but he neglects to mention that even structuralists, such as Anthony Giddens and Pierre Bourdieu, finally end up claiming that all action can be reduced to the agency of individuals.[13] Halewood himself, however, correctly argues that both structures (society) and agency (individuals) are abstractions and that no proposition about them should be regarded as having universal validity. Halewood (2011: 50) concludes: "More real and practical work must be done to establish when and where such abstractions are effective." I take that to mean that process thought should strive to help the social sciences define the specific conditions when biography is the most useful instrument for explaining how events unfold and when more institutional or structural explanations are called for. Indeed, the best biographers already understand this and shift back and forth between social and individual influences.

As helpful as Halewood's account is, it carries us only so far. To answer troubling political, economic, and legal questions about efficacy and responsibility, a clearer sense of how social causation operates in various types of human associations is needed. In other words, the most important question is what societies *do*, not what they *are*. To that end, I propose that three elements are required:

1. A clear statement about the kinds of evidence that will count in demonstrating social causation.

2. A plausible account of the precise method by which societies have causal influence.

3. Specific examples and case studies that show how important problems are solved though social causation.

In short, there is little to be gained by developing elaborate theoretical explanations of the general ontological status of societies. Such an account may not even be possible, at least not initially, because of the great diversity of social formations that have causal efficacy. Following Whitehead, we assume that there is no "essence" of social existence. We must first find operational examples, and then develop theories about how they work.

Considering human societies purely in terms of their efficacy means we do not have to ask if they exist as subjects, which is highly unlikely. There is no need to posit that a society has a "mind" or feelings or intentions or agency in order to recognize that a society exercises causal efficacy in ways that its constituent occasions do not. A tornado has qualities that its constituents lack, since the individual molecules in a tornado travel at speeds far slower than the speed of objects affected by the vacuum created by the vortex. Even the components of a rock act differently when aggregated into a society than they do when separated. Thus, even if "human society" is merely an abstraction from its constituents (individual people), the society as a whole may still have forms of efficacy that are distinctive.

A useful insight about how to think about the ontological status of societies comes from an unlikely source. Friedrich Hayek (1952: 60–62), generally considered one of the sources of modern neoliberalism, was also one of the few 20th century authors to examine in detail the origins of holistic thought and to distinguish between observable "collectives" or "wholes" (families, linguistic groups, etc.) and groups that have statistical properties in common:

The "collectives" of statistics, on which we study the regularities produced by the "law of large numbers," are thus emphatically not wholes in the sense in which we describe social structures as wholes. . . . Far from dealing with structures of relationships, statistics deliberately and systematically disregard the relationships between the individual elements. . . . In the statistical study of social phenomena the structures with which the theoretical social sciences are concerned actually disappear.

Although Hayek was adamantly opposed to considering statistical groupings as sociological wholes, which to him was one of the greatest sins of positivism, this may be the precise point at which quantum theory as interpreted by Whitehead connects with holism and emergence in social relations. While Hayek defends methodological individualism against holism on the grounds that wholes were generally regarded as the essence of observable groups (such as the spirit of a nation), Whitehead's anti-essentialist orientation would make him more open to the idea that human societies are indeed best understood as statistical configurations without obvious physical characteristics. What Hayek disavows as an ontological impossibility may in fact be streams of common experiences both inside and outside of seemingly self-contained bodies that make up multiple levels of actual occasions—from energy pulses to humans and interactions among them. A politically important society for Whitehead need not be limited to humans. The only way to make sense of it may be in terms of statistical regularities. The statistics themselves are not real, but they point to the interplay of real relations.

RESTORING THE "SOCIAL" TO THE SOCIAL SCIENCES

The term "society" is often used loosely to mean any influence by other people on individuals. That encompasses both the influence by discrete individuals and diffuse influence from sources that could not be defined precisely. Even at that level, process thought helps. Whereas common sense tells us that people are influenced by events and ideas of other people, dualism and scientific materialism fail to explain how that is possible. Hence professionals may deny that advertising negatively affects children, that alcoholism is influenced by social context, or that the "hidden curriculum" of public schools reinforces social class hierarchy. These social influences are obvious, but the standard denial that there can be nonmaterial influences often trumps evidence. Only a new ontology that regards social and individual influences as mutual can change that outlook. We have entered a "brave new world" in which pharmacology is the solution to every human problem. Even the most obvious social connections cannot be acknowledged without a new scientific framework. Whitehead can supply this framework.

Our species evolved in small bands, not as autonomous individuals alone in the wilderness. Human children cannot develop outside of a social setting, so social interdependence was the most obvious feature of human life. No special philosophy was required to explain that. Only in the past century has methodological individualism become prominent, such that individual behavior and intentions are regarded as the primary explanatory variables of social phenomena. But we cannot simply turn back the clock. To restore ideas that used to be common sense, we now have to provide a theoretical basis.

THE IMPORTANCE OF SOCIAL CAUSATION

Finally, we come to a fundamental question about the nature of human societies: do they behave in ways that one could predict by aggregating the behavior of individuals, or do societies sometimes act in ways that could not be predicted in that way? If we can find examples of social outcomes that are at variance with the predicted behavior of individuals in that society, then we can truly claim to have found evidence of social causation. At this operational level, statistical observations become especially important.

In the 19th century, the influence of Hegel led many scholars to believe that nationalities, races, religions, and other social groups are super-organisms with a mystical "spirit" (Geist) and that that spirit had causal efficacy. Critical theorists in the late 20th century named this concept "essentialism," based on the idea that various groups had a discernible "essence" that governed group behavior. In the late 19th century, it was classified as "holism" and promoted by the German "historical school," led by Gustav von Schmoller. (Max Weber and Joseph Schumpeter trace their roots to this school of thought, but they were individualists, not holists.) The Austrian school, founded by Carl Menger, reacted against essentialist historical explanation and developed "methodological individualism" as its guiding premise. Ludwig von Mises and Friedrich von Hayek popularized the ideas of the Austrian school in the 20th century. The differences between these two schools of thought developed into what was known as the *Methodenstreit*—the conflict over methods.

The mysticism and nationalism of the historical school discredited it in the eyes of later historians and social theorists. In a similar way, the view that nations were organisms undermined the later belief in any sort of organic philosophy, including Whitehead's cosmology. However, in his critique of the historical school, Menger ([1883] 1985: 143) did not claim that the historical school was wrong in its assertions. He merely insisted that the organic unity of a society should be treated as an object of scientific investigation, like any other phenomenon: "The exact orientation of research in the realm of the organic world does not thus deny the unity of organisms. It tries, rather, to explain the origin and the functions of these unified structures in an exact way, to explain how these 'real unities' have come about and how they function." What emerged from the *Methodenstreit* was not as nuanced as Menger's position. For most social scientists, the search for "real unities" was a path not taken. Methodological individualism became the default position of all social research.

French theorizing about organic unities followed a different path from its German counterparts. In the early 19th century, German thought followed the path that Menger proposed: an effort to explain the "origin and functions of these unified structures." In France, however, research on social causation began, not as grand

(Hegelian) theory in search of applications, but as an effort by Louis-René Villermé to solve very practical problems of public health: the mortality differentials among the *arrondissements* of Paris. Using statistical techniques that were being developed by Poisson, Fourier, and Laplace, Villermé showed that unhealthy social conditions, not natural factors, were the cause of differential mortality rates. By arguing against those who insisted that social problems are entirely the result of nature or individual moral failure, he introduced a new way of thinking into the analysis of human misery.

In the 1830s, a Belgian mathematician, Adolphe Quetelet, formulated a more general theory that made the concept of social causation explicit. Quetelet is considered by some to be the true founder of the field of sociology (Sarton 1935: 14). Observing the regularity of French crime statistics from 1826 to 1829, he argued that criminal behavior followed patterns similar to physical phenomena. From that, he inferred powerful social influences on individual choice that largely determine behavioral outcomes (Beirne 1987). Quetelet ([1835] 1842: 6, col. 2) attributed crime to the "social state," and regarded individual criminals as mere instruments, which meant that government intervention at the social level (not individual rehabilitation) could lower the crime rate:

> Society includes within itself the germs of all the crimes committed and at the same time the necessary facilities for their development. It is the social state, in some measure, which prepares these crimes, and the criminal is merely the instrument to execute them. Every social state supposes, then, a certain number and a certain order of crimes, these being merely the necessary consequences of its organization.

Quetelet did not deny the existence of individual volition, but he believed that individual choices tend to cancel each other out in ways that are predictable, when there are large numbers of people. (For example, if there 500 members of a group, a varying set of 45 to 50 of them might attend monthly meetings, each on the basis of free will, but collectively behaving in a consistent manner.) He did not claim to be able to predict the behavior of an individual, only aggregate behavior. Any action that might seem to be a private decision was the result of social influences, for how else could one account for the regularity of group behavior? An invisible social factor emerges out of seemingly random behavior.[14] Understanding this sort of pattern enables government to intervene in ways that will change the average number of crimes, deaths, or divorces, by modifying a *social* variable but without intervening in the lives of individuals. For that to be true, the cause of regularity must lie in a social cause that is not discernible by studying individual behavior. The relevant variable exists only at the social level.

What Quetelet discovered were patterns that could not be explained in terms of simple, direct causation. If we think in terms of the standard view of causation as a force that compels an event to occur, no such compulsion occurs. But if we think of causation, as Whitehead does, in terms of myriad influences operating among humans at every level of experience (atomic, chemical, cellular, corporeal, intellectual), then most of what shapes a pattern of events will always remain well below the threshold of conscious awareness. For that reason, social causality of this sort can only be perceived statistically. It applies only to estimates of the behavior of large numbers of people. It is equally valid to say that individuals are the cause of group behavior and that groups are the cause of individual behavior. Neither statement, taken in isolation, is correct. Social causation is constituted by a complex field of interactions that create a context in which certain outcomes occur with regularity.

There was a strong tendency in the 19th century for theorists to see causality in deterministic terms. Just as methodological individualists of the 20th century claimed that the causal influence of individual behavior was comprehensive, leaving no room for alternative explanations, many 19th century advocates of social causation claimed that it *entirely* explained certain types of behavior (such as suicide), leaving no room for individual agency. Morselli ([1879] 1882: vi) was clear on this point: "The application of the statistical method to the phenomena of the moral world . . . is the objective demonstration of modern *determinism*" (emphasis added). Social causation could be as hegemonic as individualism. To some extent, Quetelet and his student, Adolf Wagner, mitigated determinism by interpreting statistical results as tendencies and influences rather than direct causes, but their interpretations were superseded by those who took a more rigid stance in arguing against personal volition.

The promise of Quetelet's thought was never realized because he was attacked from all sides (Desrosières 1991). On the one hand, he was criticized by moralists for being a determinist, because many people interpreted him as denying free will and personal responsibility. On the other hand, he was criticized by methodological holists for proposing research classifications that cut across the boundaries of cultural wholes. Even Emile Durkheim, who made extensive (and uncredited) use of Quetelet's methods, eventually distanced himself from them to avoid charges of being a determinist. By around 1900, the statistical methods used by Quetelet were largely superseded by Karl Pearson's concept of correlation coefficients.[15] That shift made Quetelet's use of group averages seem obsolete, although difference-of-means tests are still used today. In medicine, Claude Bernard ([1865] 1927), insisted that medical progress can occur only if *direct* and observable causes can be identified. The net result was that remedies that might work in 75% of cases, but only through indirect means, were classified as unscientific because the direct cause could not be identified. That remains the dominant bias in medicine. For all of these reasons, the influence of Quetelet was cut short.

SOCIAL CAUSATION AND PERSONAL RESPONSIBILITY

Quetelet's own examples of social problems from 200 years ago explain why the idea of social causation has practical importance. Numerous articles in medical and scientific journals in recent decades have statistically demonstrated a strong effect of economic equality on crime, drug use, obesity, mental illness, illiteracy, life expectancy, and many other indicators (summarized in Pickett and Wilkinson 2009).

These studies show that the social pathology in question cannot be accounted for by individual choices, only by a social factor: income inequality. Since inequality is a pure social relation, with no physical correlate, there is only one possible meaning: social causation is at work. For that very reason, the research that demonstrates the effects of social causation is highly contentious. For the majority of scientists, social causation is as impossible as a perpetual motion machine, so they take great pains to show that there must be some methodological error in the studies that reveal social causation operative.

This evidence provides a way of moving past the impasses in social legislation, which is increasingly controversial because it requires "big government" to manage the liberal welfare state. That problem only arises because policies are based on individualist assumptions, and intervention involves efforts to manage the lives of the poor, the sick, and the aged on a case-by-case basis. Yet if social aggregates are meaningful agents of influence on individual behavior, policies aimed at modifying those social units could be much more effective than current policies. More importantly, the required policies would not be felt as intrusive by individuals because they would not be aimed at correcting personal limitations. The new policies would aim at correcting system flaws and thereby remain unobtrusive. Presented properly, this could go a long way toward resolving the central political conflicts of our time.

A necessary corollary of taking social causation seriously is a reduced emphasis on personal responsibility. This is not an either-or question. It is possible, in fact necessary, to assume that social causation and personal responsibility are both factors in creating the social order. But the emphasis has been on personal responsibility, both in terms of the accumulation of wealth and in terms of punishment for crime. The wealthy person is viewed as having achieved that status through personal effort, and the poor person is socially ostracized as a personal failure. Following the same logic, the individual is blamed in the eyes of the law for criminal behavior, even if, like Jean Valjean, he steals to save children from starvation.

Because the ontology that lies behind all political theories is based on individual causation, there has been no basis for questioning results that our intuition says are wrong. Individuals convicted of crime are treated as if they alone are responsible for their actions, letting the rest of society off the hook.

Individual responsibility remains. Proof that crime could be reduced by 80% by altering social institutions would not erase the personal responsibility of law breakers. But we can hope for a consensus that the state should act in ways that reduce avoidable harm. The implicit political philosophy would promote the search for solutions first at the level of society, and only secondarily in changing individual behavior. Social control would be managing impersonal levers that will indirectly change behavior rather than interfering in the lives of individuals.

CONCLUSION: THE NECESSITY OF PHILOSOPHICAL REVOLUTION

The problems associated with reductionism and philosophical individualism are obvious. The U.S. now spends billions of dollars to warehouse a high proportion of its citizens in prisons. Individualist economic models repeatedly cause high levels of involuntary unemployment. Social problems are ameliorated by social workers who help individuals without addressing the root causes. Environmental disasters are worsening largely because our intellectual apparatus has ignored nature and insists on individual responsibility. We should drive less and eat less meat.

There are *elements* in many philosophical systems that can advance a revolution in thought. However, most are still grounded in 17th century categories. Process thought is the only set of ideas that both interprets the paradoxes of 20th century physics and encompasses many cultural traditions. It is the only good candidate for formulating a political philosophy that gives equal weight to social and individual influences.

Only a philosophy not wedded to notions of discrete, enduring entities can do justice to the ways in which human existence is simultaneously individuated and spontaneously coordinated, separate and together, chaotic and orderly. One-sided philosophies have more popular appeal because they are readily assimilated into existing intellectual frameworks. But they leave out large parts of experience. Whitehead's polarity and chaos as necessary correlates of order adds many layers of mystery and complexity to any application of his thought. Process thought seems best suited to provide the basis for a needed philosophical revolution.

ENDNOTES

1   This economic philosophy has been inaccurately ascribed to Coase (1960). In fact, the "Coase Theorem" is an invention of George Stigler (1966: 113) and has been repudiated by Coase himself. See the interview of Ronald Coase at www.youtube.com "/watch?v=o4zFygmeCUA.

2   Actually the social sciences are far more resistant to change in this matter than the sciences, in which references to emergent phenomena already reveal cracks in the edifice of individualist or atomistic models. In some fields, models embracing emergence are becoming the paradigms with the largest number of adherents. As Wan (2011: 3) notes: "[C]ondensed matter physicists (who constitute the largest percent of practicing physicists), have for a long time regarded . . . emergent phenomena as the dominating behavior of the universe, thereby arguing against the reduction of elementary particle physics and string theory that purport to construct a 'theory of everything (TOE)'."

3   Although Rawls introduces various new terms to describe his procedure, it actually varies little from the social contract theorists of the 17ᵗʰ century who posited a state of nature (similar to Rawls's "veil of ignorance") and then proceeded to explain how common property had become private property. Rawls differs little from these 17th century theories except in terminology. The aim is the same: to justify inequality in order for liberty to prevail.

4   The same critique could be applied to Robert Nozick, Jürgen Habermas, Anthony Giddens, Pierre Bourdieu or any other 20ᵗʰ century author who attempted to construct a political theory on the basis of deductive principles about the nature of human relations.

5   I contend that different adjectives that have been used to describe
     Whitehead's philosophy (process, relational, and organic) have
     common sense meanings at odds with Whitehead's intentions
     and are thus easily misunderstood by anyone who has little
     or no familiarity with the content of Whitehead's ideas. I shall,
     nevertheless, use those same terms in this paper.

6   I shall use the term "political theory" or "political thought"
     throughout, because philosophers traditionally developed such
     a theory. The term "social theory" could also be used. Sociology,
     economics, anthropology, and political science all split off from the
     study of history in the late 19th century in universities in the United
     States, as methodology shifted from historical understanding to
     positivist analysis. There is now no overarching term that refers to
     the philosophical underpinnings of all social sciences. Whitehead's
     transdisciplinary philosophy has more in common with an older
     (pre-1870s) liberal arts tradition that brought all knowledge together
     in an effort to attain unity of thought. Thus, one might use the
     term "socio-politico-econo-anthropological thought" or some such
     concoction, but I prefer to use the older term "political theory" or
     "political philosophy" as an umbrella for all of the "human sciences."

7   Grid-group cultural theory, developed originally by anthropolo-
     gist Mary Douglas, argues that there are four or five main types
     of political orientation, each of which is based on how threatening
     or supportive people believe nature is and how tolerant they are
     of risk. For example, communitarians and social justice advocates
     tend to think of nature as delicately balanced and easily disrupted,
     whereas proponents of laissez-faire capitalism view nature as robust
     and benign, not easily damaged. For a simple introduction to this
     theory, see http://changingminds.org/explanations/culture/grid-
     group_culture.htm.

8   Just to be clear, this means that the materialist worldview regards
     all philosophical ideas as "mere opinion," in contrast to the "hard
     facts" or realism of science. This critique applies to Plato and Hegel,
     Marx and Keynes, Dewey and Whitehead, and all other efforts to
     seek a coherent interpretation of experience. Language is unreliable,
     but mathematics and logic are deemed real, even though they are
     abstractions, not material objects. For many scientists, experimental
     evidence is real, but even interpretation of evidence is questionable.

Logically, even experimental evidence should be viewed as a human construct because it is filtered through instruments derived from human ideas, but few scientists would be willing to undermine their own work in this way. The central point here is that analytic philosophy has not actually avoided the problem of being "unscientific," in the eyes of scientists, by eschewing metaphysics and ignoring the assumptions they bring to their work. All philosophy is "speculative" in the sense that Whitehead used that term. There is no neutral starting point for thought or experimentation.

9 Perhaps some of them recognize the paradox that a human designs the computer programs that enable the computer to defeat a grand master in chess. The logic of materialism and mechanism, however, would lead the scientists who fully embrace it to assume computers will outperform humans as computer programmers, and the useless human intermediary can then be dispensed with entirely.

10 After World War II, social scientists set about devising theories that would provide a stronger defense of liberalism and democracy against fascism and communism. For a couple of decades, expressing values in social and political theory was acceptable because the threats were recognized by intellectuals. When those threats receded from awareness, more value-free or positivist approaches to the study of social phenomena became prevalent. What is interesting is that almost no theory has been developed to address the threat of a complete collapse of all social norms and values and what should be done to prevent it. That threat is very difficult to even imagine. It is occasionally discernible when people have nothing left to lose, nothing to live for, and no concern about the lives of others—a situation even more extreme than the conditions that give rise to totalitarianism. At least totalitarians believe in the good of the nation or the party or the people. If the members of a society truly lost any capacity to care about anything, the results would be almost unthinkable. That was the view of anthropologist Colin Turnbull (1972) when he encountered a nomadic horticultural tribe known as the Ik, whose social world had totally collapsed when the Ugandan government displaced them from their land in the 1960s (for tourism), and they were then almost wiped out by two years of famine. Turnbull observed the following results of their induced fatalism: they lost all normal social bonds, left their children to fend for themselves from the age of 4 onwards, stole food from

other family members, and generally created a social situation that fit with Hobbes's notion of a "war of all against all."

A similar form of popular nihilism became a part of premillennialist dispensationalism (a specific type of Christian fundamentalism) in the United States in the 1970s and 1980s, when both leaders (Lindsey, Graham, Falwell, Robertson, Swaggart) and rank-and-file believers regarded a nuclear holocaust as inevitable. Indeed, many welcomed it as the means of cleansing the earth. Of course, this is the type of collective insanity that scientists claim their rationalism will avoid. Yet, if we examine the roots of dispensationalism sociologically, we find that the earth these Christians want to eliminate is a globalized, secular, commercial world, stripped of all values. The nihilism of modern science is merely the logical conclusion of the anomie that has gradually emerged from classical liberalism in which social constraints are viewed as limits on personal liberty. Initially, they are legitimate, but over time, as society recedes into the background, they are considered by anarchists and libertarians as inappropriate denials of individual freedom of expression.

11   As will be discussed below, most Whiteheadian discussions about social science still posit individuals as the locus of all decision-making, based on statements made by Whitehead and his clear indication that only individual actual occasions are real and have causal efficacy. Thus, even though Whiteheadians might critique the individualism of economics and describe the self as socially constituted, they have been committed, in practice, to forms of individualism that make impossible a thorough revision of economic theory.

12   There are passages in Marx that may transcend the dualisms of liberalism, but as a practical matter, Marxism has merely given priority to the opposite side of each duality compared with liberalism.

13   Although Giddens's "theory of structuration" might seem to lead in the direction of social causation, he explicitly repudiates that possibility. Giddens (1984: 14) argues that even in the case of actions resulting from "a non-reflexive feedback cycle," "no explanatory variables are needed other than those which explain why individuals are motivated to engage in regularized social practices across time and space, and what consequences ensue." Some examples of non-reflexive feedback cycles in a social context might include the behavior of crowds, the transformation of the racial composition of

a neighborhood, or the inflationary effects of a change in the money supply. The fact that these processes yield consequences unintended by individuals does not alter Giddens's premise that all action can be traced to individual motives. Moreover, for Giddens (1984: 26), action is constructed of "knowledgeable activities" by conscious subjects: "Human agents always know what they are doing on the level of discursive consciousness under some description."

Similarly, Pierre Bourdieu, the other major social theorist who is often believed to regard social patterns as having influence over individuals, posits that individuals organize their interactions through a slowly acquired mental structure that he calls "habitus" (Bourdieu and Wacquant 1992). He recognizes that existing networks of social relations, which he calls "fields," impinge on individual choices. But again, these fields are ultimately constituted by individual actions. His ontological presuppositions severely limit the possibility of social causation. Yet, at the same time, the "field" of social relations so thoroughly constrains individuals, they are not free in any real sense either. So, as with Giddens, Bourdieu finds himself trapped in an endless maze of reflexivity in which there is no explanation for how change can occur.

Another problem with both Giddens and Bourdieu and other general theorists in sociology is that their theories are not designed to explain anything. They do not search for causal pathways that would explain social phenomena. That shift, toward what Robert Merton called "middle range theory," is precisely what is needed if better political and social theories are to be produced. See Hedstrom and Swedberg (1996).

14 Recall that Whitehead regards life as a feature that emerges from the "empty space" (or random, chaotic interactions) within a cell. We might think of society as an organism in much the same way. In that case, the "life" of a human society does not lie in the observed regularities of behavior (eating meals together, going to school and work and religious ceremonies, birth and marriage) but in the chaos that makes no sense in our lives. If this is true, then random accidents, chance encounters, strange dreams, and erratic behavior may actually be the basis of social life that permits regularity. If this is true, it is paradoxical and perplexing, but it would seem to fit with Whitehead's conjecture about the nature of life in cells.

15   According to Desrosières (1991: 204), Pearson regarded correlations as nothing more than patterns imposed by the mind on events that are ultimately unknowable. In this way, he denied real relations. To this day, the one enduring principle that most students take away from the study of statistics is that "correlation is not causality." Desrosiere (1991: 201) expresses the same view: "The question is not 'Are these objects really equivalent,' but 'Who decides to treat them as equivalent and to what end?'" Since Derosières regards philosophical realism as "crude" and unsophisticated, it is not surprising that he does not question Pearson's "modern" view as being correct.

BIBLIOGRAPHY

Beirne, Piers. (1987). "Adolphe Quetelet and the Origins of Positivist Criminology." American Journal of Sociology 92(5): 1140–69.

Bernard, Claude. ([1865] 1927). *An Introduction to the Study of Experimental Medicine.* Trans. Henry Copley Greene. London: Macmillan.

Bourdieu, Pierre, and Loic J. D. Wacquant. (1992). *An Invitation to Reflexive Sociology.* Chicago: University of Chicago Press.

Coase, Ronald H. (1960). "The Problem of Social Cost." *Journal of Law and Economics* 3(1): 1–44.

Desrosières, Alain. (1991). "Social Science, Statistics, and the State." In *Discourses on Society: the Shaping of Social Science Disciplines.* Ed. Peter Wagner, Björn Wittrock, and Richard P. Whitley. Dordrecht: Kluwer.

Giddens, Anthony. (1984). *The Constitution of Society: Outline of the Theory of Structuration.* Oxford: Polity Press.

Hayek, Friedrich. (1952). *The Counter-Revolution of Science: Studies on the Abuse of Reason.* Glencoe, IL: Free Press.

Hedström, Peter, and Richard Swedberg. (1996). "Social Mechanisms." *Acta Sociologica* 39 (3): 281–308.

Hoffert, Robert W. (1975). "A Political Vision for the Organic Model." *Process Studies* 5(3): 175–85.

Menger, Carl. ([1883] 1985). *Investigations into the Methods of the Social Sciences with Special Reference to Economcs. (Untersuchungen uber die Methode der Socialwissenschaften und der Politischen*

Oekonomie insbesondere.) Translated by Albert Jay Nock (1963), formerly with the title *Problems of Economics and Sociology.* New York: New York University Press. https://mises.org/sites/default/files/Investigations%20into%20the%20Method%20of%20the%20Social%20Sciences_5.pdf.

Morselli, Henry (Enrico). ([1879] 1882). *Suicide: An Essay on Comparative Moral Statistics.* Trans. Henry (Enrico) Morselli. D. Appleton and Company. http://books.google.com.

Pickett, Kate, and Richard G. Wilkinson. (2009). *The Spirit Level: Why More Equal Societies Almost Always Do Better.* London: Allen Lane.

Quetelet, Adolphe. ([1835] 1842). *A Treatise on Man and the Development of his Faculties.* Translated by R. Know. With a new preface by Quetelet, translated by Thomas Smibert. Edinburgh: William and Robert Chambers. (Translated from *Sur l'homme et le developpement de ses facultés, ou Essai de physique sociale.* 2 vols. Paris: Bachelier) http://archive.org/details/treatiseonmandevooquet.

Rice, Daryl H. (1989). "Critical Individualism: Whitehead's Metaphysics and Critique of Liberalism." *The Journal of Value Inquiry* 23 (June): 85–97.

Sarton, George. (1935). "Preface to special issue on Quetelet." *Isis* 23 (1): 6–24.

Stigler, George J. (1966). *The Theory of Price.* 3rd edition. New York: MacMillan.

Sturm, Douglas. (1979). "Process Thought and Political Theory: Implications of a Principle of Internal Relations." *The Review of Politics* 41(3): 375–401.

Thatcher, Margaret. (1987). Interview for *Woman's Own.* September 23. *Woman's Own.* http://www.margaretthatcher.org/document/106689.

Turnbull, Colin. (1972). *The Mountain People.* New York: Simon and Schuster.

Wan, Poe Yu-ze. (2011). *Reframing the Social: Emergentist Systemism and Social Theory.* Farnham, Surrey, UK and Burlington, VT: Ashgate.

Whitehead, Alfred North. ([1933] 1967). *Adventures of Ideas.* New York: Free Press.

11

CULTURE IN THE INTERSTICES:

Finding Ecological Elbowroom in Whiteheadian Propositions

Luke Higgins

EDITORS' INTRODUCTION: *We have noted the central role of prehensions in Whitehead's thought. The three preceding chapters introduced the simpler forms of prehensions: physical prehensions, in their pure and hybrid forms; conceptual prehensions; and transmuted prehensions. The data of these prehensions are past entities (both physical and mental poles), eternal objects or pure potentials, and societies of these entities. We are now ready to make explicit the kinds of prehensions that constitute what is clearest in our experience. These are the more complex prehensions that integrate the simpler ones we have already dealt with. The terms for these more complex ones are also technical: "propositional prehensions" and "intellectual prehensions." The latter are where consciousness emerges. Conscious experience is largely about propositions.*

The word "proposition" often suggests logic. Whitehead was a logician and certainly did not minimize its importance. However, it will be well to keep other uses of "proposition" in mind. Women are sometimes "propositioned" by men. The sexual connotation is not entirely irrelevant. In any case, if one says "I have a proposition for you," it need not be of a sexual nature. "Proposition" can mean "proposal," and that is quite suggestive of Whitehead's use of the term. He equates "propositions" with theories. They are proposals of how things may be. He says they are "lures for feeling."

Propositions are not verbal entities or simply ideas in our minds. They exist in the world. When we prehend a proposition, we are experiencing something given to us by reality, not inventing something. Indeed, propositions are one of eight "categories of existence." They are features of reality that can be prehended by us, not created by us. Every actual entity is potentially characterized by many predicates. Of course, it is only actually characterized by one predicative pattern. But when an actual entity comes into being, that it could be characterized by all these other predicates is an objective fact in the real world. All these "impure potentials" are there for prehensions. The existence of the actual entity brings with it a host of impure potentials, or propositions, or proposals, or lures for feeling. Most of them are never felt; therefore, there are far more propositions than there are propositional prehensions. But as we are surrounded by these lures for feeling, we are encouraged to consider alternative possibilities. To be conscious of simple things, that a plate, for example, is blue, is possible only as we are vaguely aware that it could be some other color. Consciousness of the plate as blue is implicitly consciousness that it is not anything else.

We use language to articulate the propositions we prehend and to ask others to attend to them. Our statements are not the propositions, and they may lead others to attend to quite different propositions. We often talk past each other. Nevertheless, in general and overall, people who speak the same language and have similar cultural experiences are led to entertain propositions quite similar to those the speaker intends.

Whitehead is famous for stating that it is more important that a proposition be interesting than that it be true. If hearers are not interested, they will not attend. If they are interested, even if the proposition does not conform to what is actual, attention may lead to a broadening of experience and thought. It may lead to action. Indeed, "nonconformal propositions" may evoke a strong desire that in the future they will be true.

Attention to the way something may be is typically accompanied by comparison with the way it is. That comparison is what Whitehead calls an intellectual prehension. This is where beliefs and judgments come in. These intellectual prehensions have subjective forms of an emotional character. In addition to interest, the intellectual feeling may be hopeful or anxious, joyful or sad, angry or cheerful, frustrated or enthusiastic, disturbed or calm. In actual experience, the content of our feelings cannot be separated from the way they are felt. Our communications with one another are through and through evaluative and emotional. Logicians may abstract propositions from this context, but culturally the context is of great importance. The tone of voice in which a statement is made may affect the role the proposition plays more than the content of the proposition itself.

Simple events, in contrast to human experiences, do not contain propositional feelings. Physical and conceptual feelings can be integrated in what Whitehead calls "physical purposes" without involving propositions at all. There are many societies in nature in which propositional feelings play no role. But culture *is a matter of the intellectual propositions that compare possibilities with actualities. It is the world of meanings, and meanings play an enormous role in the course of individual life and history. They constitute a dimension of reality that, sadly, gets short shrift in our "value-free" universities.*

WHEN JOHN COBB INVITED ME GIVE THE LECTURE upon which this essay is based, he entrusted me with a mission of sorts. One might call it a kind of mission of "evangelization" on behalf of Whitehead and process philosophy, if this word "evangelization" did not evoke for most people a somewhat unfortunate image — that of a rather one-sided mode of communication whereby the evangelizer proclaims the unambiguously good news of a salvific "Truth." The Whiteheadian method diverges from this approach in more than one respect: First of all, for process philosophy, there is never any "good" that can be affirmed unambiguously — no path forward that is not shrouded in some degree of uncertainty. Any gain in value for life or for civilization requires experimentation with novelty, and if this experimentation never exposes itself to the risk of error and failure, there is no progress that can be made.

Second of all, Whitehead does not exactly place the quest for "Truth" at the top of his priority list, which is not to say that truth becomes irrelevant. But Whitehead's project quite definitively parts ways from what Bruno Latour has called the "sacred task of the moderns"—namely, to critically unmask illusions in order to expose an underlying bedrock, if not of truth, then of some more authentic or concrete experience.[1] As we shall see, Whitehead's task has less to do with skeptical critique than speculative, experimental construction. This, however, is in no way to place Whitehead in the opposing camp of some stereotypically relativistic postmodernism. Although Whitehead is a "constructivist" of sorts, his is decidedly not the kind that turns everything—nature included—into "just a construction" of human culture, thought or perception.[2] Indeed, Whitehead parts ways with most other 20th century philosophers in embracing a thoroughgoing—though not simplistic—realism able to incorporate the insights of scientific research, including (but not limited to) evolutionary biology and the physics of both relativity theory and quantum mechanics. He does, however, propose a shift in the way we interpret the epistemological status of these insights—one that requires us to consider scientific insights "in the same boat," as it were, as insights from other disciplines, such as aesthetics, religion, ethics, and even a nascent version of ecology.

There is one feature of this suspicious word, *evangelization*, however, that may yet be relevant to Whitehead's universe of meaning: The term indicates an act of communication in which the reality being pointed to cannot be disentangled from the value-driven aims which give it its interest and importance. The possibility for religious salvation, for example, is not a mere "fact" that we are supposed to hear in a neutral and detached way—it is aimed at evoking a specific response: awe, gratitude, personal transformation, etc. For the religious evangelizer *just as much* as for the environmental activist — matters of fact cannot be separated from matters of concern. The current carbon content of the earth's atmosphere masquerades as a dry statistic and, yet, as we know all too well — it is *anything but*. Part of what makes Whitehead's thought so radical, and also so useful for environmental advocacy, is his insistence that facts and values are inherently and necessarily entwined. In this way, his project flies in the face of what Latour has called the basic "epistemological constitution" of the moderns. For the European Enlightenment and the birth of modern science is founded on a divide — a "bifurcation" as Whitehead puts it — between the objective, immutable laws of nature, on one hand, and the subjective, shifting values of culture on the other. Human knowledge must either make its stand in the value-free zone of pure scientific research or in the groundless fabrications of human thought and feeling.

These unfortunate requirements of bifurcation go a long way towards explaining the rhetorical quagmire in which environmental advocacy seems to be stuck. If we passionately proclaim our values, we are accused of lacking factual "objectivity." On the other hand, if we ascetically whittle our case down to the "facts alone," we find that they are remarkably — indeed surprisingly — impotent in their capacity to induce any widespread transformation. We are either too shrill and fanatical on our soapbox or too elevated and detached in our sterile laboratories. Perhaps to move creatively through this impasse we need a fresh epistemological framework — one in which a diversity of insights and rhetorical strategies can work together instead of competing with and undermining one another. It is with this goal in mind that I take the opportunity to highlight certain features of Whitehead's unique framework with the hope that it might function as a kind of *lure* for feeling and thinking differently about the problems and tasks we face together at this conference.

As it turns out, this is precisely Whitehead's definition of the term *proposition*. That is, the primary role of the proposition for Whitehead is to function as a "lure for feeling" — to convey matters of interest and importance. They are that element of experience whose expression is, in Whitehead's words: "Have a care! Here is something that matters!"[3] The proposition's role as a vehicle for truth is secondary. In Whitehead's famous words, "In the real world it is more important that a proposition be interesting than that it be true. The importance of truth is that it adds to interest."[4] This statement is all the more remarkable coming from a scholar who spent the first three decades of his academic career at Cambridge University studying propositions in their more conventional habitat of logic and philosophical mathematics. Luckily for us, Whitehead seems to have grown tired of the narrow parameters of these questions, and in 1924 was invited to the other Cambridge — the one in Massachusetts — to expand his work on a new kind of speculative philosophy.

Following the lead of William James and others, he now took up the much broader task of constructing a philosophical schema aimed at *integrating* the full range of human knowledge and experience. The problem that Whitehead now fixed his mind on was that of *coherence*: How could a philosophy of nature simultaneously affirm not just the internal perceptions and experiences of the subject, but the external realities with which these experiences seem to put us in touch? To pass this test of coherence, our aesthetic appreciation of "the red glow of the sunset" should be considered as much part of nature as "the molecules and electric waves by which men of science would explain the phenomenon."[5] Whitehead fervently asserts that the major challenges our civilization faces can only be addressed if our diverse disciplines of knowing are able to cross-fertilize and revitalize one another. Conversely, the myopic entrenchments of further disciplinary turf-war can only result in cultural paralysis. The ecological framework that permeates virtually every level of Whitehead's philosophy thus in some ways begins with his commitment to a diverse *epistemological* ecology — one that he found sorely lacking in his contemporary educational and cultural institutions. It is one that we similarly lack today, as professions and disciplines of study become increasingly specialized and detached from a sense of connection to, and concern for, our living world as a whole.

Consistent with this expansion in his thinking, in his later work Whitehead concludes that "handing over propositions for theoretical considerations to logicians, exclusively," is a prime example of the kind narrow-minded specialism that was stifling genuinely creative thought and cultural progress.[6] He instead redefines propositions in far broader terms than they had ever been considered before: For Whitehead, propositions are not limited to language. And, as previously mentioned, their primary role has less to do with conveying truth than proposing a "lure for feeling" capable of providing "immediacy of enjoyment and purpose."[7] Propositions are not primarily to be judged in their capacity to convey the truth or falsity of some state of affairs, but simply to be "felt" or entertained as possibility. As Whitehead puts it, "But its own truth, or its own falsity is no business of a proposition."[8] Its truth status can, however, impact the type of interest or importance that a given proposition holds for those who entertain it.

The feeling of novel propositions is what opens the inexorability of the past to the possibility of becoming or meaning something *new* in the present. Within Whitehead's evolutionary cosmology, then, the feeling of propositions marks one of the key entry-points of *novelty* into the becoming of reality. In Elizabeth Kraus's words, "Propositions . . . initiate feelings which can transcend the givenness of the past and open the door to novel futures."[9] As the role of propositional feelings expands in importance, so does the cosmos grow in complex and diverse order. This is all to say that, for Whitehead, the proposition is far more than a mere construction of the human mind — it is an ontological "existent" of its own; one that comes to play an especially prominent role in the evolution of living organisms. Propositions "propose" potential modes of togetherness. And the realization of these modes, or "predicates" as Whitehead calls them, does more than passively reflect the *facts* of some external reality — it actively conveys a particular set of *values*.

By this point in my discussion of Whitehead's unique approach to propositions, I am hoping that those readers for whom philosophical logic feels like an alien discourse will be resting a bit easier. Feats of logical acrobatics will not be on my agenda for this essay, though perhaps I will ask the reader to envision plans for the provisional construction of a zigzagging path of tightropes that propose potential links between the domains of science, story-telling, ethics, political efficacy, and maybe even some old fashioned "evangelizing" on behalf of the planet. For I believe that the best preachers do not rely on some arrogant presumption that they alone are "right." The really effective preachers — or activists or educators or shamans or prophets — are the ones that tell the best stories, the ones that perform the most imaginative feats of cultural bridge-building, including those between different species. This may or may not be considered a religiously significant task but, for my part anyway, I consider it part and parcel of the sacred "work of the world"—what Thomas Berry has called the "Great Work" (Berry).

"EVERYTHING IS SOCIOLOGY": THE OVERLAPPING ECOLOGIES OF WHITEHEAD'S PHILOSOPHY OF ORGANISM

This may be a good opportunity to sort through some process philosophy fundamentals. For if we are going to explore what implications Whiteheadian propositions have for "reinventing culture" (the original assignment for this essay) we should probably get a more solid grasp on how Whitehead conceives of culture to begin with. And while he talks relatively little about culture per se, he does spend a great deal of time talking about "societies." Societies, as it turns out, make up just about everything we can point to in our day-to-day lives — whether it is mailboxes, academic societies, trees, or planets. Clearly then, this is a far broader use of the term society than its standard usage would suggest. But what also distinguishes Whitehead's approach is how he defines what counts as a member of any given society. The most basic units of reality — individual members of societies — are not substances that self-subsist through time. They are *events* which arise through the relations that precede them, and perish into a new set of relations that succeed them. In this, Whitehead follows James' notion that reality grows in droplets or buds. What Whitehead calls "actual occasions" are the events through which reality constructs itself. The becoming, or "concrescence," as Whitehead puts it, of each and every actual occasion takes place in phases, of which we will primarily concern ourselves with two — the "physical pole" and the "mental pole."

Like many of the key terms in Whitehead's philosophy (including, as we have seen, the proposition), we have to expand these words' meanings beyond their conventional usage. For Whitehead, all events or occasions are initiated into existence by their physical pole: This pole consists of no more and no less than the entirety of the past world within which they find themselves. (The world that is physically prehended includes, incidentally, a divine element; however a discussion of that is beyond the purview of this essay). That is, each event's physicality is expressed by the necessity that — one way or another — it takes its whole past *into itself.* Thus we are not externally but rather internally related to our world. Whitehead's word for this internal mode of relationship is "prehension," though he also uses the more familiar term "feeling" more or less interchangeably with it. The physical pole is Whitehead's way of accounting for what Aristotelean philosophy would call "efficient causality" — the vectoral force exerted on one thing by another. Our physicality encapsulates the sense in which we cannot choose our past — we inherit a world that is what it is or, rather, is what it has "chosen" to become. The environmental inheritance handed to us by the last few centuries of human civilization has left many of us in this day and age feeling quite sober, if not downright traumatized. Certainly, there is much grieving to be done over what has been irretrievably lost. But in the final analysis, what should concern us most is not what we have inherited, but what our descendants — both human and nonhuman — will inherit in the decades and centuries to come. Fortunately, that has not yet been fully decided.

This brings us to the second phase of concrescence — namely, the mental pole. If the physical pole expresses the inevitability of being influenced by a settled past, the mental pole points to the open window of opportunity with which each moment presents us. For although we cannot choose *what* we inherit, we can choose *how* we will inherit it. It is through the mental pole that each event decides how it will receive or prehend its past and, in turn, what it will become through that past. The mental pole (roughly) corresponds to what Aristotelian philosophy would call a thing's "formal cause." It is also the basis for what Whitehead refers to as the "elbowroom" of the universe—that degree of indeterminate self-creativity built into the becoming of each and every occasion.[10] As the occasion's potential for freedom increases, so does its potential for value—or loss of value as the case may be. Freedom thus allows events to express new forms of value-seeking, but also exposes an event—and the society of which it is a part—to the risk of degrading or squandering values that have already been achieved.

Having clarified the operations of individual events or occasions, we are able to now step back and appreciate the more macrological level of Whitehead's analysis. As theorist Didier Debaise has pointed out, descriptions of process philosophy can often overemphasize the role of occasions at the expense of societies, which, as it turns out, are the real things we encounter and experience in the world—including ourselves.[11] A society is no more and no less than any grouping of occasions united by some common mode of prehension—primarily of one another, but also of everything else. Whitehead uses the term "mutual immanence" to describe the relation of a society's occasions to one another. Simply put, societies are united by some common way in which they *feel* one another and their larger world. Michael Halewood, drawing on the work of Debaise, observes that a society is what it is, not because of some static quality or essence that inheres within it, but because of the mode of experience to which its members are prone.[12] The best description of societies would then not be adjectival but rather adverbial. In his words, "Societies should not be considered as primarily noun-like—that is, as having some inner core of which qualities are predicated. Instead, societies come to be and endure through the shared manner in which their constituents regard one another."[13] So, for example, if a chunk of granite can be called a society, it is not because it possesses the quality of being solid. It is because the members of that society both experience and express themselves *solidly.* Solidity describes the way this grouping of occasions *feel themselves,* and thus what they become through these mutual feelings. Insofar as they shape the becoming of events immanent to them, societies both organize and direct particular trajectories of events through time.

Keep in mind, of course, that events are not limited to membership in just *one* society; rather, there are a near infinite number of societies, ranging from the most general to the most specific, that overlap in both space and time. One implication of this is that there is nothing in Whitehead's cosmology that is not ecological through and through. Events are constituted in and through their relations, and patterns in these relations interweave the cosmos in ways that both conserve complex orders and give rise to astounding innovations. Furthermore, Whitehead's framework allows for no definitive dichotomy between the natural and the social. What makes societies social is their capacity to express nature's patterns of order. Halewood points out that, unlike most analyses of culture and society in the social sciences, "Whitehead places the social at the heart of the natural. For, as far as nature is ordered, it is social; it exhibits 'social order.'"[14] Whether it is a grove of redwoods, a guild of artisans, or the enduring trajectory of one person's thoughts, these same basic dynamics apply. Moreover, if everything in the universe consists of societies of events, and every event has *both* a physical and a mental pole, it quickly becomes clear that *mentality,* and hence, *value-seeking,* is an essential feature of everything that actually exists. In one fell swoop human civilization is denied the conceptual apparatus that for centuries warranted its subjugation of our planet. For if mentality is no longer restricted to the human soul, and value-seeking is no longer restricted to human societies, then how can we justify using nonhuman nature as mere fodder for human culture? The world can no longer be divided among those beings that have intrinsic value and those that have mere instrumental value. It is not that everything possesses consciousness per se, but everything does have some intrinsically valuable *experience* of its world. It is in this vein that David Ray Griffin has — quite accurately I believe — described Whitehead's philosophy as "panexperientialist."

What is so helpful about Whitehead's metaphysical rebranding of the term "society" is that, even as its applicability is radically broadened, the concept also continues to shed light on societies in their conventional sense — namely, human societies. For one thing, it might help us through some of the theoretical quagmires that have marked contemporary social and political theory — for instance, debates over individual agency versus social enculturation: Whitehead would observe that, on one hand, individual members cannot be reduced to the society in which they belong. Since there is real agency expressed in each unique member of a society, persons cannot be considered mere passive vessels for cultural encoding. (The fact that each person's life is itself composed of a multiplicity of events makes it that much more unlikely.) On the other hand, a society is far more than a simple collection of individuals. Each member is essentially composed of its relations, and the pattern of those relations is shaped first and foremost by the societies to which it belongs. To understand ourselves and the various challenges we face is to understand our constitutive societies, which includes both their intersections and their exclusions.

Whitehead's framework also opens a fresh approach to the nature vs. nurture debate: He would point out that we inevitably inherit the past trajectories of a number of different societies to which we belong. Some are part of our human cultural inheritance; others are part of our biological inheritance. Neither of these, however, can be understood as determinate chains of causality; both evolve along an unfixed path. It may be that certain of these trajectories are more or less stabilized and thus more or less capable of yielding to abstract modes of analysis, i.e., scientific "law." Whitehead's mode of analysis would actually be quite comfortable with the ambiguity of this word's double meaning as it is applied to human society on one hand (legal institutions or agreements) and nature on the other (law as unchanging fact). He would not demand that we impose a metaphysical dichotomy on biological evolution as compared with the historical unfolding of human culture—memes vs. genes. Rather, the only substantive difference between the two lies in their relative rate of change—an insight at which contemporary thinkers in science studies and the posthumanities are only now arriving. In this vein, it may be helpful to follow thinkers such as Latour[15] and Timothy Morton[16] in suggesting that there *is no nature*, at least if you define nature in terms of static substance and mechanistic determinism. Rather, there are only ecologies of culture—whether it is cultures of humans, cultures of cellular life, cultures of ecosystems, or even the culture of a universe with its unique electro-magnetic constants.

Where this gets even more interesting is in the overlap and mutual transformation of these various societal trajectories. Keep in mind that each trajectory operates on its own scale of temporality or rhythmic duration. Societal trajectories can sometimes reinforce one another and sometimes cancel one another out, not unlike the wave interference patterns studied in physics.[17] If enough of them come into play all at once, as tends to happen in any ecological milieu of a sufficient degree of complexity, systems can start exhibiting some strange and unpredictable patterns. These "strange attractors," as they are called in complexity theory, can cause systems to behave in ways that appear "self-organized"—a kind of emergence of new order at the border of chaos. Indeed, these dynamics are the basis for some of the most compelling scientific explanations for the emergence of life itself—see the work of Stuart Kauffman for instance.

It is no surprise that one of the pioneers of complexity theory in chemistry and physics, Ilya Prigogine, was deeply influenced by his reading of Whitehead. Indeed, his key partner in theorizing this work, Isabelle Stengers, has gone on to contribute some of the most original contemporary scholarship on Whitehead, in particular her landmark volume, *Thinking with Whitehead: A Wild and Free Creation of Concepts,* whose approach to Whitehead informs this essay in ways that cannot be captured by a few citations. Political theorist William Connolly has also brought attention to the impact of these "far from equilibrium" dynamics for political ecology. Connolly examines the trajectories of capitalism and religion insofar as they intersect both with one another and with the massive changes being wrought on our biosphere.

These overlapping trajectories of thought suggest that there are no unchanging structures that underlie all societies—no transcendent plan or code—whether defined theologically or scientifically—that can determine once and for all what a society is capable of. All we can say is that a society is what it is because of its modes of mutual immanence. These patterns of immanence include not just what societies have in *common*—but also their ordered *contrasts* with what they exclude. To return momentarily to the world of the actual occasion—while every event must physically prehend the entirety of its past, its becoming is also shaped by the potentially novel way it mentally draws these prehensions into *ordered contrasts*. In this way, some influences are reduced to a vague background while others are drawn into a more vivid foreground. In some cases, a particular combination of contrasting prehensions or feelings can give rise to an utterly original experience of becoming. When a set of interlocking societies, what Whitehead calls a "structured society," is able to channel or, in Whitehead's terms, "canalize" a thread of intensely novel occasions, Whitehead calls it a "living person."[18]

This brings us to Whitehead's startlingly unique definition of life, which is really more of a non-definition. Life is synonymous with the origination of novelty, what Whitehead calls, "a bid for freedom."[19] This novelty allows the society to integrate (positively prehend) more diverse features of its world so as to interact with that world more flexibly. In Whitehead's words, "The purpose of this initiative is to receive the novel elements of the environment into explicit feelings . . . [that] conciliate them with the complex experiences proper to members of the structured society. Thus, in each concrescent occasion its subjective aim originates novelty to match the novelty of the environment."[20] Instead of having to filter out the multifarious elements of its world (as negative prehensions), a living thread of events is able to constructively integrate more of them as creative contrasts. This allows it to respond to its world in more proactive and innovative ways.

Since freedom is what defines life, and freedom requires what Whitehead calls elbow-room, he comes to the fascinating conclusion that life is a characteristic not of space *occupied* by any particular kind of society, but rather of *empty* space. In Whitehead's words, "Life lurks in the interstices of each living cell and in the interstices of the brain."[21] A structured society can thus be identified as living to the extent that its constituent member occasions are living. But an occasion's status as living in turn depends on the interstitial space that the society offers it. In the case of organisms that have central nervous systems, there is a unique opportunity for some thread(s) of occasions within it to entertain a striking degree of relational novelty. These threads of richly novel experience constitute what we call consciousness (more on this below).

There is a certain paradoxical logic at work here: An event belongs to some particular society insofar as it conforms to that society's pattern of social order—namely, its repetition of some mode of prehension. And yet a *living* society culminates in precisely that which *subverts* these patterns of conformity—that which is, in important respects, "non-social." In other words, a living society is specifically aimed at cultivating a thread of events whose paradoxical "purpose" is to break the very patterns of social order that defined that society in the first place. This creative non-sociality is made possible through the shelter of an organism's interstitial spaces, spaces which enable threads of living occasions to construct themselves of a more diverse and open-ended palate of contrasts. To honor this strangely non-social mode of relationality, Whitehead rejects the idea of defining life in itself as a kind of society, instead employing the term, "entirely living nexus."[22] As indicated above, the freedom of non-conformity is actually what allows living occasions to be more present to their environment — to be more *interestingly* social.

Stengers appropriates Whitehead's odd use of the word "infection" to describe a kind of relationality in which events are drawn into a shared mode of feeling, without necessarily conforming to one another.[23] Debaise expands on this element of Stengers' work, describing the "dynamics of infection" as a relationship in which it can never be finally determined which member is the infectious agent, and which is its effect.[24] Although this word tends to carry negative connotations of sickness, Stengers appropriates it in a more positive sense: Whitehead, for instance, talks about Wordsworth being "infected" by the "ancient brooding presence of the hills."[25] In common speech, we can also be infected with joy or excitement. For Debaise, this forms the basis for a unique philosophy of the living: "The living is what infects, and what lets itself be infected."[26] Debaise sees these dynamics as inseparable from life's constitutive interstitiality. For interstitiality is not just a spatial but also a temporal phenomenon — it is the interval or pause between one set of events and another that allows for a heightening of intensive contrasts between them. In his words, "Everything happens in the zones in between bodies and their environments, in what we have described as the 'interstices.' Bodies and environments are 'infected' in their non-occupied spaces."[27] Tracing the etymological roots of the term "infection" back to an earlier word which meant "to stain," Debaise continues: "The environment 'stains' the living, affects it by introducing itself into each of its parts — in its interstice — and obliging it to renegotiate its endurance throughout internal as well as external variations."[28] Perhaps we can provisionally identify the word "culture" with any ecology of living societies whose members are able to both infect and be infected by one another.

Cultures are, in Debaise's words, "transformed by what lurks in their interstices and in return, integrate these new elements into their historical trajectory."[29] Perhaps, then, a *healthy* culture will necessarily be engaged in the work of "sheltering" within its between-spaces some significant degree of non-conformity. This would be something like what Stengers calls a "culture of interstices."[30] I suggest that it is only from this place that we can begin to re-imagine what a truly ecological culture might look like. It is only now that we can truly appreciate the significance of the quote from Stengers on Whitehead with which I started this section of the essay: "Everything is sociology."[31]

It will probably come as little surprise that propositions are one of the key components of this elbowroom lurking in the interstices of our planetary ecology. Propositions are a kind of hybrid intermediary between the physical and mental poles—a provisional link between the physical reality of some given nexus—the proposition's "logical subject"—and some set of abstract or "pure" possibilities—the proposition's "predicative pattern." As I indicated earlier, the primary role of a proposition is not to be *judged* as true or false, but simply to be *felt*, or *entertained*. It is a proposal that something in our experience—some logical subject—might be experienced in a certain way—that it might be prehended according to a certain predicative pattern. Propositional feelings are able to integrate conceptual feelings and physical feelings in such a way that, in Stengers' words, "could be associated with a 'mobilization.'"[32] In the words of Nicholas Gaskill and A. J. Nocek, the logical form of a proposition is not "S is P" but "S *could be* P."[33] The feeling of a proposition can, in this way, point us toward a "different way of being interested in, of paying attention to . . . what experience offers."[34]

Unlike propositions of the more traditional variety, Whitehead's propositions are not at the foundation of knowledge. Rather, they arise in the middle of things; they are hybrids that allow an experience of something that merely *is*, to be considered in the light of what it *could be*. For Whitehead, the ability to hold a contrast between some physical feeling, on one hand, and some propositional feeling, on the other, constitutes what he calls an "affirmation-negation-contrast."[35] These most rarified of feelings—what Whitehead calls "intellectual feelings"—are, in Whitehead's view, the basis for consciousness itself.[36] It is important to keep in mind, however, that the basic elements composing intellectual feelings and, in turn, consciousness, are the same that underlie every occasion in the cosmos—namely, physical feelings and mental feelings.

PROPOSITIONAL EFFICACY IN A LIVING CULTURE OF INTERSTICES

With these physical-conceptual tools in hand, we are more than ready to revisit the original task of this paper: to investigate how Whiteheadian propositions can help us reinvent our ecologically sick culture. A Whiteheadian diagnosis of this sickness would point to the way our various societal trajectories have rigidified into overly conformal patterns of specialized professionalization. As Whitehead puts it, "Effective knowledge is professionalized knowledge, supported by a restrictive acquaintance with the useful subjects subservient to it. This situation has its dangers. It produces minds in a groove."[37] This remains an all too accurate description of our culture today: The engineer works in isolation from the biologist, who in turn works in isolation from the poet and the minister. Even communities of environmental activism have developed their own incestuous patterns of cultural self-replication, complete with dress code and musical playlist. This is not to say that we should not seek out like-minded souls with whom to forge communities of mutual support and advocacy. It is just a reminder that getting caught in any one groove, any one set of propositions for entertaining interest in the world, is likely to cut ourselves off from the wider contrasts that give vitality and efficacy to our work. For the really dramatic transformations of culture take place not in its grooves but in its shifting interstices.

The one set of social processes that *has* radically succeeded in knitting society together is, of course, capitalism. But the neoliberal version of it that holds sway today tends toward a crass reductionism in its calculation of value. Its idolatrous embrace of the fallacious dogma that the "best of all possible worlds" can be equated with the growth of financial markets has crippled our capacity to envision a higher, more inclusive ideal for ourselves. Instead of cultivating interstices within which we might shelter one another, each of us is sent out to brave the wilds of the market on our own. As someone who has spent his fair share of time wandering in the wastelands of our enervated academic job market, I've had a strong dose of this bitter pill. But challenges such as these, of course, pale in comparison with the contingency and vulnerability faced by the vast majority of this planet's inhabitants — both human and nonhuman — who eke out their survival on the margins of a world parsed up and mutilated by the post-industrial capitalist machine. This cultural context provides very little opportunity, let alone incentive, to do much of anything other than conform to the professional requirements of some sector of our economy. The idea of allowing our own path to be "infected" by the concerns and interests of diverse members of our ecosystem can feel dangerously un-pragmatic. Certainly we do not want to avoid danger entirely, for where there is risk, there is also potential opportunity. But perhaps there are ways to nurture new openings, shelter new interstices, within which we might feel these diverse life-paths without either getting washed out by despair, or paralyzed with fear. What might help mobilize us to both *feel more*, and respond to these feelings with concerted expressions of care and resistance?

As you might guess, this question is not easily answered. But the framework we have explored in this essay might at least outline the form such an answer would take. This answer will have something to do with what might be called false propositions — possibilities that have not yet been realized. Given Whitehead's insistence that it is more important for a proposition to be interesting than to be true, it makes sense that it would be false or "non-conformal" propositions that would take the most important role in the quest for a more ecologically healthy world. This quest, of course, will not be without its risks. In Whitehead's words, "When a non-conformal proposition is admitted into feeling, the reaction to the datum has resulted in the synthesis of fact with the alternative potentiality of the complex predicate. A novelty has emerged into creation. The novelty may promote or destroy order; it may be good or bad. But it is new . . . In their primary role [non-conformal propositions] pave the way along which the world advances into novelty."[38]

We have plenty of other, more common words for what Whitehead calls non-conformal propositions. For instance: *stories, visions, dreams.* Modernity's insistence on the bifurcation of nature into facts and values, non-fictions and fictions, has pushed this category of propositions to the sidelines of what can really "matter" in regards to the nonhuman. But as many of us are finding out these days, what is really needed are not more "facts" to beat over people's heads, but better stories and visions with which to lure communities toward change. Whitehead's late work, *Adventures of Ideas,* traces one particular propositional "dream"—namely, universal human freedom from bondage—through some of its "adventures" in the history of Western civilization. What distinguishes Whitehead's historical-sociological analysis here is his refusal to define human societies in terms of any universal structures. Human culture, like all structured societies, must be understood in terms of the specific set of propositions that shape and bend its trajectories.[39] Societies change and evolve as the role, expression, and importance of these propositions also changes. Whitehead points out that this particular propositional dream of freedom from bondage—one that would be most famously expounded on by Martin Luther King Jr.—was entertained in the imaginations of ancient philosophers and mystics long before its "truth" could be realized. In Whitehead's words, "The world dreams of things to come and then in due season arouses itself to their realization. Indeed, all physical adventure which is entered upon of set purposes involves an adventure of thought regarding things as yet unrealized."[40] King himself studied Whiteheadian theology at Boston University, and one might speculate that this conceptual framework echoes through his evocative claim that the "arc of the moral universe is long, but it bends toward justice."

Of course the story of humanity goes much further back than the ancient Greeks—scientific cosmologies trace our biological roots back to the origination of life in the primordial oceans of a far younger planet, and our cosmological roots back to the Big Bang. On their own, however, scientific descriptions of our origins seem to offer little more than a dry statement of facts stripped bare of any normative implications they might have for the way we live today. But as *The Universe Story* (Berry and Swimme)—and, more recently, the film, *The Journey of the Universe* (Swimme and Tucker)—have been so successful at highlighting, the larger narrative of scientific cosmology—our "common creation story"—both can and should have a powerful impact on the way we feel our participation in this unfolding and unfinished drama. Thanks to our patron saints of religiously tinged ecology and cosmology—Thomas Berry and Brian Swimme—we have a fresh telling of our origin story that remains faithful to scientific insights, while "mobilizing" them into a predicative dream or vision for what we might become. Facts and values are cross-fertilized; neutral, disenchanted observation gives way to interstitially animated vectors of change. We are no longer in the realm of propositions that merely state bald truths, but closer to what Catherine Keller calls a "truth event."[41] This type of propositional truth is not "certainty or conformity, but the pledge of trustworthiness within the field of relation; the more interesting the truth at hand, the more it opens into the unknowable future, and the more its trustworthiness must prove itself, come true, make free, take place in that opening."[42]

The truth event called into being by an interesting and trustworthy proposition is inherently ethical in its nature, but this is a different kind of ethics than moral law-seeking. Whiteheadian ethics are not a declaration of what we *should be*, so much as experimentation with what we *might become*. Ethics follows the lure of a moving target; indeed, sometimes the target transforms itself completely. No final, eschatological goal is offered, after which achieving we could say, "It has been accomplished." Neither is there some universal formula with which we might consistently discern the difference between right and wrong. As Keller reminds us, an ethical truth event asks for trust, and trust would not be needed if there were no risks involved. Real progress, however, is possible; ancient society *was* legally and economically founded on slavery, contemporary society is not (at least not officially). The point is — the imaginative ventures of hopeful, trustworthy dreamers can make a difference, even if these dreams are only actualized a long way down the road.

Of course, as writers like Bill McKibben keep on reminding us, climate change has dramatically shortened the time-frame within which certain *kinds* of change can make the key difference that is needed. I am thus in no way counseling philosophical detachment in our goal-seeking. Leveling off carbon emissions is not just a hopeful dream, it is a necessary reality if we are to stave off an ecological holocaust and civilizational collapse. I am, however, saying that we have to work with the world we are given — our physical inheritance, in the Whiteheadian sense, is not something we can choose. It is healthy and life-giving to hope for a better future — but hoping for a better past can only bring paralysis and despair.

This is one of the features of Whiteheadian discourse I find most helpful — that it operates primarily in a constructive rather than critical mode. It pragmatically experiments with the consequences of particular strategies rather than mapping out some utopia *ex nihilo*. Stengers has been particularly insightful in drawing out this feature of the Whiteheadian method. Following a Spinozan ethical arc, she uses the term "propositional efficacy" to designate those propositional feelings that make a difference, or, in her words, "mark an epochal change."[43] This efficacy can only be rooted in a thoroughly contextual discernment of the openings to which any given society at any given moment might be prone. In Stengers words,

> Each society should be approached from the point of view of what it is capable of, in the form of speculation, and this capacity does not designate its judgments but the interstices that society shelters. The question is how to 'infect' these interstices.[44]

The cultural traction that propositional efficacy seeks is not based on the unmasking of illusions — the preferred method of modernity. This is not to say that denouncing the false idols of anthropocentrism will not continue to have an important role in ecological discourse. But Whitehead and Stengers would encourage a set of tactics focused less on the pride that comes from being right — either factually or morally — than the hope that comes from being wrong — in the sense of entertaining a "false," non-conformal proposition. Culture will be transformed far more efficaciously by the crafting of hopeful lures than either the declamation or the deposing of verities. The name of the conference section for which this essay was written, "Reinventing Culture," reminds us that it is primarily *inventors* we need if we are to bring about real change: Not necessarily technological inventors — though let us bring them on board too — but the inventors of new propositions.

The process of inventing propositions necessarily carves a circuitous path — there is no foolproof method that can guarantee forward movement. The best we can do is place ourselves at the interstitial crossroads of our world's sometimes scary, sometimes wondrous trajectories of becoming. Then we must experiment with the consequences of infecting these interstices with new contrasts of feeling. While we must be familiar with the conformal habits of these trajectories, we should not assume that these habits cannot be redirected toward some new end. In Stengers' words:

> Thought is then no longer the 'exercise of a right [or wrong] but becomes an 'art of consequences,' of consequences that leap from domain to domain, or more precisely that make interstices zigzag through places where a homogenous law seemed to reign.[45]

Proposition-making is all about the art of connection, and what is ecology, really, other than that?

The inventing of propositions is unlike other forms of invention in that it does not leave the inventors the same persons they were before the propositions were entertained. Placing ourselves in the hands of this indeterminately creative process requires a certain "letting go," a certain trust. For it is more accurate to say the propositions possess us than that we possess propositions. In this way, identifying propositions with "dreams" may be more apropos than we even realized. For dreams are mysterious experiences that *come to us*—they "take over" our reality and reorient our sense of who we are, and what can be connected with what. Stengers thus likens propositional efficacy to the process of modifying the dreams of others.

> Dreams do not abstract from their means. On the contrary, they dissolve the identity of the dreamer in adventures which give back to the means their effective modes of existence: that of propositions which possess the individual much more than the individual possesses them.[46]

I will close with this hope: That, together, we can modify one another's dreams. Indeed, the work of the Center for Process Studies and the Whitehead Research Project have already been modifying my dreams for years. So: May you dream sweetly, may you dream efficaciously, and may you dream in a spectrum of technicolored hope that has yet to be seen by any eye, or felt by any heart.

ENDNOTES

1 Bruno Latour, *We Have Never Been Modern*, 44.

2 Isabelle Stengers, "A Constructivist Reading of Process and Reality," 2008, in *The Lure of Whitehead*, 44–46.

3 Alfred North Whitehead, *Modes of Thought*, 116.

4 Alfred North Whitehead, *Process and Reality*, 259.

5 Alfred North Whitehead, *The Concept of Nature*, 29.

6 Alfred North Whitehead, *Adventure of Ideas*, 244.

7 Whitehead, *Process and Reality*, 184.

8 Ibid., 258.

9 Elizabeth M. Kraus, *The Metaphysics of Experience: A Companion*

to Whitehead's Process and Reality, 96.

10 Whitehead, *Process and Reality*, 201.

11 Didier Debaise, "The Living and Its Environments" *Process Studies* 37.2 (2008): 129.

12 Michael Halewood, "The Order of Nature and the Creation of Societies" 2014, in *The Lure of Whitehead*, 366.

13 Halewood, 366.

14 Ibid.

15 Bruno Latour, *Politics of Nature: How to Bring the Sciences into Democracy*, 4–5.

16 Timothy Morton, *The Ecological Thought*, 3.

17 Indeed, feminist science studies theorist Karen Barad uses the phenomenon of wave interference or "diffraction" as the root metaphor through which she unfurls her "intra-active" theory of "agential realism"—a relational approach to "onto-epistemology" that shares many essential characteristics with process philosophy.

18 Whitehead, *Process and Reality*, 107.

19 Whitehead, *Process and Reality*, 104.

20 Whitehead, *Process and Reality*, 102.

21 Whitehead, *Process and Reality*, 105–6.

22 Whitehead, *Process and Reality*, 103–5.

23 Stengers, *Thinking with Whitehead*, 157–63.

24 Debaise, 134.

25 Whitehead, *Science and the Modern World*, 92.

26 Debaise, 134.

27 Debaise, 135.

28 Ibid.

29 Debaise, 133.

30 Stengers, *Thinking with Whitehead*, 367.

31 Stengers, *Thinking with Whitehead*, 363.

32 Stengers, *Thinking with Whitehead*, 414.

33 Nicholas Gaskill and A. J. Nocek, *The Lure of Whitehead*, 14.

34 Gaskill and Nocek, 14.

35 Whitehead, *Process and Reality* 24, 243.

36 Whitehead, *Process and Reality*, 266.

37 Whitehead, *Science and the Modern World*, 197.

38 Whitehead, *Process and Reality*, 187.

39 Halewood, 376.

40 Whitehead, *Adventure of Ideas*, 27.

41 Catherine Keller, "Uninteresting Truth? Tedium and Event in Post-modernity," in *Secrets of Becoming: Negotiating Whitehead, Deleuze, and Butler*, edited by Roland Faber and Andrea M. Stephenson, 208–9.

42 Keller, 212

43 Stengers, *Thinking with Whitehead*, 409.

44 Stengers, *Thinking with Whitehead*, 517.

45 Stengers, *Thinking with Whitehead*, 572.

46 Ibid.

BIBLIOGRAPHY

Barad, Karen Michelle. *Meeting the Universe Halfway: Quantum Physics and the Entanglement of Matter and Meaning*. Durham: Duke University Press, 2007.

Berry, Thomas. *The Great Work: Our Way into the Future*. New York: Bell Tower, 1999.

Connolly, William E. *Capitalism and Christianity, American Style*. Durham: Duke University Press, 2008.

Debaise, Didier. "The Living and Its Environments." *Process Studies* 37.2 (2008): 127–39.

Gaskill, Nicholas, and A. J. Nocek. *The Lure of Whitehead*. Minneapolis: Univeristy of Minnesota Press, 2014.

Halewood, Michael. "The Order of Nature and the Creation of Societies." In *The Lure of Whitehead*. Edited by Nicholas Gaskill and A. J. Nocek, 360–78. Minneapolis: University of Minnesota Press, 2014.

Kauffman, Stuart A. *The Origins of Order: Self-organization and Selection in Evolution.* New York: Oxford University Press, 1993.

Keller, Catherine. "Uninteresting Truth? Tedium and Event in Postmodernity." In *Secrets of Becoming: Negotiating Whitehead, Deleuze, and Butler.* Edited by Roland Faber and Andrea M. Stephenson, 201–13. New York: Fordham University Press, 2011. .

Kraus, Elizabeth M. *The Metaphysics of Experience: A Companion to Whitehead's Process and Reality.* New York: Fordham University Press, 1979.

Latour, Bruno. *Politics of Nature: How to Bring the Sciences into Democracy.* Translated by Catherine Porter. Cambridge, MA: Harvard University Press, 2004.

Latour, Bruno. *We Have Never Been Modern.* Translated by Catherine Porter. Cambridge, MA: Harvard University Press, 2002.

Morton, Timothy. *The Ecological Thought.* Cambridge: Harvard University Press, 2010.

Stengers, Isabelle. "A Constructivist Reading of *Process and Reality.*" 2008. Reprinted in *The Lure of Whitehead.* Edited by Nicholas Gaskill and A. J. Nocek, 44–46. Minneapolis: University of Minnesota, 2014.

Stengers, Isabelle. *Thinking with Whitehead: A Free and Wild Creation of Concepts.* Translated by Michael Chase. Cambridge, MA: Harvard University Press, 2011.

Swimme, Brian, and Thomas Berry. *The Universe Story: From the Primordial Flaring Forth to the Ecozoic Era — a Celebration of the Unfolding of the Cosmos.* San Francisco, CA: HarperSan Francisco, 1992.

Swimme, Brian, and Mary Evelyn Tucker. *The Journey of the Universe.* Performed by Brian Swimme. Shelter Island, 2011. DVD.

Whitehead, Alfred North. *Adventure of Ideas.* 1933. New York: Free Press, 1967.

Whitehead, Alfred North. *The Concept of Nature.* Cambridge: Cambridge University Press, 1920.

Whitehead, Alfred North. *Modes of Thought*. 1938. New York: Free Press, 1968.

Whitehead, Alfred North. *Process and Reality*. 1929. Corrected Edition. Edited by David Ray Griffin and Donald W. Sherburne. New York: Free Press, 1978.

Whitehead, Alfred North. *Science and the Modern World*. 1925. New York: Free Press, 1967.

$\approx$ 12 $\approx$

CREATIVITY, IMAGINATION, AND THE ARTS:

Marjorie Hewitt Suchocki

EDITORS' INTRODUCTION: *The introduction of Whitehead's thought in the first seven chapters was largely nontechnical. In the last five chapters of the book, however, we introduced some of Whitehead's technical philosophy in a more systematic way. We think that his idea of "prehension" is his single most important contribution to the history of thought; so we have focused on it, beginning with its simplest forms and moving to the complex integrations of simple prehensions in propositional and intellectual prehensions.*

The most problematic part of our procedure has been to tie particular fields of thought closely to particular prehensions. We focused on pure physical prehensions in the chapter on education, although it is obvious that education involves intellectual prehensions of the most complex sort. And, of course, pure physical prehensions are necessary for culture. Every part of Whitehead's philosophy is important for every other part, and the relevance to particular problems cannot be separated from the whole. Nevertheless, we cannot say everything at once, and we hope that the arbitrary elements in the exposition have had their value.

These comments are particularly relevant in this final chapter. Whitehead uses "creativity" as the name for that activity that most fundamentally constitutes all that is actual. To be actual is to be a moment of creativity, which, in every instance, is the occurrence of "the many" becoming "one." Creativity is the process of synthesizing prehensions. Each synthesis becomes an actual occasion of experience — and it is these occasions that make up the world.

Still we have reserved the thematic discussion of creativity for the chapter on the arts. We think of art as exemplifying creativity in its fullest and most developed form, but, for Whitehead, art should not be separated from other spheres of activity. When speaking of spirituality, he talks about the art of the inner life. We could think of education as the art of teaching, and of governance as the art of political rule. These are all highly developed forms of creativity. But highly developed forms depend on the creativity of myriads of much simpler events.

Whitehead locates "creativity" in the category of the "ultimate." One avenue to understanding this part of Whitehead's philosophy is through Buddhism. Buddhists have also been keenly interested in identifying the ultimate. For them the purpose is to overcome attachments to what is not ultimate, but then to understand that the ultimate is not something to which one can attach oneself. Since Buddhism, like Whitehead's philosophy, is a form of "process" thought, their understanding of ultimate reality is remarkably similar. Like Whitehead's creativity, the Buddhist ultimate, sometimes called Buddha-nature, sometimes, Dharmakaya, can be understood as the many becoming one.

Nevertheless, there is a difference. Buddhism has not focused on the issue of individual freedom and responsibility, so important in the West. If one brings that question to Buddhists, the answers usually give the impression that Buddhists do believe that each of us has responsibility for what we make of ourselves. But Buddhist thinking about ultimate reality does not usually include an explanation of how this can occur. Accordingly, the many becoming one can seem to be a process determined by the many. For Whitehead, it is an act of synthesizing, so that however much is determined by the many, the becoming actual occasion makes the decision as to exactly what the synthesis will be. The term "creativity" suggests this element of self-determination that is so important for Whitehead.

The closest analogue in traditional Western philosophy is "being." From Thomas Aquinas to Martin Heidegger, Being Itself has been seen as "ultimate." That is, to be or exist at all is to be a being, and a being is an instantiation of being itself. There has been a tendency to think of this as an underlying substance, but some Thomists stress that Being Itself is the dynamic act of being, not a substance. This brings some Thomists close to Whitehead. If they can also assert that the act of being is an act of synthesizing what is given from the past, and if that includes the prehension of potentialities as well as actualities, Whitehead can be seen as a further development of the Thomist tradition.

This raises the question of theology. Sometimes "God" is defined as "Ultimate Reality." When Thomas clarifies that ultimate reality is Being Itself, he assumes that it is, for that reason, God. For him, Being Itself is not sharply separated from God as the Supreme Being, but in the course of time, that separation has occurred. Heidegger affirms Being Itself, but since it is not a being, he denies that it is God. Tillich affirms Being Itself as the ultimate, and he recognizes that it is very different from the biblical God. His judgment is that Christians should re-think God as Being Itself, giving up the idea that God is the supreme instance of being. Some, who are influenced by Whitehead in other respects, follow Tillich's example and re-think "God" as "creativity." Whitehead agrees with Heidegger that the ultimate, being itself or creativity, is not God, but unlike Heidegger and Tillich, he holds that there is a supreme and unique instantiation of creativity that can be identified with God, if we focus on what he called the Galilean vision. In this chapter, Marjorie Suchocki deals briefly with Whitehead's account of God as one of the many that creatively become each new actual occasion. Whitehead attributes the "initial aim" of each occasion to the immanence of God.

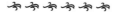

ALFRED NORTH WHITEHEAD, IN THE BEGINNING PAGES of *Process and Reality*, included a brief and somewhat astonishing section called "The Category of the Ultimate." In this tersely worded category he named not one, but three notions involved in the ultimate:

one, many, and creativity. For Whitehead "the ultimate" is not a simple category, but a complex category. Its ultimacy has nothing to do with a supreme status of either "creativity," "one," or "many," as if each existed in some ultimate transcendent state, distant and far above ordinary existence. He called "one," "many," and "creativity" ultimate simply because everything whatsoever that exists can only be adequately understood through these three notions taken together. Every existent entity is what it is because it is a coming together (which is to say, creativity) of multiple actualities and possibilities (the many) into the single thing that it is (the one). As such, "creativity," "one," and "many" are triadic: each is a necessary part of anything that exists. They are also abstractions, naming what is essential to any and every actual entity as analyzed by Whitehead. No reality can be adequately described without reference to all three, which is why together they constitute the Category of the Ultimate. The danger entailed in calling them "ultimate" is our penchant for projecting extraordinary transcendence onto anything given metaphysical ultimacy, as if it must then be somehow godlike in its transcendence. But there is no godlike "otherness" involved; neither element in the category exists apart from its instantiations.

There is no finite entity, nothing whatsoever, no particle of existence, that does not emerge from the many; there is no entity, nothing whatsoever, that does not selectively integrate the many into a relatively new way of being, and no entity, nothing whatsoever, that does not in the process of this creative selectivity become a new "one." As a new one, it changes the nature of the many, which now, including the new one, calls for yet a new integration creating a new one, hence a new many, calling again for a new one: and the process, repeated infinitely, yields the reality of the ever-expanding universe. One, many, and creativity are abstractions describing this never-ending process. As Whitehead says, there is no meaning to creativity apart from creatures; he might just as well have said that there is no meaning to many apart from creatures, and there is no meaning to a singular one apart from creatures.[1]

While Whitehead applies the dynamics of creativity, many, and one to the most minute aspect of existence, it is also the case that these dynamics apply at the macro level of complex organisms such as persons. Consider your own experience for a moment; think about who you are. How would you describe yourself to someone else — how would you even introduce yourself? It could be in terms of your profession, or where you work, or whom you represent, the sort of thing that's on your nametag. "Hello, I'm Marjorie Suchocki, I'm connected with the Center for Process Studies and Claremont School of Theology." It might be in terms of your relationship: "I have the immense privilege of naming John Cobb as my mentor and friend," or in terms of where you live: "I currently live in California, but I'm actually moving to Texas to be closer to family," or in terms of your interests, "oh, you like film? So do I! Have you heard of the Whitehead International Film Festival?"

It's so obvious that we just take it for granted, but it's actually metaphysically important that every single item that you or I name, even in something so brief and commonplace as an introduction, refers to something beyond ourselves. Our profession? We were taught by others, institutions and persons; we are not self-made. To name myself as a theologian drags in a 2,000-year-old tradition that gives the profession its meaning, both positive and negative; it implies working through an enormous body of texts under the initial guidance of teachers and mentors. Likewise, with any profession: we do not invent it all ourselves; it has its antecedents in immediate or long-term history. A place? We did not invent that place; it pre-existed our arrival and continues to exist when we leave. Our dear relationships? Our interests? All are defined not simply by ourselves, but by that which is other than ourselves. I defy you to find any meaningful presentation of yourself that does not depend in part on that which is more than yourself — there is a "many" that has contributed to the one who you are.

Of course, how you relate to the many is influenced by, but not determined by, the many. You are not passively formed by others.

Moment by moment, there is a process to becoming yourself, and this process includes your decisions, your choices. These are not only about how you relate to the many, but even how you choose those elements that you allow to influence you the most. You exist in a deeply interrelational universe, where everything actually has some effect, however miniscule or major, on everything else. But how all these things affect you, and which are more important than others, rests to some degree with your own cumulative choices. You are an active participant in the process. In your formative years, it might seem that an entire future is before you, but you cannot be an entire future. You are forced to decide, even if that decision is to avoid decision by drifting. The sense of the future, immediate and long-term, guides what you do with what you have received from your past. Thus, in every moment you are confronted with two forms of the many: the many influences of the past, the many possibilities for the future. Your response to these past facts and future possibilities is your own creativity, weaving the two together, becoming one: yourself. All along the way, you are integrating influences into who you are at every single moment. In and through this selective process, you become yourself. I say "to some degree" because there are always some elements that are simply given as primary constituents of who you are and who you can be. You are born into a particular nationality, a particular family, with particular genes, particular strands of DNA, and particular challenges of various sorts. These are your givens; you must deal with them. But how you deal with them rests to some degree within your own creative process, a process in which there is always a modicum of freedom. Nothing is ever 100% predetermined.

So let me now take you from illustrations of the creative process at the personal level to Whitehead's technical analysis of the creative process at its most fundamental level, the basic drops of experience from which all things are formed. To follow this you need to add three words to your vocabulary: "conformal prehensions," or the first phase of an actual occasion, the way the past is received;

"concrescence," which is the phase in which the becoming entity integrates its prehensions, and "satisfaction," that final phase toward which the becoming occasion aims, and which the occasion finally achieves. A Whiteheadian understanding of creativity is nothing other than the analysis of the prehensions, concrescence, and satisfaction that describe the constitution of an actual entity; creativity is the essential dynamism that qualifies the whole process of becoming from inauguration to conclusion.

Remember that Whitehead's "category of the ultimate" has a triadic character: one, many, and creativity. Every instance of creativity within an actual occasion also has a triadic character. It emerges as a responsiveness grown out of the appetitions from the many in its past: many elements in the past push the nascent entity into its becoming — and its becoming *is* its creativity. Creativity begins in the nascent occasion through feelings emerging as a forced conformation to a past, feelings which naturally include tensions since the many disparate feelings must be unified so that the new occasion can become a subject unto itself. Apart from some sense of what the emerging entity can become there would be paralysis, a sort of still-born nothingness. Thus the initial emergence of creativity brings about a subject that feels not only the multiple appetitions of its past, but also some sense, whether vague or clear, of just how it might become: it senses possibility. For Whitehead, since everything and every feeling that exists must be grounded in either the becoming entity or another, this sense of possibility must come from an entity that grounds all possibilities, which leads to Whitehead's unconventional notion of the relational God — but that is clearly a subject too complex to include in this chapter. So now we consider the three phases of creativity within an actual entity, "conformation," "concrescence," and "satisfaction." Conformal prehensions are the feeling of otherness, both the otherness of the many entities within an emergent occasion's finite past actual world, and the otherness of God, through whom the occasion feels its initial impulse toward unification.

The many prehended feelings that the nascent occasion must unify are competitive, since no prehended finite entity had to deal with precisely these feelings. Occasions which were contemporaries for what is now experienced as past formed no part of how that past became itself—but they do form a part of what the becoming entity feels. Thus the new entity must find a way of unification unlike that of any entity before it. It emerges from feelings of many that have never before been unified from precisely this perspective. It also emerges from its feeling of God's own unification of that past, which provides the guidance Whitehead calls the "initial aim" that, together with the feelings of the past, launches the emerging entity into the adventure of its becoming. God has felt the entire past world of the becoming entity, and hence has the wherewithal for envisioning ways whereby that world might achieve forms of unification in numerous becoming standpoints. Each emerging occasion feels possibilities for its own perspectival unification of its past, resolving the incompatibilities also felt within its past. But it is not God who resolves the problem of each emerging entity's unification; it is that entity's own dynamic responsiveness to God and its past that inaugurates the further process of concrescence.

How is satisfaction creative? The question should rather be, how can satisfaction be anything other than creative? Satisfaction is the final holding together of what has been done with the many prehensions received, supplemented, and integrated into unity. Whitehead says that an occasion of existence is an "all-at-onceness," indivisible. For purposes of abstraction we speak of such occasions temporally: first they prehend, then they concresce, then they achieve satisfaction, in a 1-2-3 fashion, and so we must speak, given the temporality of our understanding. But Whitehead calls us to intuit the deeper unity of an occasion beyond the successiveness of our understanding. There is an all-at-onceness to prehension, concrescence, satisfaction. Through this complex unity, we come to understand the dynamism rather than static nature of satisfaction. The resolution of concrescence is no resolution if it is not a sort of holding together of the achievement, and holding disparate parts together is itself a dynamic process, a creative process. But just as the inaugurating phase of the becoming entity had both external and internal components, even so the concluding phase has both internal and external components. Both require the dynamism of creativity. The inaugurating phase looked outward in order to progress inward; the concluding phase looks inward in order to progress outward. That is, the inward progression of the beginning was an appetition from the many toward unity; the outward progression of the ending turns appetition from the unity achieved toward a new many yet to come. To put it another way, creativity at the beginning and ending of the actual occasion is rather Janus-faced. It is outward/inward at the beginning, and inward/outward at the end. The push toward concrescent creativity at the beginning becomes the push toward transitional creativity at the ending. What I am calling "transitional" Whitehead calls "transcendent creativity," meaning it is creativity pushing beyond its location in the subject. Whitehead indicates this in his double naming of the actual occasion as the "subject-superject." By "transcendent creativity" and "subject-superject," Whitehead simply signifies the sense in which the subjective satisfaction of the occasion pushes beyond itself toward what will become the prehensive phase of creativity in its successors. We can describe prehension through the phrase, "from the many, one" and we can describe satisfaction as being "from the one, many," with concrescence being the middle phase, the process of unification.

This final act of becoming in satisfaction is not a simple cessation of the entity's brief emergence into actuality, for creativity is not left behind in satisfaction. If it were, there would be no further emergence, no further evolution, no further world. Just as the category of the ultimate is triadic, and the phases of creativity are triadic, even so there is a triadic form to the final satisfaction that concludes the entity. This is because the emergent satisfaction is qualified by the process undergone to attain it; satisfaction has reference to the intensity from which it grew. But satisfaction is also at the same time (if time there be in this miniscule world) a dynamic holding together of the elements finally chosen as self-definition. The satisfaction is what it is because of the unique combination of influences now concretized; thus satisfaction has a tensile strength in which all the elements are held together as a whole. More than this, the satisfaction has within it what Whitehead calls "appetition," a sense of what is now possible in the world beyond the entity because of what this entity has now added to that world — a new many, created through the emergence of precisely this one — multiplied a billionfold. Through the transcendent creativity of satisfaction, the entity, reaches beyond itself, turning the subject into that which is no longer just the subject, but subject-superject.

There is a sense, then, in which the actual entity is outside of time — a kind of all-at-onceness within its own experience — while at the same time these droplets of existence, with their triadic form of creativity, ground what we in our larger world call the experience of time. Note that the responsiveness of the entity relates to a past — not just an immediate past, but all the pasts successively contained in the creative surge of entity after entity, each retaining and transforming that which it has received, grounding as it were the larger process called evolution. The past is created in and through successive emergences of that which is newly present. Creativity in the form of responsiveness to the energies forcing its emergence is a foretaste of time itself in the constant creation of a past.

But creativity is also analogous to the pervasive form of time we call the present. The intensity of the inward process of creativity, the whirl of selective energy that weighs and judges and negates and accepts and decides is the deeply subjective experience of the entity, immersed in the necessity of what it must do and how it might do it. Is not our own experience of the present similar? We have that with which we must deal, and we do so sometimes in a seemingly automatic fashion, but actually there is a constant below the surface — and sometimes not so below the surface — energy of becoming ourselves in and through how we deal with what we are given in light of our larger goals and hopes and desires. The deeply internal concrescent creativity is analogous to our own deepest sense of who we are in the present moment.

Yet again, the satisfaction of the entity, that triadic miracle of becoming, holds within it a dynamic hope for the future. Analogously, the very conference for which this was prepared was an action unto itself, that which drew us together for a creative time of hearing and speaking and contrasting and judging. But its major purpose looks beyond itself, with some hope that as we hold the dynamism of this time together it will propel us into a new future; that its appetition toward a greater good than that which we have been able to achieve thus far will, with some imperative, invite a new future, a new way of being responsive and responsible to one another and to this good earth that we call our home. The present gains its depths not simply by its relation to a past, but even more deeply by the hope it contains for a future. Even so, the satisfaction of an entity in Whitehead's analysis creatively holds together the triadic experience of past achievement, present decision, and future hope.

Creativity, then, in Whitehead's world, is a momentary experience of becoming that includes that which precedes it and that which might follow it. As such, each momentary experience grounds time—and even more than that, creates time as bit by bit by billions and billions of bits, there becomes something instead of nothing in the macro world. Creativity is a dynamic, triadic process. It yields the world.

Two further aspects of this creative becoming of existence need to be emphasized: the first is that while each droplet of experience is an intensive immersion in the process of becoming, seeds of transcendence pervade that process. The second is that the primary feelings that define each entity are not left behind in the element of transcendence: transcendence includes feelings that in a unique way combine otherness with subjective identity. Transcendent feelings within the emerging actual entity become, in the larger world that is created through complex combinations of entities such as persons, the ground of empathic self-transcendence, and this quality becomes an essential ingredient in imagination and all art forms.

To summarize, the entity is immersed within itself as it pulls its experience of the otherness of the past and the otherness of the future into its own form of becoming, yielding its final actuality. But even while the entity is immersed within itself, its necessary inclusion of otherness within the self provides the seeds of transcendence, of motions beyond the self that can reach full attainment not within the momentary form of the actual entity, but within the more complex forms that emerge through societies of actual entities. The ground of transcendence is within the instantaneous entity; the actuality of transcendence occurs minutely as the appetition of one entity forces the emergence of successors. The process is replicated on a grand scale with composite creatures such as ourselves.

Because the originating form of transcendence is accomplished through feeling, even so the forms of transcendence that obtain for us are accomplished through feelings. These feelings express themselves as emotive relations to that which is beyond the self, creating the possibility for empathy. Empathy, in turn, is the capacity to recognize the other as also subjective, also feeling, also dealing with the experience of becoming a self through time. Can you begin to see, then, how creativity becomes the ground of imagination? Imagination is the ability to think beyond the present, whether that "beyond" be the past or the future. Imagination is the capacity to transcend present experience through visions of alternatives. Imagination is the capacity to place oneself empathically in situations that are other to ourselves, with persons and places and cultures and customs that are other to our own, not with fear of difference, but with appreciation for difference, for widened horizons. It involves deeper empathy with the lives and loves of others, with their tragedies and burdens, with worlds and ways somewhat like our own, and somewhat unlike our own. Imagination is the capacity for loving the world beyond ourselves. Imagination finds its ground in the transcendent aspect of creativity, and it finds its expression in the creation of beauty and in deeds of love and compassion.

Think now of ourselves as persons—compilations of many series of actual entities, if you will—but persons. Analogously to the emergence of a single actual entity, we also emerge moment by moment from a past, some of which is retained within ourselves as memory, most of which is more like a hidden bombardment of influences from our family, our religion, our profession, our culture, our politics, our nation—even our solar system, our galaxy, our place in the universe. Our very emergence, our existence relies on a vast network of interrelationships, other to us, but effective on us and within us, contributing to who we are. Analogously to the single entity, we have the seeds of transcendence of the self within us through a relation to the past that precedes us, but internally affects us. We read histories to understand our past beyond the immediate world of families of origin; beyond our ethnicity, our nationality. We read histories and stories, we watch films and hear music, and through doing so we increase the breadth of our understanding. More intimately, we each have a complex personal past of relationships both positive and negative, and we have developed a history of dealing with those relationships. The wider and narrower breadths of the past constitute the stuff of memory. And, indeed, in each moment we become ourselves in the context of those memories, whether submerged into our subconsciousness, or pushing at the edges of our awareness, or filling us with present feeling. We are beings partially made through memory: our relation to the past. In and through memory, there is a sense in which we escape from the mere intensity of our present immersion in ourselves, for memory takes us beyond the present, offering a multitude of stories from the past.

Just as each occasion begins with a sense of the past, even so each entity is an immersion in its own presentness. As are we. But we have within us a very common way of escaping from self-absorption in our own creative processes, and this is the way of empathy. We are subjects, present to other subjects; we have histories and stories, but so do others. And in and through hearing the stories of others, through the act of truly listening to another, we learn empathically what it is like to be that other. We perhaps begin to appreciate a point of view not our own All such acts of empathy constitute a kind of transcendence over immersion in ourselves. Participating in community, whether a religious or academic or political or other form of persons coming together, is at the same time an action of self-transcendence, moving beyond immersion in one's own preferences, one's own ways, one's own self.

We transcend the immediacy of ourselves by being able to reach into a past no longer present, accessible only through memory and through recorded histories. We transcend the immediacy of ourselves also through our capacity to empathize with others, feeling with them, and growing our own capacity for understanding. And we also transcend ourselves by our ability to dream a future not yet here. We project ourselves imaginatively into the way possibilities might realize themselves, letting that vision of what might yet be become a part of us, and consequently become part of our actions.

Creativity is what undergirds our capacity for self-transcendence in these three modes—and these three modes, in turn, become the stuff that makes possible the power of imagination. This whole process is not simply creativity, but creativity with a purpose; it is the ground of imagination itself. In and through openness to the past in multiple dimensions, woven into empathic understanding of others in the present, oriented toward possibilities not yet realized in the future, imagination is born. Imagination, then, is the work of weaving: selecting alternative strands from the near or distant past, weaving them into one's own immediacy with an eye to what might yet be. Imagination emerges in and through the metaphysics of creativity itself. It replicates on the macro level the dynamics already present in the miniscule level of the actual occasion.

I need only add that just as feeling is the fundamental basis of existence in the actual occasion, even so our own replication of that level through these three modes of transcendence—the past, the present, the future—is grounded and accomplished through feeling. Feelings give rise to thought, to conceptualizations emerging from feelings and codifying feelings in ways that formulate that which might be, in a kind of a weaving that holds past, present, and future in formulations newly possible: imagination.

For example, I recently attended a concert at Disney Hall; Gustavo Dudamel was conducting Bach's Toccata and Fugue in D Minor, as orchestrated by Igor Stokowsky. At least three geniuses were at work: in 1703 Bach wrote the Toccata, reputedly as a device to show his own amazing dexterity with the organ. Two hundred years later a young Stokowsky loved the Toccata, and imagined it not as a piece for the organ, but as an orchestrated work of art. Out of his deep empathy with Bach's work, he felt the ways in which the Toccata could be orchestrated; he found how the sounds of each different instrument could give expression to the original sound of the reverberating organ. He memorably gave the result to the world through his collaboration with Walt Disney, for Stokowsky's version of Bach's Tocatta is the opening music in Disney's *Fantasia,* heard by countless numbers of children as well as adults, inspiring many. Nearly a century later, Gustavo Dudamel selected the piece for the Los Angeles Philharmonic, presenting it in the magnificent Disney Hall—and I listened. Bach's creative genius; Stokowski weaving that genius with his own, Dudamel building upon both as he adds his own distinctive interpretation to the music: imagination! The result is a beauty that defies description—feeding one's soul, pervading it with feelings of beauty.

The art of film shows the same dynamics. I served on a film jury for the Washington, D.C., Film Fest, and was delighted to watch a film with the unlikely name of *Me and Earl and the Dying Girl.* If Stokowsky reached two centuries back to interact with Bach, the directors of this film had a shorter time span for their inspiration—but this light-hearted film is what it is through its interplay with film history. The viewer begins to get the clue during an early scene: at the insistence of his mother the 17-year-old has gone to the house of his classmate, who has been diagnosed with leukemia. As he enters the home, the single mother of the girl, drink in hand, begins making up to the boy, and images of Mrs. Robinson from *The Graduate* nag at the edges of one's mind. Meanwhile, our young protagonist and his best friend, Earl, are novice filmmakers themselves, using a video camera to stage shots using whatever materials are to hand. The comic films they produce bear titles such as *Sockwork Orange*, and *2:48 Cowboy*. And music from Truffaut's classic film, *400 Blows*, keeps appearing as background in the film. Weaving their way through film history, the writer/director projects characters that invite our empathy, then brings the film to a fitting conclusion. Imagination: envisioning a future that appreciatively appropriates a past for the sake of present fulfillment.

In this conference the music and film track offered was the singular work of filmmaker Jason Starr. Like Stokowski finding Bach, Starr finds Gustav Mahler. Moved by the symphonies of this great composer, Starr envisions them not simply for the magnificence of sound, but for the magnificence of sight and insight. Feeling the emotive force of Mahler, he translates the emotion communicated in sound into images that, through the power of film, accompany the music. Music and image together powerfully communicate the depth of the music, and, at the same time, they transform the music by virtue of its different context. We are given additional "Starr-power" in that Starr adds commentary to the music, selecting different artists, philosophers, and ecologists to interact with the music. Through their interactions, we are invited to join our own interactions as well. Out of the many, Jason Starr creates a new "one," offering it to us for further creative use. Imagination! The singular art of music joins the singular art of film joins the singular art of commentary; drawing us deeper into the power of music and imagery. Utilization of a different medium allows profound new ways of accessing the music.

I was fortunate to know an artist in the 20th century; his name was Irwin Lachmann, and he managed to escape Nazi Germany in 1939. He painted. I have one of his pieces in my home; it is four panels, each in a different color using acrylics and sand. The name of the painting is, "In Praise of Ancient Walls." But one does not see walls when looking at the painting—instead there is merely color and texture. One panel is red, one maroon, another golden brown, another gold. There is something in the juxtaposition of the panels, with their color and texture, that moves my soul. And where are the ancient walls? There are memories painted into each panel; memories of historical walls, of fear, of pain, of survival, of hope. A past of fear and repression horrendously repeated in the present merge together in these panels. There is empathy in the panels—a call to see, to understand, to identify. And there is imagination in these panels for a different future, a place where walls shelter, where differences can abide appreciatively side by side, where ancient good can find its own transformation in a new present. There is much to be said in this painting, this praise of ancient walls. Creativity and imagination; memories of pain and visions of hope woven into panels of paint and sand.

Poetry: we have a beautiful poet in our midst here in Claremont; her name is Patricia Patterson. Listen to her poem, Body of God:

> **Glimpsing** the body of God in the rounded dark of arching sky and starry night/sitting on the edge of our galaxy with images of our true blue planet permanently implanted on our minds by explorers beyond.

> **Touching** the body of God in damp spring soil prepared for the sowing, awaiting the rising of germinating seed to stem to flower to vegetable to tree, aware of fruitfulness of path through hunger of satiated appetite, of divine body in our body.

> **Hearing** the body of God alive in the liveliness of millions of creatures living striving thriving throughout the earth and sea and sky; a cornucopia of life in birdsong, whale cry, rustling of insects in grass and tree.

Spiriting the body of God through minds and hearts feeling the translation of material to soul, meeting the divine in every aspect of our breathing, knowing, loving our enlivened beings, filled inside and out with over-flowing life.

Do you hear the creative transformation happening in these verses? There are echoes of the Christian communion service of Eucharist in this poem, but the presence of God cannot be confined to bread and wine; it is here surpassed by a divine presence that permeates all things. This real presence is given to all, to glimpse, to touch, to hear the ever-given fecundity of God, the ever-given beauty of God, the ever-giving life of God in all the wonder that is earth and earthy. This glimpsing, touching, and hearing is at the same time a joining of spirit with Spirit, and in the union the whole earth is alive with joy. Transcendence, creativity, imagination, empathy combine to offer us such a vision of our world.

And what of the imagination that produces the great works of literature throughout all ages and cultures, sometimes oral only, often written in flowing scripts that are in themselves works of beauty? All of our languages become the stuff through which stories come to expression, whether plays or novels; our languages also become the means of formulating the deepest questions, striving for understanding. Imagination, working through the capacity to transcend narrow concerns to embrace our widest humanity, yields the literatures of our world.

Creative imagination works with the world as it is to suggest ways that it can be. It may well be that the various arts are the ultimate modes through which creative imagination takes hold, expressing what has been, what is, and what may yet be. In many respects, the purpose of art is simply itself, offered to whoever will receive its gift. And the gift is perhaps an invitation to openness? a possibility of wisdom? of discovering depths of the human spirit we intuited but could not fully grasp til the artist puts it before us?

Perhaps it is the case that the progression of humanity, driven so often by greed and self-aggrandizement, can almost be stopped in its tracks through the great gifts of the artists among us. They show that there is more in the past than we had thought, that our private immersions in our respective pasts can be enlarged as we feel the impact of others in the past with different visions. And perhaps they show that an empathic identification not only with the past, but with contemporary humans in all our diversity, shows us to ourselves, calls us to a wider more empathic awareness. Perhaps, as well, in doing both, they open our eyes to visions of beauties that still might be: beauties of relationships based in kindness and appreciation; beauties of a world not sacrificed to human greed, but honored and cared for in all its splendors; beauties of a miraculous planet that still might be preserved for the sake of life.

Creativity involves a necessary reaching into the past that blends it with empathic understanding in the present, leading to visions of a good that might yet be. This very basic metaphysical process is grounded in the dynamics of existence itself. Out of the many a new one emerges, creatively unifying the many in order to generate a new one, which in turn calls forth a shadowy future waiting to be born.

Whitehead's imaginative description of creativity in conjunction with the one and the many as fundamental to existence per se is also descriptive of that creative process that we call imagination. Through imagination, we receive one of life's greatest gifts, the arts. It is not philosophies alone that can rescue us from our greed and guide us to a more generous future, not rationality alone that serves us, not politics alone that can make our world a safer place. Only as we open our hearts and ourselves to the empathy embedded within the arts is there power for the hope we have of a habitable world where all manner of things can survive and thrive. The arts, emerging from imagination, rooted in the creativity that pervades the world, are our harbingers of hope in a world otherwise gone amok.

ENDNOTES

1   Alfred North Whitehead, *Process and Reality*, 1929, Corrected Edition edited by David Ray Griffin and Donald W. Sherburne, (New York: Free Press, 1978).

CONTRIBUTORS

CLIFF COBB is the editor of the *American Journal of Economics and Sociology,* a journal devoted to analyzing the roots of contemporary social, economic, and environmental problems. He is an active supporter of the Institute for Postmodern Development of China and its efforts to promote ecological civilization in China and the U.S.

PHILIP CLAYTON is Ingraham Professor of Theology at Claremont School of Theology and affiliated faculty with Claremont Graduate University. A constructive Christian theologian, Philip has been a leader in dialogues with science, contemporary philosophy, and religious traditions East and West. He is particularly interested in the evolving understanding of Christian faith in the 21st century, and the societal changes that are necessary for establishing sustainable forms of civilization on this planet.

LUKE B. HIGGINS received his doctorate in Theology and Philosophical Studies from Drew University's Graduate Division of Religion. He currently teaches courses in philosophy at Armstrong State University in Savannah, Georgia. Process philosophy and theology occupy the center of a web of interdisciplinary research interests that includes environmental ethics, cosmic Christologies (ancient and modern), Continental philosophy (especially Gilles Deleuze and Henri Bergson), feminist science studies, and various "New Materialisms."

NANCY R. HOWELL is Professor of Theology and Philosophy of Religion and Poppele Professor of Health and Welfare Ministries at Saint Paul School of Theology in Kansas City. She received her Ph.D. from Claremont Graduate University in 1991. Howell is associate editor of the *Encyclopedia of Science and Religion* (Macmillan), and her research examines the impact of primate studies on theological understandings of humanity. She is a member of the International Society for Science and Religion and serves on the Broader Social Impacts Committee of the Human Origins Initiative of the National Museum of Natural History at the Smithsonian Institution.

CATHERINE KELLER is George T. Cobb Professor of Contructive Theology in the Graduate Division of Religion of Drew University. Her publications include: *From a Broken Web: Separation, Sexism and Self; Apocalypse Now & Then; God & Power; Face of the Deep: a Theology of Becoming; On the Mystery: Discerning God in Process; Cloud of the Impossible: Negative Theology and Planetary Entanglement;* and *Intercarnations: Exercises in Theological Possibility.*

SANDRA LUBARSKY founded one of the first graduate programs in sustainability (the M.A. Sustainable Communities at Northern Arizona University) and chaired the Department of Sustainable Development at Appalachian State University. She is the author of several books and many articles on process thought, interreligious dialogue, beauty, and sustainability.

JAY MCDANIEL is Professor of Religion at Hendrix College, where he is the Director of the Steel Center for the Study of Religion and Philosophy. McDaniel has written and lectured on a number of topics including, religion and ecology, religion and interreligious dialogue, and spirituality in an age of consumerism. His recent publications include, *What is Process Thought? Seven Answers to Seven Questions; Gandhi's Hope: Learning From World Religions as a Way to Peace; Process Theology: A Handbook* (co-edited with Donna Bowman); and *Living from the Center: Spirituality in the Age of Consumerism.*

MARY ELIZABETH MOORE is Dean of the School of Theology and Professor of Theology and Education, Boston University. She has also been a professor of religion and education at the Claremont School of Theology, and Emory University, where she served as the Director of the Women in Theology and Ministry Program. Moore has written on topics of socio-economic justice, and socio-ecological renewal, and throughout her career has significantly contributed to the dialogue between theology and education. Her recent publications include, *Teaching as a Sacramental Act*; *Ministering with the Earth*; *Covenant and Call*; and *Teaching from the Heart*.

FRANZ RIFFERT is Professor at the Department of Educational Science at Salzburg University, Austria; he is a certified psychotherapist and has studied theology, philosophy, psychology and educational science. He received grants and invitations to do research at the Center for Process Studies (Claremont, USA), the Catholic University Eichstätt (Germany), and the Harvard Graduate School of Education (Cambridge, USA). His research focuses on philosophy of science, anthropological aspects of education, interdisciplinary relations between philosophy, education, and psychology as well as on educational topics such as instruction (learning cycles), self-governance in school development, and the impacts of subconscious processes in problem solving.

WM. ANDREW SCHWARTZ is a scholar, organizer, and nonprofit administrator. He is Executive Director of the Center for Process Studies, Co-Founder and Executive Vice President of EcoCiv, and Adjunct Professor of philosophy and theology at Claremont School of Theology. Andrew received his PhD in Philosophy of Religion and Theology at Claremont Graduate University, and was a principal organizer of the *Seizing an Alternative* conference, from which this book emerged. His recent work has been focused on high-impact philosophy and the role of big ideas in the transition toward ecological civilization.

MARJORIE HEWITT SUCHOCKi is Professor Emerita at Claremont School of Theology, where she held the Ingraham Chair of Theology and also served as Dean. She is a Co-Director of the Center for Process Studies and is the founding director of the Whitehead International Film Festival, begun in 2002 (now Common Good International Film Festival). Suchocki serves on ecumenical juries in places as varied as Montreal, Berlin, Washington, D.C., and Miami, and often lectures on film and theology in churches, colleges, and seminaries.

JOHN SWEENEY, author of *I'd Rather Be Dead Than Be a Girl*, retired as Managing Director, Center for Process Studies, in 2013. During his long academic career, Dr. Sweeney taught introductory philosophy classes at three California Community Colleges, as well as teaching several different introductory process theology courses at the Claremont School of Theology. In retirement, John has volunteered at the Philadelphia Zoo and currently volunteers at the Big Bear Alpine Zoo. Dr. Sweeney is married to the Rev. Dr. Sharon Graff and actively supports her progressive ministry.

Made in the USA
Middletown, DE
14 March 2019